EDUCATION AND SOCIETY

Studies in the Politics, Sociology and Geography of Education

EDITED BY L. BONDI AND M.H. MATTHEWS

ROUTLEDGE
London and New York

First published in 1988 by
Routledge
11 New Fetter Lane, London EC4P 4EE
29 West 35th Street, New York NY 10001

© 1988 L. Bondi and M.H. Matthews

Printed and bound in Great Britain by Mackays of Chatham PLC, Kent

All rights reserved. No part of this book may be reprinted or reproduced or utilised in any form or by any electronic, mechanical, or other means, now known or hereafter invented, including photocopying and recording, or in any information storage or retrieval system, without permission in writing from the publishers.

British Library Cataloguing in Publication Data

Education and society : studies in the
　politics, sociology and geography of
　education.
　1. Education. Sociopolitical aspects
　I. Bondi, L. II. Matthews, M.H. (Michael
　Hugh), *1948-* .
　370.19

ISBN 0-415-00451-9

CONTENTS

Contributors
List of Figures
List of Tables
Preface

Introduction Liz Bondi   1

Part One: The Politics of Educational Provision

1. Consulting for Change: the political
   geography of school reorganisation in
   Portsmouth Alan Burnett   19

2. Delegation and Community Participation:
   an alternative approach to the problems
   created by falling primary school rolls
   Michael Adler and Liz Bondi   52

3. Rezoning: an exercise in compromise
   Alison Petch   83

4. A Tale of Two Cities: the impact of
   parental choice on admissions to primary
   schools in Edinburgh and Dundee
   Gillian Raab and Michael Adler   113

5. Educational Policy Innovation: a
   conceptual approach Frank Burdett   148

v

Contents

6. The International Recruiting Game: foreign
   student-athletes in American higher
   education John Bale   178

Part Two: Social Issues in Education

7. Black and White Young People and Employment
   in Britain John Eggleston   213

8. Educational Attainment in Glasgow: the
   role of neighbourhood deprivation
   Catherine Garner   226

9. Catchments, Schools and the Characteristics
   of Teachers M.H. Matthews, Anthony Airey
   and Lesley Tacon   257

10. Technical and Vocational Education
    Initiative: criticism, innovation and
    response
    Les Bell   285

Conclusion Liz Bondi   306

References   310

Index   330

CONTRIBUTORS

Michael Adler is Senior Lecturer in Social Policy at the University of Edinburgh.

Anthony Airey is Senior Lecturer in Geography at Coventry (Lanchester) Polytechnic.

John Bale is Lecturer in Education at the University of Keele.

Les Bell is Senior Lecturer in Education at the University of Warwick.

Liz Bondi is Lecturer in Geography at the University of Edinburgh.

Frank Burdett is Lecturer in Geography at Bath College of Higher Education.

Alan Burnett is Senior Lecturer in Geography at Portsmouth Polytechnic.

John Eggleston is Professor of Education at the University of Warwick.

Catherine Garner is a Research Fellow at the Centre for Educational Sociology, University of Edinburgh.

M.H. Matthews is Senior Lecturer in Geography at Coventry (Lanchester) Polytechnic.

Contributors

Alison Petch us a Research Fellow at the Social Work Research Centre, University of Stirling.

Gillian Raab is Lecturer in Medical Statistics at the University of Edinburgh.

Lesley Tacon is a Research Assistant in Geography at Coventry (Lanchester) Polytechnic.

FIGURES

1.1	Official and Unofficial Organisations Involved in Decision-making over Sixth-form Provision in Portsmouth	20
1.2	Secondary Schools and Catchment Areas in Portsmouth	26
3.1	Secondary School Catchments in West Fife	88
4.1A	Placing Requests out of Edinburgh Primary Schools, 1982-5	126
4.1B	Placing Requests into Dundee Primary Schools, 1982-5	127
4.2A	Placing Requests across Adjacent Boundaries between Primary Schools in Edinburgh in 1984	130
4.2B	Placing Requests across Adjacent Boundaries between Primary Schools in Dundee in 1984	131
4.3	Distributions of Six Variables derived from the 1981 Census for Primary School Catchment Areas	132
4.4A	Characteristics of Primary School Catchment Areas in Edinburgh	140

Figures

4.4B	Characteristics of Primary School Catchment Areas in Dundee	141
4.5A	Inter-school Movement between Schools in North-west Edinburgh	142
4.5B	Inter-school Movement between Schools in North-east Dundee	143
5.1	Secondary Expenditure per Pupil	149
5.2	Percentage of Schools in each LEA with at least one Microcomputer	150
5.3	Concepts for the Analysis of Policy Innovation	156
5.4	Tiers within a Local Education Authority	159
5.5	Details of Policies on Computers in the Four LEAs	162
5.6	Stages of Policy Innovation in the Four Case Studies	168
5.7	Timing and Duration of Initiation	170
5.8	Implementation: Duration to Policy	172
6.1	A Three-tier Format for the Study of Top-class Sport	182
6.2	Numbers and Continental Origins of Superior Foreign Track and Field Student-athletes	188
6.3	Number of Foreign Student-athletes in Soccer and Track and Field squads, Clemson University, 1970-85	189
6.4	National Origins of Superior Foreign Student-athletes (male, track and field), 1973-85	191

Figures

6.5	Campus Destinations of Superior Male Track and Field Student-athletes from (a) Kenya, (b) Nigeria, (c) the United Kingdom and (d) Republic of Ireland	192
6.6	Destinations by State of Superior Male Track and Field Student-athletes Recruited from Overseas, 1973-85	198
6.7	Global Origins of Superior Women Track and Field Student-athletes Recruited to US Colleges and Universities, 1977-85	200
6.8	Destinations by State of Superior Women Student-athletes Recruited from Foreign Countries, 1977-85	201
9.1	Classification of Schools by Location and Social Priority Status	264
9.2	Teacher Characteristics and the School: an Interactive Model	282

xi

TABLES

1.1	Non-denominational Secondary Schools	24
1.2	The Results of the First Ballot	32
1.3	The Results of the Second Ballot	38
3.1	Number of First-year Pupils Opting out of and into Local Secondary School Catchments in West Fife	89
4.1	Number of Placing Requests Received by Stage of Schooling, 1982-5	120
4.2	Proportion of Placing Requests Granted (initially or on appeal) by Stage of Schooling	120
4.3	First-year Placing Requests as a Proportion of Total for Primary and Secondary Schools, 1982-5	120
4.4	Placing Request Rates by Region, 1984	122
4.5	Placing Requests at P1 Entry, 1982-5	124
4.6	Variables Derived from the 1981 Census Data	134

Tables

4.7	Logistic Regressions of Predictors on Placing Request Rates to Adjacent Schools	137
6.1	Numbers of Foreign Recruits to Big 8 Conference Institutions, 1979-83	187
6.2	Major National Donors of Superior Foreign Track and Field Student-athletes (male), 1973-85	190
6.3	Principal College Destinations of Superior Foreign Student Track and Field Athletes (male), 1973-85	199
8.1	Deprivation Score: Constituent Variables	238
8.2	Pearson Product Moment Correlations for Background Variables with SCE Attainment and Neighbourhood Deprivation for School Leavers in Glasgow	240
8.3	Regression of SCE Attainment on Home, School and Neighbourhood in Glasgow: Contributions of Variable Groups	242
8.4	Regression of SCE Attainment on Home, School and Neighbourhood in Glasgow: Tests of Significance	243
8.5	Regression of SCE Attainment on Home, School and Neighbourhood Variables in Glasgow	244
8.6	Contribution of Neighbourhood Deprivation to Differential Attainment in Glasgow	246
8.7	Probit Analysis of Attaining/Not Attaining Three or More SCE Highers Passes in Glasgow (summary)	247
8.8	Probit Analysis of Attaining/Not Attaining Three or More SCE Highers Passes in Glasgow	249

xiii

Tables

8.9	Definition of Advantaged and Disadvantaged School Leavers and their Probability of Qualifying for Entry to Higher Education	250
9.1	Selected Social and Economic Characteristics of School Catchments in Coventry	262
9.2	Similarities in Selected Characteristics of Teachers Working in Inner- and Outer-City Schools	266
9.3	Differences in Selected Characteristics of Teachers Working in Inner- and Outer-City Schools	268
9.4	Differences in Selected Characteristics of Teachers Working in Social Priority and Other Schools	269
9.5	Composition of the Teaching Force at Each School	272
9.6	Experience of Teachers at Each School	274
9.7	Attitudes of Teachers towards their Schools	275
9.8	Attitudes of Teachers towards the Profession	276
9.9	Correlation Matrix: Catchment Area Data and the Characteristics of Teachers	278

PREFACE

This book arises from a conference entitled 'Education and Society: geographical perspectives', organised by the editors under the auspices of the Social Geography Study Group of the Institute of British Geographers. We are grateful to the Institute of British Geographers for their generous grant, which enabled us to organise a multi-disciplinary conference focusing on contemporary issues in education. We also wish to thank Woolton Hall of Residence at the University of Manchester for providing accommodation. In the production of this volume we owe particular thanks to Dr Michael Bradford for his advice and encouragement, and to Elizabeth Clark for her painstaking preparation of the figures for Chapters one, three, four and six.

Liz Bondi
M.H. Matthews

Introduction

THE CONTEMPORARY CONTEXT OF EDUCATIONAL PROVISION

Liz Bondi

INTRODUCTION

In Britain, education is 'in recession' (Hewton, 1986a). Three elements of this recession, each originating in the 1970s, can be identified. First, 'education is in an economy which is in recession' (ibid., p. 7) or, more accurately, in an economy in which public expenditure has been strongly curtailed. Secondly, demand for education has receded because the decline in the birthrate (commencing 15 to 20 years ago) has reduced the numbers entering the education system. Thirdly, belief in education as a means by which social and economic problems can be overcome has been seriously eroded: this is a trend captured by (but pre-dating) the Conservative Party's 1979 election slogan 'Educashun Isnt Wurking'. These forms of 'recession' are not unique to Britain but are evident to varying degrees throughout the Western world (Eversley and Kollmann, 1982; Neave, 1984).

Each element of 'recession' is itself dynamic: although all three senses of 'recession' have been integral to the context of education in Britain for at least a decade, there are marked contrasts between 1977 and 1987. Further, these three elements do not operate as wholly independent, or external, constraints; rather there is a complex web of interactions between education and its contemporary economic, social and political context. Several recent studies have focused primarily upon the interaction between education and the economy, emphasising particularly the role of economic recession (Dennison, 1984; Dale, 1985; Hewton, 1986a). This volume seeks to redress the balance by presenting a series of studies concerned primarily with

Introduction

social and political aspects of contemporary educational provision. The empirical chapters are based on original research in the form of local case studies. The aim of this chapter is to provide a broad framework on the contemporary social and political context of educational provision, within which these detailed studies can be located.

THE POLITICS OF EDUCATIONAL PROVISION

In most countries, the state is directly responsible for the bulk of educational provision and regulates any part of the service provided privately. Consequently, the influence of politics on education and the character of educational policy-making have attracted considerable research interest. This section provides an overview of three aspects of contemporary British politics that have particularly influenced education provision. These are the impact of public expenditure restraint, the role of political ideologies in recent educational developments, and the relative power and influence in education of different governmental agencies.

Education and public expenditure restraint

Since 1979, central government grants to local authorities have been reduced, penalties for overspending and more recently rate-capping, have been introduced (Hunter, 1983; School for Advanced Urban Studies, 1983; Boddy, 1984). Because education is the largest spender among local services (accounting for 50 to 60 per cent of current expenditure) it was inevitable that these stringent economic measures would affect the resources available. Other elements of the context, including falling pupil numbers and the erosion of confidence in education, ensured that the service was at the forefront of cuts in local government spending. Hewton (1986a, 1986b) considers the consequences of this for local education policy-making. In particular he poses the question whether 'the idea of planning for contraction (has become) part of the organisational culture in local authorities' (Hewton, 1986b, p. 304). He characterises an 'emergent cuts culture' as one in which defensive, pragmatic and reformist elements compete,

Introduction

respectively, to resist cutbacks, to search for solutions minimising damage, and to pursue radical changes. Fowler (1981) described the adjustment to the new economic constraints of the late 1970s as a process of 'disjointed decrementalism', which involves

> what is sometimes called 'grazing'; that is to say you 'take the skin off' every element in the system. This procedure, though hurtful, is fair to all elements of the system ... (p. 19)

This approach is typical of education policy-making that has not adapted to contraction but instead adopts what Hewton terms a defensive posture. As possibilities for uniform 'grazing' have been exhausted (see Department of Education and Science (DES), 1986) the reformist element identified by Hewton has gained strength. The reformist element is evident, for example, in the more ambitious programmes of rationalising school provision that have been adopted by some education authorities (see Audit Commission, 1986). Chapters 1, 2 and 3 examine in depth a number of examples of the political issues arising in individual education authorities responding to the combined effects of economic and demographic contraction. The issue of policy innovation in education authorities is taken up in Chapter 5, which, like Hewton (1986a, 1986b) utilises concepts drawn from organisational theory.

Education and political ideologies

Public expenditure restraint has been central to the policies of the Conservative governments of the 1980s, led by Margaret Thatcher. At the same time, political debate about education itself has shifted onto new ground: new political ideologies have come to the fore, and these have transformed discussions about the provision of education and other services. This transformation has been possible because of the gradual breakdown of the post-war social democratic consensus (Birmingham Centre for Contemporary Cultural Studies, 1981; see also McNay and Ozga, 1985). In education this breakdown of consensus is generally linked to the erosion of belief in the service during the 1970s, although Kogan (1985) is sceptical about the existence of cross-party consensus during the 1950s and

3

Introduction

1960s. Nevertheless, it is clear that 'Thatcherism' ushered in a new form of Conservatism in the 1980s, which has been characterised (by, for example, Stuart Hall) as 'authoritarian populism'. Moreover the growing disquiet about education during the previous decade ensured that

> (t)he opportunity and the desire to implement key precepts of Thatcherism can rarely have combined more favourably than they did in education at the beginning of the 1980s. (Dale, 1983, p. 233)

Various elements of 'Thatcherism' are evident in recent debates about education policy, including those addressing educational standards, moral education, vocationalism and parental choice, each of which is examined below.

First, concern over 'educational standards' has been voiced repeatedly during recent decades, frequently in the context of criticisms of 'progressive' teachers and 'child-centred' pedagogy. Within the ideology of 'Thatcherism' the issue has also been used as an attack on 'universalism' in education, which, it is argued, has led to a 'levelling down' of standards (Dale, 1983). Secondly, moral education has also been a topic of debate for many years, but, as David (1983) argued, since 1979 the position of the right-wing has been consolidated through the harnessing of popular opposition to liberal ideas about sexuality and parenthood. Thirdly, through youth training, the Technical and Vocational Education Initiative (TVEI) and plans for city technology colleges, a 'new vocationalism' is emerging in which training takes precedence over liberal education (Dale, 1985; see also Chapter 10).

Turning fourthly to parental choice in education, various initiatives have been implemented or are being planned that are designed to enhance another theme central to 'Thatcherism', namely individual choice. These include the assisted places scheme (see Tapper and Salter, 1986), legislation to permit greater parental choice within the state sector (see Stillman and Maychell, 1986; Adler, Petch and Tweedie, 1987) and plans now in hand to enable schools to opt out of local authority control and receive funding direct from central government. In addition to championing 'Thatcherist' definitions of individual choice, these initiatives have the negative aim of curbing the pursuit of collective social goals (often dubbed 'social engineering') exemplified by comprehensive secondary reorganisation and

Introduction

policies of positive discrimination (discussed further below). Although the education service in Britain was ripe for change at the onset of the 1980s, Conservative ideas have not always had smooth passage into policy. For example, Sir Keith Joseph abandoned plans to introduce a voucher scheme, where parents would have been able to choose between state and private schools, subject to their ability to find the difference between the value of the voucher and the cost of fees. In other instances, initiatives have been implemented but the results have not necessarily been of the kind expected. This is illustrated in Chapter 4, where the operation of parental choice legislation in two Scottish cities is examined.

Power and influence in education policy-making

The 1980s has also seen significant changes in the balance of power between the various bodies involved in education policy-making. Most obviously, the powers of the education authorities have been reduced relative to those of central government. This has been achieved through public expenditure policies and, increasingly, through initiatives to enhance parental choice. The actions of central government appear to have been motivated by a desire to bring recalcitrant, Labour-controlled local authorities under control. However, the theme of individual choice and freedom from state regulation has provided a powerful counter-argument: within 'Thatcherism', curbing local authority powers has been advanced as a key means of 'rolling back the state' and liberating people from dependence on the state.

Considering education more specifically, Ranson (1980, p. 10) has argued that

> (T)he balance of power between the partners in education had at the end of the sixties and early seventies swung very much towards the local authorities and to heads and teachers in schools ... But the context was beginning to change. The economy was moving into recession, the political climate was sharpening, and the scrutiny of public expenditure in general and education's performance in particular was growing ... The Secretary of State and the DES moved to arrest the decline in its influence and reassert

Introduction

control.

The recovery of control by central government has proceeded along several paths. The professional autonomy of teachers has been challenged in relation to the curriculum, conditions of service, deployment and so on (Broadfoot, 1986). Legislation has affected the relative powers of central government and the education authorities in contradictory ways. For example, the authorities now have greater responsibility for decisions about closing schools but have less discretion because of financial constraints. Chapter 2 demonstrates how this has intensified conflict between education authorities and the local communities they serve, without necessarily reducing conflict between local and central government. Meanwhile, the pursuit of individual freedoms, rather than collective goals, through the parental choice legislation threatens to further erode the powers of education authorities. As the balance of power between central and local government has shifted the powers of schools, local communities and individual parents have become more variable: the position of some has been enhanced; that of others has deteriorated. Conflict between the different 'scales' of individuals, schools, communities, education authorities (and divisions within them) and central government is apparent in several chapters in Part One. The issue is pursued at the international scale in Chapter 6.

Cuts in public expenditure and tightening controls on local authority expenditure have also affected the balance of power within central government. Thus, Hunter (1983, p. 87) has argued that 'it is the Department of Environment, not the DES, which is making the decisions with regard to education.'

Another challenge to the authority of the DES is apparent in the emphasis on vocationalism, which has been pursued primarily through the Manpower Services Commission (MSC) under the aegis of the Department of Employment, although some schemes do operate via schools. Thus, the school-based TVEI is funded by the MSC rather than via local education authorities (LEAs) or the DES (see Birmingham Centre for Contemporary Cultural Studies, 1981; Parkes, 1985; as well as Chapter 10).

Introduction

EDUCATION AND SOCIAL ISSUES

The social role of education has attracted research interest for several decades. Within this research, education has been viewed both positively, as a means of overcoming or alleviating social problems, and negatively, as a factor maintaining or intensifying social inequalities. Both perspectives inform interpretation of contemporary education systems. This section outlines the development of ideas concerning three themes (equality of opportunity, unequal cultures, and education and unemployment), which are taken up by contributions to this volume in relation to issues of the 1980s, and which illustrate both positive and negative views of the social role of education.

Equality of opportunity

Positive appraisals of its social role regard education as a key means of reducing social divisions, whether those of class (a particular concern in Britain) or those of race (a particular concern in the United States). From this perspective, Western societies may be viewed as meritocracies, within which education plays a key role in facilitating social mobility. In a perfect meritocracy, individuals are allocated to different social positions according to their merit. Merit is defined in terms of ability and is measured through performance and qualifications. Education is crucial in this process because high levels of educational achievement give access to positions of high social status. Indeed, education is viewed as the principal mechanism of social mobility. Although social differentiation is integral to the notion of meritocracy, under ideal conditions there would be no correlation between the social status of children and the social status of their parents. Equality of opportunity is essential if education is to fulfil satisfactorily its role in promoting this degree of social mobility.

In practice, it is recognised, that no meritocracy functions perfectly (see Jencks and associates, 1973), but there is no agreement regarding the degree of social differentiation appropriate to a meritocratic society, or what strength of correlation between the social status of parents and children would be acceptable. Nevertheless, reformers and researchers alike have expended a great deal

Introduction

of effort in pursuit of increased social mobility. Because of the important role of education, much of this attention has focused on the issue of equality of opportunity. However, just as opinions regarding the limits of meritocracy vary, so the concept of equality of opportunity has been subject to different definitions (Coleman, 1968). In particular, there has been a shift in the meaning of the term during the postwar period, as the difficulty of removing impediments to social mobility became increasingly apparent.

In Britain, the Education Act 1944 sought to remove inequalities arising from the inability of some parents to pay for the education of their children. In particular, the Act committed the state to providing universal, free, secondary education, in place of a system in which most children received only elementary education. The architects of the Act envisaged what became known as the tripartite system: children were to be selected for one of three kinds of secondary school on the basis of intelligence tests conducted at the age of 11 years (Mortimore and Mortimore, 1986). The assumption was that children could be provided with 'equal but different' secondary education according to their aptitudes for abstract, concrete and practical learning (provided by grammar, secondary modern and technical schools, respectively). However,

> (f)ew technical schools were established and the secondary moderns became the Cinderellas of the education service despite providing for the majority of the population. (Mortimore and Mortimore, 1986, p. 3)

Increasingly, the validity of intelligence testing was called into question and its bias in favour of children from middle-class homes was demonstrated (Floud, Halsey and Martin, 1956; Jackson and Marsden, 1963; Douglas, 1964).

The policy of reorganising secondary education along comprehensive lines was aimed at eliminating both the need for testing and the bias associated with selection; in so doing, it sought to increase equality of opportunity. This policy implied an interpretation of the concept 'equality of opportunity' in terms of equality of access for all social groups. By this time (the mid-1960s), however, a new meaning of the concept, in terms of 'equality of achievement' was also emerging:

> (o)n this basis, equality of educational opportunity

Introduction

comes about if the proportion of people from different social, economic and ethnic categories at all levels of education is more or less the same as the proportion of these people in the population. (Burgess, 1986, p. 51)

This new interpretation recognised that some groups were unable to reach the same level of educational achievement as others because of various forms of social disadvantage. These disadvantages were assumed to be associated with the home background of the children concerned, including material factors (such as poverty, unemployment, housing and health) and cultural factors (such as child-rearing practices, language and parental attitudes). Policies of positive discrimination were devised to offset or compensate for such disadvantages and were directed chiefly at the early years of a child's education (see Mortimore and Blackstone, 1982). In Britain, Educational Priority Areas (EPAs) were the most thoroughly researched of these initiatives (see, for example, Halsey, 1972; Morrison, 1974; Payne, 1974; Barnes, 1975; Smith, 1975; Mortimore and Blackstone, 1982). Other aspects of positive discrimination have attracted less attention although they have more widespread application. In particular, the DES makes provision for LEAs to identify individual schools considered to serve areas of educational disadvantage: these are designated 'social priority schools'. Teachers at these schools qualify for a supplementary allowance. The effect of this policy, together with other factors, on the composition of the teaching force at schools in Coventry is explored in Chapter 9.

Policies of positive discrimination have operated on a more or less explicit areal basis. This was most marked in the EPA initiative, which tackled the problem of educational disadvantage by channelling extra resources to schools in five designated areas. Although Social Priority schools may be located in any LEA, they are also designed to serve local areas, where social disadvantage is great (see Chapter 9). The areal basis of these policies have been criticised on the grounds that the majority of socially disadvantaged children do not live in disadvantaged areas and that most children in disadvantaged areas are not themselves disadvantaged (Barnes and Lucas, 1975). However, these policies can also be defended, in that most schools serve particular neighbourhoods so that the social composition of a school is a factor affecting all its pupils

9

and its staff. This implies that the neighbourhood may affect the educational achievement of children. This possibility has long been recognised (Douglas, 1964; Robson, 1969) but firm evidence has been difficult to obtain. The issue is examined in Chapter 8, where a detailed analysis of variations in attainment among schools in Glasgow provides support for the notion of a neighbourhood effect.

Education and unequal cultures

Despite the various policies designed to enhance the 'strategy of equality' in the UK (Le Grand, 1982), class differences in educational attainment remain marked; racial differences in educational attainment in the United States have proved similarly resistant to compensatory policies (Herbert, 1976; Rogers, 1986). Attempts to explain the persistence of these differences have followed a number of avenues. Some researchers have sought to re-evaluate the relationship between education and the social structure (Bowles and Gintis, 1976; Apple, 1982a); others have sought to identify more subtle mechanisms within schools that may account for under-achievement among particular social groups.

As shown in the foregoing section, concern with equality of opportunity in education has been underpinned by the assumption that education makes a positive, if less than perfect, contribution to social issues. This assumption has not gone unchallenged: while some commentators have argued that education can reduce inequalities, others have argued that a more important role of education is to perpetuate existing social divisions. From this perspective, equality of opportunity in education is less of a solution to social problems than a device to legitimate and justify social inequalities. The foremost proponents of this approach, Bowles and Gintis (1976), have argued that the relations of authority associated with the workplace are recreated and taught in schools as part of the 'hidden curriculum'. For example, the deference to a teacher expected of children is similar to the deference expected by an employer of his (or her) employees; the hierarchy created by prefect and age-related systems within schools is similar to the hierarchies between employees created by skill and supervisory systems in the workplace. In addition, there are hierarchies of certification, which reflect (as well as give

Introduction

access to) varying job opportunities. Through these various mechanisms, the authors claim, the education system shapes future workers to the occupational structure, fitting some for unskilled jobs without career prospects and others for professional or managerial posts with well-structured careers.

In its original form, this approach has been widely criticised. For example, Finn, Grant and Johnson (1978) found the 'correspondence principle' overly deterministic and pointed to the many ways in which education has failed to provide industry with the workforce it requires. There is, however, considerable evidence that schools do influence the aspirations of pupils, albeit in more subtle ways than suggested by Bowles and Gintis. For example, Bernstein (1977) has shown how linguistic codes differ between social classes and how these differences may influence educational achievement because of the dominance of 'middle-class' language in schools. Similarly Labov (1972) has demonstrated the 'logic of non-standard English' used by Negro children in New York. These writers strongly resist the view that these differences make working-class or black children deficient: their cultures, linguistic and otherwise, are merely different from those of white, middle-class children. Similar themes have been taken up in ethnographic studies of class, racial and gender divisions in schools, which show how particular groups are alienated by the schooling they receive and respond in ways that restrict their future opportunities (Willis, 1978; Stanworth, 1981; Troyna and Smith, 1983; Davies, 1984; Roberts, 1986). Stated generally, this approach attributes under-achievement to the devaluation of certain cultures (working-class, non-white, female) within education systems dominated by professionals from, or assimilated into, the white, middle class. The issue is pursued in Chapter 7, which provides graphic illustrations of how social processes within schools curtail the aspirations of young black people.

In addition to this shift of focus from correspondence between school and workplace to more subtle mechanisms operating within the social milieux of schools, this critical approach to educational provision has been revised in other ways. In particular, several authors have stressed that the perpetuation of social and cultural divisions is not directly determined by economic factors, as Bowles and Gintis implied (Bourdieu and Passeron, 1977; Apple, 1982b). Thus, the notion of 'cultural reproduction' has been employed to

Introduction

analyse the ways in which the values of certain groups dominate the educational process (see, for example, Bernstein, 1982). This is illustrated in Chapter 6, where the nature and consequences of this kind of cultural dominance is examined in the context of the recruitment of foreign student-athletes to American universities.

Education and unemployment

A major social issue in contemporary Britain is unemployment, especially youth unemployment. Many initiatives addressing this issue are designed for those who have left school and are organised separately from the education service. However, the issue has also provoked renewed discussion and new initiatives concerning technical education. The Education Act of 1902, assimilated a pre-existing dichotomy between 'secondary' education (generally recognised as being for the elite) and 'technical' education (generally recognised as being inferior) into the state system (McCulloch, 1986). Four decades later, the Education Act 1944, attempted to reconcile secondary with technical education in the new context of the tripartite system of 'secondary education for all', but, as noted above, the technical sector was never effectively established. The question of technical education came to the fore again in the 'Great Debate' launched by James Callaghan in 1976 (DES, 1977). In this, as in earlier contexts, the issue was couched in terms of how the education service could most effectively meet the needs of industry. Initiatives in the 1980s reflect a new social and economic context: technical education (and training) has been offered in various guises as a palliative or panacea for the problems of rising youth unemployment as well as the rapid changes in skills required by industry. Thus, as Dale (1985, p. 7) argues, the aims of these new initiatives

> differ somewhat from those typically found in education-employment discussions due to the shadow of extremely high levels of youth unemployment and the possibility that they may be permanent. The aims are not confined to training young people for jobs but also include the need to adjust them to a new status, somewhere between work and non-work.

Introduction

Within schools, the TVEI, which is examined in Chapter 10, has been particularly significant.

EDUCATIONAL PROVISION, GEOGRAPHY AND THE USE OF CASE STUDIES

Although focusing primarily on Britain, the contributions to this book deal with a context that is far from uniform. For example, education authorities may be controlled by a political party that differs from the one in power nationally. Moreover, during the 1980s, the geography of these political variations has become more sharply delineated. This volume illustrates three aspects of the geography of education (also see Bradford, Bondi, Burdett, Peck and Quirk (forthcoming) for a discussion of education, space and locality). First, case studies from both England and Scotland are included, which demonstrate some of the differences and similarities between two educational systems that have separate histories and separate systems of administration and legislation, but which co-exist within one nation-state (also see Bell and Grant, 1977). Secondly, it is clear that the pressures for educational change do not develop uniformly over space. This issue is examined explicitly in Chapter 5, where the question of why some LEAs innovate earlier and more rapidly than others is addressed. Chapter 2 also utilises the comparative method, while several other chapters focus on single, unique places. The outcomes identified cannot be expected to be replicated elsewhere, but these studies attempt to identify underlying processes that operate in a variety of contexts. Thirdly, spatial patterns are important at a finer scale because systems of educational provision interact geographically with social patterns. For example, schools serve more or less well-defined residential areas the social composition of which varies. Consequences of this interaction between social and spatial patterns are explored in Chapters 4 and 8.

STRUCTURE OF THE BOOK

All the contributions to this volume are based on research papers presented to a conference organised under the auspices of the Social Geography Study Group of the Institute of British Geographers, which was held in

Introduction

Manchester in September 1986. The book is divided into two sections; the first focuses on political issues in the provision of education and the second on social issues in education. Falling school enrolments and financial constraints have prompted many education authorities to reassess and rationalise existing school systems. Examples of such responses are examined in Chapters 1, 2 and 3. Chapter 1 discusses the issue of provision for the 16 to 19 age-group with particular reference to Portsmouth, whilst Chapter 2 draws upon examples of current practice to suggest new ways in which the contentious issue of closing primary schools might be approached. Parental opposition to changes in provision is also highlighted in Chapter 3, which discusses the rezoning of secondary school catchment areas in Fife. Chapter 4 explores a related theme, namely the impact of parental choice legislation on school admissions in Edinburgh and Dundee. The analysis reveals, contrary to expectations, that the new legislation has been utilised to a greater extent by working-class than middle-class parents. These four studies explore, in different ways, the interaction between education authorities and local communities. Chapter 5 approaches policy-making in education from a different perspective, illustrating the relevance of concepts drawn from organisation theory in a comparative study of policy innovation. Following this study of new ideas and organisational structure among education authorities, Chapter 6 adds an international perspective in a study of foreign student-athletes recruited to American universities, stressing the importance of universities as organisations through which 'cultural colonialism' is propagated.

Turning to the second section, Chapter 7 presents a provocative study of the school experiences of ethnic minority groups, arising from a recent study sponsored by the Department of Education and Science. It is demonstrated that low achievement of black pupils is very frequently a consequence of social processes within schools. The question of variations in attainment among school-leavers is also pursued in Chapter 8, which demonstrates the effect of multiple deprivation in local residential neighbourhoods in a study of Glasgow. Policies of positive discrimination designed to counter the consequences of deprivation have enabled education authorities in Britain to identify 'social priority schools', where teachers' salaries are enhanced. Chapter 9 examines variations in the teaching forces at different schools in Coventry, considering the

Introduction

effects of Social Priority designation, location in the inner or outer city and the characteristics of catchment areas. Inadequacies of post-war secondary education underlie recent initiatives emphasising technical and vocational education including TVEI, which is examined in Chapter 10. The concluding chapter of the collection identifies gaps in existing research and sets out an agenda for the future.

NOTE

My thanks to Dr Michael Bradford and Dr Roger Cornish for their comments on an earlier version of this chapter, together with their encouragement in the preparation of this volume.

Part One

THE POLITICS OF EDUCATIONAL PROVISION

Chapter One

CONSULTING FOR CHANGE: THE POLITICAL GEOGRAPHY OF SCHOOL REORGANISATION IN PORTSMOUTH

Alan Burnett

INTRODUCTION

Perspectives on school reorganisation

Schools are being reorganised and closed in many British cities but there are relatively few studies of either the mechanics or political processes by which these changes are (or are not) being accomplished, (but see Brown and Ferguson, 1977, 1982; Bailey, 1982; Thomas and Robson, 1984; Bondi, 1987; and Adler and Bondi in this volume).

During 1981 and 1982 parents in Portsmouth were consulted over the future shape of sixth-form education. The local education authority (Hampshire County Council), faced with falling school rolls, declining numbers in sixth forms of several secondary schools, and the need to make savings, proposed that changes be made to sixth-form provision in the city. The local Area Office was charged with investigating the problem and, having consulted those potentially affected, recommending changes. Figure 1.1 shows the numerous organisations involved in making decisions or influencing them. The education committee of Hampshire County Council was the locus of municipal responsibility, with its decentralised Portsmouth Area Office officials and their advisory committee playing a key role. Governing bodies of schools and parents were consulted through official channels and other organisations and groups made their views known in other ways.

Discussions on the issue took place over a period of 18 months and a two-stage consultation exercise was mounted over (1) what form future sixth-form provision should take,

Figure 1.1: Official and Unofficial Organisations Involved in Decision-making over Sixth-form Provision in Portsmouth

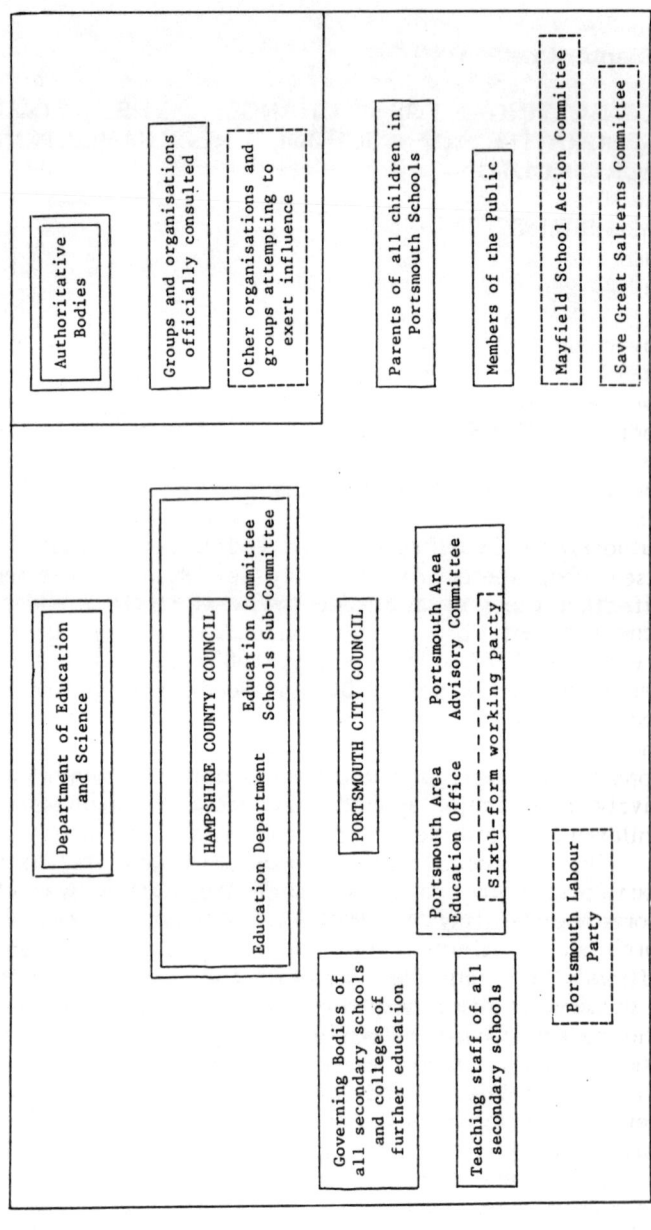

and (2) which existing secondary school should be closed to make way for a sixth-form college. Parents of all schoolchildren in the city were consulted as well as school governors, teachers and the public. The involvement of parents and the public over this issue provided an opportunity to explore the extent and efficacy of public involvement in an aspect of educational policy-making in one British city. As Boaden, Goldsmith, Hampton and Stringer (1982) have noted, it is over such administrative questions in education that public involvement is frequently encouraged.

Although there is one parent-representative on the governing body of every school in the city, parents are heavily outnumbered by political appointees, including the nominees of the majority Conservative Party. Governing bodies have been characterised by Packwood (1984, p. 271) 'as something of a catspaw; convenient at different times for promoting different purposes'. He argues that they are merely 'talking shops', with ambiguous objectives, uncertain authority and only indirect accountability. In Portsmouth, as elsewhere, political decisions of the authority (Hampshire) affecting the size of the education budget, the pattern of schooling, the pupil/teacher ratio, and curriculum planning, are beyond their scope. Although many schools have thriving parent-teacher associations, parents are rarely given any real authority on decision-making bodies and spend much of their time fund-raising and organising social events. Thus, opportunities for parents to be directly or even indirectly involved in major educational decisions affecting their children are limited.

This chapter focuses on the role of parents in this particular aspect of educational policy-making. Initially, Portsmouth's secondary school system is described, and the 'problem' of sixth forms, as defined and presented by officials, is noted. The main part of the chapter consists of a detailed analysis of the form, functions and outcome of the consultation process that was undertaken. The extent and pattern of involvement on the part of parents is noted, as are the roles of county councillors and officers who were centrally involved in the consultation process and its outcome.

As Honey and Sorenson (1984) have noted, closing schools is often very traumatic, not only for those whose school is in jeopardy but also for those making the decisions. Such proposals arise out of population loss or shifts, a decline in the birthrate, obsolete buildings, a prevailing attitude among educational administrators that learning is enhanced in schools large enough to provide curricular and staff flexibility, and fiscal retrenchment. School reorganisation and, in particular, school closure is an acute spatial political problem because benefits and costs that are not geographically uniform, are altered; for example, proximity to a school means a quick and safe journey for pupils and quiet weekends for neighbours. Thus '(c)losing schools destroys benefits while imposing additional costs on children and their parents when children are reassigned to more distant schools' (Honey and Sorenson, p. 119). The potential for conflict is therefore high.

The procedures for making school reorganisation and closure decisions are likely to be crucial. In Britain, central government legislation and guidelines (particularly the Education Act 1980 and subsequent Circulars) have ensured that parents are informed and consulted and have the right of appeal to the Secretary of State. One strategy employed by officials to reduce conflict is to present the causes as technical rather than political, thereby increasing the role of experts. But even the expert assessment of buildings, costs and pupil re-assignment, and the preparation of an array of alternatives with supporting background data, does not result in what Honey and Sorenson (p. 123) call 'a politically antiseptic result'.

A case study of this sort can, of course, be interpreted from one or more of the numerous theoretical approaches currently employed by social scientists and human geographers. In this study, locational conflict and managerialist perspectives are favoured. Thus, for example, there are reasons for anticipating that education officers will manage any public consultation in the interests of gaining acceptance for policies they believe in and (coincidentally) are in the interests of organisations to which they belong. It is also likely that participation by parents will revolve around individual schools that are threatened, and will only occur if parents see their children being adversely affected. Members of the public who live close to schools may also protest if a change in the status of a school is thought to adversely affect the amenity value of their neighbourhood.

CASE STUDY - PARENTS IN SCHOOL REORGANISATION

Secondary education in Portsmouth

Following major reorganisation in 1975, nine maintained comprehensive secondary schools were established in the city. In 1981, a total of 10,439 pupils were being taught in the secondary sector, of which only 750 were in sixth forms. While the two denominational and two single-sex schools drew their intake from broader areas of the city, entry to the remaining five mixed comprehensives was primarily from neighbourhood, feeder, middle schools. The city operated a 'designated area' system whereby parents were permitted to send their children to a school other than the one designated, only if there were 'extra' places available. Details of non-denominational secondary schools in the city are presented in Table 1.1 and the location of schools and their catchment areas is shown in Figure 1.2. Clearly, schools in Portsmouth vary in previous status, total enrolment, sixth-form enrolment, and (in so far as the number of 'enforced' pupils is a measure of unpopularity and the percentage of pupils from outside the catchment area is a measure of their popularity) the esteem in which they are held. Priory and Mayfield each had sixth forms of over 100, while there were between 50 and 100 sixth formers at Springfield, City Boys and City Girls, and Great Salterns.

It was estimated by local officials that all schools would have spare capacity by the end of the decade. Two (King Richard and City Girls) would, if parents continued to select schools for their children as they had in the past, be left with tiny intakes. Whereas in January 1981 the 15+ age-group in the city totalled 2,513, by 1993 it was estimated that it would decline to 1,470. Given a 20 per cent staying-on rate, it was feared that most, if not all, sixth forms could not be sustained.

Figure 1.2 shows that all but the two single-sex schools had catchment areas based largely on a neighbourhood principle. In the north-west of the city, King Richard serves the predominantly local authority housing estates of Paulsgrove and Wymering; to the east of the A3, Springfield's catchment area covers Cosham, Farlington and Drayton as well as Highbury (where the city's largest further education college is situated). Great Salterns caters for children in the east of Portsea Island, and Priory is the only non-denominational state secondary school in the south of

Table 1.1: Non-denominational Secondary Schools

	King Richard (KR)	Spring-field (S)	City of Portsmouth Boys (CB)	City of Portsmouth Girls (CG)	Mayfield (M)	Priory (P)	Great Salterns (GrS)
Former status (pre 1975)	Secondary Modern	Secondary Modern	Boys Technical High School	Girls Secondary Modern	Grammar School	Girls Grammar School	Boys Grammar School
No. pupils 1982	1032	1105	1588	899	1633	1218	1057
1981	1110	1088	1568	937	1637	1229	1124
No. in Sixth Form 1981	25	62	76	53	177	137	71
Sixth Form as percentage of total roll	2%	6%	5%	6%	11%	11%	6%
'Enforced' pupils (not first choice)	107	-	34	65	10	-	-

24

Table 1.1: continued

Pupils from outside designated area as percentage of places offered (1981)		1	12	54	36	27	20	16
Estimated intake (based on parental choice)	1981	194	241	360	175	363	259	217
	1985	14	200	307	88	312	260	156
	1988	76	152	260	71	282	250	150

Source: Area Education Office

Consulting for Change

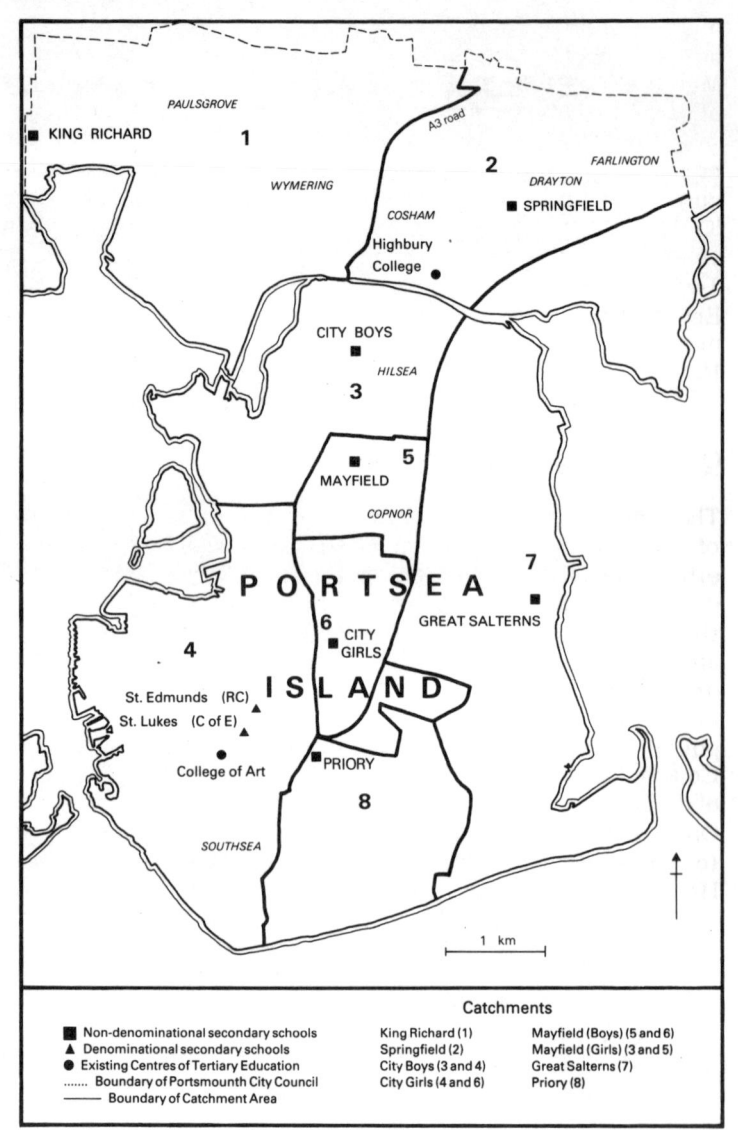

Figure 1.2: Secondary Schools and Catchment Areas in Portsmouth

the city. The catchment areas of Mayfield and the two single-sex schools (all more 'centrally' placed in the city) are more complex. Pupils are allocated to these schools by sex and by where they live. Thus, in Hilsea girls went to Mayfield and boys to City Boys, whereas Copnor boys were allocated to Mayfield and girls to the City Girls School.

This, then, was the spatial structure of secondary education in the city in 1981. Turning to the sixth-form curriculum, schools offered a varying range of both 'A' and 'O' level and less academic courses. In addition, many 16-year-olds attended courses at Highbury College of Technology, and the College of Art, Design and Further Education. Some travelled outside the city: substantial numbers living in the north-east of the city, attended Havant Sixth-Form College.

Official definition of the problem

There is no evidence that any concern regarding the quality of sixth-form provision in Portsmouth was articulated by either parents or teachers in the city. Nor, indeed, was it county councillors or school governors who put the issue on the agenda. Rather, it was education officials at Winchester and in the local Area Office, prompted by the Department of Education and Science (DES), who began to look critically at the size of some school sixth forms in the early 1980s. A policy to cope with future falling school rolls was required. County officials had already confronted the problem elsewhere in Hampshire, for example, in the Gosport area. Once officials had raised the issue, elected members began to voice their concern. Thus, in 1981, the chairman of Hampshire Education Committee was quoted as saying that

> while comprehensive schools in Portsmouth had done an excellent job and the results in sixth forms are very creditable indeed ... nonetheless it is easy (but undesirable) to shut one's eyes to the impending storm and let matters drift on in cost complacency. (Portsmouth News, 12 December 1981)

The projected falling school rolls, the small size of several existing sixth forms and the limited range of 'A' level courses being offered, the apparent success of sixth-form colleges and tertiary colleges elsewhere in Hampshire, combined to convince officials and councillors that structural changes in the school system were necessary. The possibility of a solution involving ad hoc arrangements whereby sixth-form pupils could transfer on a full-time or shared basis between schools, was rejected at the outset. Officials argued that there was no way of achieving an acceptable level of sixth-form provision, and making the necessary economies, if they retained the existing pattern of secondary schools.

Whilst clearly impressed by the need to take action, councillors evidently viewed the prospect with some trepidation. In Gosport, the loss of the sixth form of certain schools had been vigorously and successfully opposed and county councillors feared that the public might not readily accept the need for yet another major alteration in the school system, especially if it involved the closure of any schools. The chairman of the County's education committee was at pains to point out that

> these predictions (of falling rolls) were not the work of bureaucrats playing with theoretical calculations but were based on actual births and children in schools. (Portsmouth News, 12 December 1981)

Thus, the question of sixth-form reorganisation was initiated, highlighted and framed by officials. County councillors, mindful of the potential acrimony of such an issue, were already attempting to rally public support for change.

Aims of the consultation programme

Parents, and others, were to be consulted over any future changes in sixth-form provision. The local newspaper reported the issue under the headline 'Parents are to have a say in sixth form college plan' (Portsmouth News, 12 November 1981). The County's education committee resolved, in September 1981, to hold consultations (in accordance with the authority's normal practice) with members of governing bodies, the staff of all schools for 12- to 18-year-olds and the two further education colleges, teacher representatives, parents, the public and members of the local area advisory committee. Thus, while the views of parents and members of the public in the city were solicited, they were not the only ones with a stake in the issue whom the authority was anxious to consult. The outcome of the process was to be reported 'for consideration' by the Portsmouth Area advisory committee and the county authorities. There was no doubt, however, that the public and parents were to give their views within parameters laid down by the authorities. This feature was particularly evident in the case of the first questionnaire survey. The reply slip attached was for parents to express their opinion 'within the alternatives now under consideration'. Thus, the organisers of the consultation process (the Area Office) were constraining and focusing the debate. Precisely who was deciding what, was left ambiguous. They explained that they hoped that 'a majority opinion' could be obtained for consideration by the Portsmouth Area advisory committee, who then would advise the LEA. Official forms stated that governors, teachers, parents and the public were to be consulted. The order in which these groups were listed may or may not have been significant. However, ambiguity was also apparent in terms of the purpose, precise status of the exercise (particularly the significance of the results of the survey) and the mechanisms to be used.

Initial stages of consultation

As already noted, education officials at The Castle in Winchester and in the Civic Offices in Portsmouth, mindful of the Circulars emanating from the DES, saw the spare capacity and small sixth forms of certain secondary schools in the city as financially unacceptable and educationally undesirable. From the outset, the twin issues, of reducing the number of secondary schools (and thereby filling up those remaining) and providing a broader based curriculum for sixth formers, were interlinked. Alternative solutions, such as ad hoc arrangements to allow transfers between sixth forms (already taking place on a small scale), were ruled out. Nor was it thought feasible to solve the twin problems by closing one, or more, secondary schools. This 'fewer-secondary-schools-but-with-larger-sixth-forms' solution, was rejected by the Area advisory committee's working party on the advice of the Area education officer. Although it would have solved the problem in accommodation terms, this solution would not have provided large enough sixth forms to offer a broad range of subjects. By linking the two problems (half-empty secondary schools and small sixth forms), a strategy of 'killing two birds with one stone' could be pursued. In the minds of officials, creating a sixth-form or tertiary college on the site of an existing secondary school was a neat and probably a politically acceptable solution.

Tertiary and sixth-form colleges had been established as alternatives to traditional sixth forms in other parts of Hampshire. However, the Hampshire County Council Schools subcommittee did not publicly specify a preference for sixth-form college education in the city of Portsmouth at this stage. They certainly did not wish to be seen as forcing a particular solution onto one of their eight area subdivisions. Consultation with the local Area advisory committee, parents and teachers was, therefore, politically convenient as well as being a statutory requirement.

The officials in the Area Office defined four options. The first, preserving the status quo, was all but excluded in official documents and discussions. In explanatory notes accompanying the first questionnaire, the disadvantages of such a course of action were strenuously stressed, and the advantages minimised; elsewhere, it was described as 'unrealistic'. At public meetings, officials told audiences of the educational dangers of falling school rolls and the consequent reduction in the numbers of pupils in schools particularly in their sixth forms.

> Every effort must be made to point out the seriousness of the situation - falling rolls, size of sixth-form classes, restricted range of 'A' level choices and the non-viability of secondary schools in future. (Minutes of the Portsmouth Area advisory committee's working party)

The Area education officer and her colleagues duly availed themselves of every opportunity to demonstrate this point with the aid of graphs and statistics. Their views were echoed by councillors.

Nonetheless, retaining the status quo was included on the list of options in the first questionnaire. The three additional options were: (1) a mixed system of some secondary schools with sixth forms, and some without, (2) provision of a sixth-form college (replacing one existing secondary school), and (3) a tertiary college. The demerits of (1), the hybrid system, were also fully emphasised in both educational and social terms. It was also stated that

> such a system was in direct contradiction to the attitude of the authority in adjacent parts of the county since it created a first and second class division of schools. (Minutes of the Portsmouth Area advisory committee's working party)

There was no doubt that (2) and (3) were thought to have many more advantages to administrators not least because they involved the removal of one secondary school, thereby easing the problem of declining pupil numbers.

The advantages and disadvantages listed in the paper presented to the Area advisory committee were far from balanced in terms of the number of points made for and against each solution (see Appendix). It is also apparent that 'strength' of the arguments varied as between the options proposed. Some of the merits of options (1) and (2) - the least desirable scenarios, in the authority's view - can barely be seen as advantages at all. In other words, the authority, represented by the Area Office, took a far from neutral stance. Change was needed and the favoured solution was a sixth-form college located on the site of an existing secondary school, with all the remaining secondary schools catering exclusively for 12- to 16-year-old pupils.

Considerable effort was made to provide this information to as many parents as possible and to circulate the questionnaire. Attendance of the public at a series of meetings varied enormously, from 18 at King Richard, 60 at Great Salterns, to over 300 at Mayfield. Any reference to the closure of schools was studiously avoided (the public notices advertising these meetings noted merely that their purpose was to discuss the future sixth-form provision in the city). Inevitably, however, the issue of which school would provide the site for a college, was raised in questions put to officers and councillors at the public meetings. Some parents and the press interpreted the answers given by officials as suggesting that Mayfield School was a strong candidate to become the sixth-form college and, not surprisingly, Mayfield parents and Copnor residents were alerted at an early stage in defence of their school. Other parents, including those with children at Great Salterns, saw no threat to their own schools.

Governors were ambivalent about the need to make

Consulting for Change

Table 1.2: The Results of the First Ballot

	Parents	Teachers	Public	Total Votes cast for each solution	
Status quo	102	10	3	115	(24%)
Mixed system	81	3	5	89	(19%)
Sixth-form college	164	19	7	190	(41%)
Tertiary college	69	1	4	74	(16%)
Total votes cast	416	33	19	468	

(95 votes were in favour of more than one option)

Votes cast by catchment area	M(a)	GrS	KR	P	S	CB + CG
Status quo	86	7	1	1	15	5
Mixed	76	2	0	2	8	1
Sixth-form college	58	25	4	29	67	7
Tertiary college	29	5	1	10	24	5
Total votes cast	249	39	6	42	114	18
Votes cast as a percentage of total	(53%)	(8%)	(1%)	(9%)	(24%)	(4%)

(a) See Table 1.1 for school abbreviations

Source: Area Education Office.

alterations to a system that had been reorganised only just over a decade ago. Governing bodies of schools with large sixth forms, for example those of Mayfield and Springfield, were not convinced of the need for change. Some voted for the status quo; others, such as those at Priory, reluctantly, for a sixth-form college. Teachers also expressed reservations about structural changes. Most expressed a preference for a sixth-form college rather than a tertiary college, fearing school job losses if sixth-form pupils were taught in the further education sector. On balance, many were unimpressed, at the outset at least, by the case for such a radical change.

As Table 1.2 shows, relatively few parents and members of the public returned questionnaire ballot reply slips. Indeed, the low response rate, generated by this first consultation exercise, was startling. Only 468 completed forms were returned, a pitiful number given that there were 25,000 parents with school-age children in the city. Even taking into account that only 20 per cent of children in the city stay on at school after 16, the response rate was still very low. The response rate did, however, vary considerably between school catchment areas, with parents and public in the Mayfield area providing over one-half of the total. Apart from the 114 Springfield parents, the rest of the city chose largely to ignore the survey, presumably feeling that it did not directly affect them or their school. Many parents, other than those with children at Mayfield, either did not realise that establishing a sixth-form college would entail the closure of a secondary school, or assumed that it would not be 'their' school that closed.

As Table 1.2 shows, while there was some support for all four options, the sixth-form college option was the most popular. Mayfield parents were the only group to vote differently. Scrutiny of the Mayfield replies revealed that some 95 respondents stated categorically that Mayfield should not be chosen as the site of any college established. In comments accompanying the ballot, a number of parents indicated that they found it difficult to decide between the status quo option or the mixed system solution. Between these two possibilities, the vote was finely balanced with 43 per cent favouring sixth form in schools and 57 per cent a college system (tertiary or sixth form).

Comments made by parents and the public on the ballot papers gives an indication of the thinking behind the votes. Many agreed with the sentiments expressed by a Mayfield parent who wrote, 'the idea of a sixth-form college is marvellous but (should) not be based on an existing school'. More than 50 Mayfield parents cited educational and amenity reasons why Mayfield School should not be chosen as the site of a college. Another Mayfield parent stated, 'the school with the lowest success rate should be converted if this is to happen at all, at least the children would be offered a better education in compensation for their travel which would not be the case if Mayfield was to close.' Several cited specific objections based on a perceived threat to amenity: 'where would sixth formers park their cars ... not outside my house I hope'; 'the community life of the area will be cut to shreds'; 'this entirely residential area will be flooded with young adults with all the consequent problems especially of traffic and parking'. Many of those opposed to any change gave equally specific reasons in support of the status quo. Some parents did little to hide the fact that they thought the whole consultation exercise was a waste of time.

The results of this consultation were discussed by the local Area advisory committee at their meeting on 1 February 1982. They interpreted the results as a narrow but firm mandate for change and resolved that a sixth-form college could be established on the site of an existing secondary school. Lingering doubts about the wisdom of altering the system so radically remained in the minds of some members of the advisory committee, but they were reminded of the forecasted fall in school numbers. The result of the consultation exercise was interpreted as showing that a majority of the few parents and the members of the public who had participated (in addition to governors and teachers) favoured the sixth-form college option. It should be remembered that the advisory committee is a diffuse body comprising majority and opposition party councillors, teachers, governors and assorted other co-opted individuals. (The author was the sole parents' representative on this body.) Conservative Party councillors, evidently, had been convinced of the case made by officers. No organised opposition emerged, either in the Area advisory committee or, indeed, in the city as a whole. The Area education officers relayed their recommendation to the Schools subcommittee, who duly confirmed the recommendation in March 1982. County councillors requested that further consultations be held to resolve which school would provide the most suitable site for a college.

It is pertinent to speculate on what the result of a poll would have been had the closure of a secondary school (specified or not) been explicit in the four initial options. Many parents, it seems, thought that a sixth-form college could and would be set up alongside an existing secondary school or on a completely different site. It is quite possible that, if school closure had been mooted as a prerequisite for the college options, then the first two options would have received more support. What would have happened if a majority had voted against the college proposals is anybody's guess but (with the benefit of hindsight) it seems likely that the county would still have pressed ahead with a college plan.

The second stage in the consultation process

Having agreed in principle to establish a sixth-form college, there remained the thorny problem of which existing secondary school should be closed to make way for it. As already noted, no other site had been seriously considered, although plenty of such possibilities were advocated by parents. The working party of the Area advisory committee had meanwhile (during the initial consultation exercise) undertaken detailed 'feasibility' studies of the accommodation requirements of a sixth-form college catering for a notional 750 students. They reviewed the available premises and facilities at each of the non-denominational secondary schools in the city. This exercise identified only three schools suitable for conversion to a college. As the only state secondary school in Southsea, Priory was ruled out. The City Boys School was deemed inappropriate because it had a dual site, and the City Girls School because the cost of conversion was thought to be prohibitive. Springfield was too small and ill-equipped. Thus, by a process of elimination, the search focused on a short list of King Richard, Mayfield and Great Salterns. It is probable that the Area education officials had felt all along that Mayfield was the best site: at earlier public meetings they had inadvertently given the impression they favoured this school. Nonetheless, to justify their statutory duty, and for political reasons, a second round of consultations with parents and the public was planned.

More meetings were arranged with parents and the public. These were held at each of the three schools in question, during May 1982. (Not a timely calendar, given that the World Cup Football matches were being televised at the time.) Questionnaires were again distributed to parents at meetings and via their children. Messages written on the forms suggest that at least some of them reached the homes of pupils, but what happened to them thereafter is debatable. On one form was the message, 'Mum, gone swimming with Kev, see you later, Rob'. Governors and teachers at the three schools were also consulted. Suggestions as to the impact of the alternative proposals on the system and detailed guidance of consequent changes in catchment areas, accompanied the questionnaires. Respondents were asked to indicate the school they felt would be the most suitable for use as a sixth-form college. Space on the reply slip was left for additional comments.

This time, a greater response was forthcoming, though it was not always positive. Nearly 100 parents refused to vote for any one school and indicated their opposition to any major change, with comments such as, 'the phrasing of the paper precludes any choice of not having a sixth-form college ... I regard this as a cynical public relations exercise ...'; 'let the present system continue with minor alterations'; 'I don't wish any school to close ... if there must be a college ... build one'; 'I don't know the facilities of each ... whatever public opinion feels is sure to be totally disregarded ... the faceless ones at The Castle always know what is best for the rest of us'. One parent wrote, '... this is participation in decision-making gone mad ... the education authorities and teachers are better equipped to solve this problem, that is what they are paid for'. A variety of alternative sites for a college were suggested, including sundry buildings at Portsmouth Polytechnic, the Portsmouth High School, and Highbury College of Technology. Opposition to change, especially when it involved closing an existing school, was evident in many of the replies. 'I see this as a cynical application of the have-you-stopped-beating-your-wife variety, and further by naming three schools your obvious intention is to split your opposition and force them to defend their own schools and hence cancel each other out', was the comment of one parent. Many Mayfield parents clearly felt that their school had already been chosen: 'the choice of Mayfield is a <u>fait accompli</u> ... I conclude that this paper is some kind of whitewash exercise'.

The 98 parents who took part in the exercise, but refused to select a school for a college site, were a small minority. The results of the overall voting in this second ballot are subsumed in Table 1.3. In Table 1.3A, the total votes for different schools are shown by 'family' votes and individual parents: both totals are recorded by the Area Office, since there was no indication on the reply slip whether parents should vote jointly or individually. However the results are analysed, Mayfield came out as the site favoured by the majority of parents. Other members of the public were evenly divided between Mayfield and Great Salterns, while governors of the three schools overwhelmingly preferred Mayfield, including those at the school itself. Parents who declined to select a site did so for a number of reasons. Several stated that they did not know sufficient about the schools to make a choice, and others that they had just moved to the area, or were about to leave it, or intended sending their children to private schools. Teachers (voting either as members of the public or parents) favoured Mayfield, although polls organised in individual schools were less conclusive. Staff at King Richard were asked to rank their preferences (the only case in the entire survey of such a procedure being adopted) and the outcome clearly favoured Mayfield. At Mayfield, 95 papers were issued to teachers in an opinion poll organised by the staff association; however, 67 abstained, while 15 voted for Great Salterns and 13 for their own school. Teachers, in general, cited the centrality, size and educational record of Mayfield to justify their choice. One claimed that the vote against Mayfield was purely 'emotive and special pleading'.

One noticeable feature of the response by different sections of the community was that very few (85) members of the public who were not parents, governors or teachers, actually voted. Thus, in spite of the public meetings being advertised in the local newspaper (mistakenly under the heading of social announcements), only those who had a direct interest in the proceedings involved themselves to any significant degree. The general public, of course, did not benefit from having forms delivered to them via their children.

The turnout varied between school catchment areas (Table 1.3C) from 23 per cent in the case of Mayfield (already recognised as the most likely candidate), to 7 per cent in the King Richard School catchment area. In contrast, Great Salterns' parents had never been led to believe their school was threatened, and King Richard School, although advocated by the Portsmouth Labour Party as its choice, was declared a virtual non-starter at an early stage by virtue of its peripheral location (Figure 1.2). However, when comparing the turnout for different schools, it should be noted that the 'staying-on' rate and, thus, the number of parents of actual and potential sixth formers, varied considerably between schools.

The most significant results are that, although over

Consulting for Change

Table 1.3: The Results of the Second Ballot

A Total votes by different groups

Votes cast by:	Great Salterns	Mayfield	King Richard	Total
Individuals	1129	1452	450	3031
Families	896	1205	373	2474
Other members of the public	35	36	13	85

B Votes analysed by catchment area (family votes)

Catchment Area	Percentage voting for site of college to be at:		
	Great Salterns	Mayfield	King Richard
Mayfield	58%	27%	15%
Great Salterns	25%	62%	13%
King Richard	16%	46%	38%
City Boys/Girls	25%	67%	8%
Priory	30%	65%	5%
Springfield	29%	67%	4%

C Turnout by school catchment area (family votes)

King Richard	7%
Great Salterns	17%
Priory	5%
City Boys/Girls	5%
Mayfield	23%
Springfield	13%

D Proportion of family votes for each site

Site	Total votes cast	Source of Votes		
		Great Salterns	King Richard	Mayfield
Mayfield	1205	23%	9%	21%
Great Salterns	896	13%	4%	57%
King Richard	373	17%	24%	45%

Consulting for Change

	City Boys/Girls	Priory	Springfield
Mayfield	16%	11%	20%
Great Salterns	8%	7%	11%
King Richard	7%	3%	4%

E   Comments given in support of preferences

For Mayfield
32% commented. Of these 66% cited centrality, 39% cited accessibility, 14% cited building/facilities and 3% cited educational record.

For Great Salterns
33% commented. Of these 24% cited safety/accessibility for older children, 20% cited facilities, building, parking, 18% cited centrality, 5% cited scope for future expansion and 8% cited less deleterious effect on neighbourhood (than Mayfield).

For King Richard
24% commented. Points raised included buildings/facilities, schools vulnerable to closure, it was wanted by the estate (boost to area and should encourage school leavers to continue into a sixth form), King Richard pupils would be 'spread out' and this would improve their chances.

Source: Area Education Office

one-quarter of parents in the Mayfield catchment area favoured Mayfield, nearly 60 per cent voted for Great Salterns. Parents in all other catchment areas were in favour of Mayfield by substantial majorities (Table 1.3B). One can conclude from this analysis that, while a majority of the Mayfield parents who voted preferred Great Salterns, elsewhere in the city, as a whole, parents voted for Mayfield. It is clear that support for Great Salterns was substantially boosted by the votes of parents in the Mayfield catchment area. The distribution of support for Mayfield, on the other hand, was evenly spread throughout the remaining catchment areas (Table 1.3D). King Richard School drew little support from any part of the city, although a large minority of Paulsgrove parents voted for it.

One-third of parents taking part in this second stage of

the consultation exercise completed the section inviting additional comments. Some parents wrote at great length. The main reasons given for choosing Mayfield and Great Salterns are outlined in Table 1.3E. Not surprisingly, Mayfield was favoured because of its centrality and accessibility, but parents also viewed its buildings and facilities, and good educational record as advantageous. While some also thought Great Salterns was sufficiently accessible, it was its spacious site in a non-residential area that attracted parents (not least those of children attending Mayfield). The relatively few parents who voted for King Richard School, cited the vulnerability of the school, its capacious buildings, and the fact that the sixth-form college option had been welcomed by ward councillors.

For Mayfield parents, the prospect of having 'their' school disrupted (some pointed out they had moved to the Copnor area to ensure their children went to Mayfield) evidently caused a high 'turnout' and contributed to the size of the vote for Great Salterns and, to a lesser extent, King Richard. Written comments indicated that some local residents feared the amenity value of their neighbourhood would be threatened by parking congestion, noise, and anti-social behaviour. One local resident wrote to the chairman of the Area advisory committee's working party: 'the proposal will turn the Mayfield area from a high rateable value neighbourhood into a car and motorcycle park'. A number of parents in the Mayfield catchment area were frank enough to explain their preferences in terms of 'anywhere-but-here' arguments.

Official recommendations and decisions

Having received a report containing the results of this second consultative exercise from the area education officer, the Area advisory committee voted by a large majority (20 to 5) for Mayfield as the site of a future sixth-form college. The resolution was proposed by Councillor N (chairman of Great Salterns Board of Governors) and seconded by a teachers' representative. Opposition came from a few Conservative Party councillors. These included Councillors H and J (the chairman) who had previously faced a stormy public meeting at Mayfield School. Thus, the committee followed the recommendations of its working party, which had identified three schools as suitable candidates for the site of a sixth-form college. They were also influenced by the fact that the majority of the parents, who responded in the consultation exercise, favoured Mayfield.

Three weeks later (July 1982) the Schools subcommittee of Hampshire's education committee meeting in Winchester voted (17 to 3) in favour of <u>Great Salterns</u>. At this meeting, neither the Portsmouth area education officer nor the chairman of the Area advisory committee spoke in favour of Portsmouth's choice, that is, Mayfield. In defence of his actions, the chairman was quoted as saying, 'the impression was given that public and professional opinion had been unanimously or near unanimously in favour of Mayfield but statistics proved that their opinions were only marginally in favour of that school ... we looked at Great Salterns and thought it would make an ideal American-style campus' (<u>Portsmouth News</u>, 15 September 1982). County councillors of the majority party, taking their cue from one or two influential Portsmouth councillors, opted for the public's second choice.

Several explanations of this decision were provided by those involved and, also, by those whose initial recommendation for Mayfield had been overturned. Councillor J stated, 'closing a school requires much soul-searching ... both are fine schools and the case was finely divided' (minutes of Portsmouth Area advisory committee meeting). What actually seems to have happened is that several members of the Schools subcommittee visited Portsmouth prior to the committee's decision. They were shown the three schools and were convinced by their hosts (local Conservative councillors, including J and H) of the wisdom of choosing Great Salterns. One of those involved in this successful lobbying maintained that, 'on balance, Great Salterns was the only logical choice ... the subcommittee visited these schools, had all the evidence available locally and made their choice on the basis of fact' (<u>Portsmouth News</u>, 3 September 1982). Mrs B (the parent of a child at Great Salterns School who subsequently organised a petition objecting to the choice of that school) wrote to the local newspaper: 'while allowing for difficulties of members who may have scant knowledge of the school and its position in Portsmouth we cannot understand their reasons for suddenly choosing Great Salterns for closure' (<u>Portsmouth News</u>, 26 October 1982). Several letters to the editor also expressed surprise and indignation that the views of the advisory committee had been disregarded and the ballot, to ascertain the views of parents and others, had apparently been ignored. Mr O'N of Copnor, commenting on Councillor H's justification of the decision, wrote: 'according to the votes submitted by parents it is not their choice and this included the parents of the present and future pupils of Mayfield School who were afforded the same opportunity of voting' (Portsmouth News, 15 September 1982).

A Conservative county councillor, also a member of the Schools subcommittee, told a newspaper reporter that, 'consultations were important but it was up to the education committee to make the decision. I agree Mayfield is geographically ideal for a sixth-form college but older children will be able to travel longer distances than younger children' (Portsmouth News, 15 September 1982). Councillor M, Leader of the Conservative-controlled Portsmouth City Council, claimed that his view that Mayfield should be retained in its present form was 'shared by many residents and parents in the north-west of the city' (Portsmouth News, 28 October 1982). He suggested that the results of the survey did not reflect the view of the majority of parents and local residents.

In response to those who defended the decision to choose Great Salterns, the president of the National Union of Teachers in Portsmouth (who was also a member of the Area advisory committee) maintained that the issue had been 'bedevilled by the actions of local politicians', and that the much-publicised activities of a minority of parents living in the immediate vicinity of Mayfield had further 'muddied the waters'. One of the advisors to the Mayfield action committee was a local clergyman who was quoted as saying, 'the thought of destroying Mayfield is terrible ... it will kill the community ... I will be liaising with councillors' (Portsmouth News, 23 May 1982). This liaison, and the vociferous opposition of Mayfield parents and Copnor residents, was the key to the success of the action committee. County councillors in the north of Portsea Island certainly all advocated, and voted for Great Salterns. A letter to the local newspaper stated: 'it is obvious that Great Salterns was chosen as a sixth-form college so that councillors of the Mayfield catchment area can avoid disfavour with their electors' (Portsmouth News, 11 August 1982). This comment focused on the possible electoral aspects of the decision.

In September, 1982 the County education committee

Consulting for Change

formally ratified the recommendation of their Schools subcommittee, despite sustained last-minute lobbying by Great Salterns' parents. In July, the City Council had voted for a sixth-form college 'somewhere in Portsmouth but not at Paulsgrove'. Labour Party councillors argued the case for King Richard School. This was ruled out, but resolutions in favour of Mayfield and Great Salterns were also defeated (8 to 28 and 16 to 17, respectively). Thus, stalemate prevailed amongst city councillors who, in any case, had no authority over the matter. Elected representatives could not bring themselves to make, or support, an unpopular choice.

By this time, a 'Save Great Salterns' group had been formed. Leaflets had been distributed in the east of the city, and a petition with 4,207 signatures been raised. Parents of children at Great Salterns School who organised the petition had little difficulty in obtaining signatures: they encountered only two refusals. A detailed dossier was compiled and presented to the Department of Education and Science in London. The parents' group argued that Great Salterns had a good educational and extra-curricular record, excellent community ties and that parents had been misled during the consultation exercise by the fact that only Mayfield had been mentioned as a likely site for a sixth-form college, creating a sense of false security.

Criticism continued within official bodies as well as in the local press. At their October (1982) meeting, members of the Area advisory committee made some forceful comments about the lack of leadership shown by their chairman, who had voted against his committee's recommendation. The Area education officer, who had chosen (or had been instructed) to say nothing in defence of the Mayfield plan at the relevant Schools subcommittee meeting, also came in for criticism. A resolution, proposed by Councillor N, expressing surprise and indignation that the recommendations of the Area advisory committee had been rejected without explanation, was passed. The charge of political expediency was levelled at those councillors who represented wards in the north of the city and who had, despite the results of public consultation, acceded to the demands of the Mayfield parents and Copnor residents. The chairman of the County education committee defended the decision: 'I am aware that the Area advisory committee, after extensive research, found that figures of opinion were marginally in favour of Mayfield but ... the decision was finely balanced ... Great Salterns is an attractive campus and older children will be able to travel to it' (Portsmouth News, 14 May 1982).

Both statutory and non-statutory objections to the County decision were submitted under Section 12(3) of the Education Act 1980. As already noted, the organisers of the 'Save Great Salterns' campaign also visited Elizabeth House in London and were received by Under Secretary Dr Rhodes Boyson. They reported a 'sympathetic' hearing to their plea that Great Salterns Secondary School should not be closed. They claimed that on no occasion had the County Council advanced a clear and logical argument in favour of their decision. Despite these protests, the Minister confirmed the decision and a sixth-form college is now established on the site of Great Salterns School. It received its first intake of 350 sixth-form pupils in September 1984.

CONCLUSIONS

The education authority had a duty to consult those affected by any proposed sixth form reorganisation. They gave overall responsibility for the mechanics of consultation to the Portsmouth Area Office. The local Area advisory committee constituted the major channel of communication between the LEA and the public, and its working party did most of the detailed background investigations. It is clear that the public were not sure if they were making decisions or merely taking part in the process by which decisions were being made (Richardson, 1983). The main function of the consultation exercise, from the officials' viewpoint, was to mobilise support for a major change in sixth-form provision. The disadvantages of the status quo and a mixed system of secondary schools (some with sixth forms and some without) were stressed to governors, teachers and parents. Had this not been done, and had the intended closure of an existing school been emphasised in the first round of consultation, then a vote for such a radical change would not, in all probability, have been secured. As it was, support for such a change was achieved without difficulty. The lack of concerted political opposition on the part of those representing schools with relatively large and successful sixth forms, allowed the proposal to be pursued.

The separation of the two rounds of consultation is open to varied interpretation. Was it a genuine and logical attempt to first seek the views of parents on the need for change and the type of solution preferred and then to seek views on the location of the sixth-form college? Or was it a cynical tactic to keep opposition weak and divided? The evidence suggests a mixture of both. If the primary aim of officials and Portsmouth Area advisory committee members was to consult, the conduct of the consultation exercise could certainly have been improved. The timing of polls, publicity for public meetings, design of the ballot forms and wording of background information, and method of distribution forms to parents and members of the public, are all open to criticism.

The evidence supports the view that it is those members of the public, whose interests were directly affected, who participated (i.e. Mayfield parents and local residents in the first and second ballots, and Great Salterns parents thereafter). Neighbouring residents, fearing for their amenity, attended public meetings, and parents responded to the consultation exercise. Some went to a great deal of effort to write long and closely-argued comments in their replies.

Why, having gone to the trouble of consulting teachers, parents, governors and the public in Portsmouth, did county councillors not accede to the wishes of the majority? The answer may well be that (Conservative) city and county councillors, representing wards in the north of the city, wished to show they possessed political clout. They avoided opposing the vociferous demands not to close Mayfield as a secondary school. The fact that their colleagues from elsewhere in the county on the Hampshire Schools subcommittee apparently took their advice and voted for Great Salterns, was due to their personal influence and party cohesion. A belief that Portsmouth councillors 'knew best' also seems to have prevailed at Winchester.

In one sense, therefore, the decision in favour of Great Salterns over Mayfield was a re-assertion of the views and authority of elected representation over officers and the teaching profession. This was in direct contradiction to what had appeared to be the likely balance of influence at the start of the exercise. An intuitive, and essentially ward-oriented, assessment of public opinion over the issue was relied on by certain key councillors. Councillors J and H, in particular, were reluctant to accept the results of the consultation exercise in the face of concerted, albeit localised, public pressure. Education officials did not intervene when it mattered. They did not defend the results of a consultation programme that they had framed and which had been agreed by elected members and representatives of teachers and parents.

This case study has provided an opportunity to compare and contrast the various forms of consultation and participation that took place over the issue of sixth-form provision in Portsmouth between 1981 and 1983. Parents in the city, and others who took part in the official consultation exercise, preferred a sixth-form college at the site of Mayfield School. Influential councillors, pressurised by a well-organised campaign by parents and residents associated with this school, successfully hijacked the carefully-laid plans of their officials. Parents with children at Great Salterns School (which eventually became the sixth-form college) belatedly petitioned, and made statutory objections, in vain. The majority of parents behaved naively, officials manipulated public opinion and some councillors treated it cynically. Some teachers and governors were disenchanted by what they saw as the 'political' motives of those who had the ultimate authority to choose a new college site. In the decision-making process, the officials won the first round by placing the issue on the agenda and by securing a majority for a sixth-form college at Mayfield. However, the majority was slim. Local politicians were able to use the finely-balanced result to justify switching to a more vulnerable target, that is, Great Salterns where parents had not been alerted to a possible threat to their school. The Secretary of State endorsed the County Council's proposal and in a sense, therefore, sealed the victory for local Conservative Party councillors. Those who argued, or thought, that the views of a majority of parents, expressed in an officially-organised programme of consultation, should prevail, were defeated. Thus, the influence and connections of a few elected members of the majority party ensured that a sixth-form college opened on the site of Great Salterns School in September 1984.

Boaden et al. (1982) have suggested that experienced politicians and administrators may use consultation to manipulate a consent that would otherwise be withheld. This is exactly what happened in Portsmouth. A contentious issue was, in part, defused by giving the impression of moving the locus of decision-making from the LEA (in Winchester) to the city. The mechanics of consultation were manipulated to attain the result that officers, from the outset, thought was best. Only at the last minute did certain influential elected members upset this solution. Although they subsequently incurred the wrath of one group of parents, the secondary school system was 'altered' accordingly.

This case-study of consultation over the creation of a new sixth-form system in the city can also be viewed from different theoretical perspectives. In the introduction, it was suggested that educational officials (and councillors, unless they had powerful and specific electoral reasons for acting to the contrary) managed participation in order to minimise dissent, and to legitimise the goals and policies to which they were committed. This is congruent with the managerialist thesis. Thus, the conduct of consultation over sixth-form provision served to divide and rule potential opposition. In addition to the two-stage consultation, this goal was pursued by the selective dissemination of information and the ambiguous presentation of the consequences the proposals raised.

The conflict depicted by Honey and Sorenson is also evident in the disagreements and arguments that were generated in Portsmouth over secondary school reorganisation. Mayfield School, in particular, was defended by local parents and residents by virtue of its educational merits and the perceived loss of amenity that would follow if it was designated as a sixth-form college. The existing school was deemed to be a 'salutary' facility and the proposed changes would entail the introduction of a 'noxious' one.

In this case, changing the school system, and in particular closing a school, altered the balance of perceived benefits and costs to the public in different neighbourhoods. The extent and pattern of response by parents and residents to these proposals for educational change reflected fears about loss of amenity and educational disadvantage.

APPENDIX

Extracts of final paper from working party to area advisory committee for 1st February 1982

This paper summarises the findings of the Working Party set up by the Area advisory committee to examine factors involved in the future education of pupils aged 16 to 19 in Portsmouth. The advantages and disadvantages of each of four solutions to the problem are set out below.

Solution 1

Make no change: all nine secondary schools to continue to try to build up sixth forms

Advantages
1. No further action would be required at this stage.
2. Certain schools would continue to offer reasonable sixth forms during the 1980s.
   Mayfield
   Priory - probably
   City Boys - possibly
   Springfield - possibly

Disadvantages
1. It seems inevitable that some schools would fail to keep their sixth forms. As numbers in the main schools drop they will be less able to 'subsidise' their sixth forms with staff time from the main school. This is likely to be the case at:

   King Richard   In order of possible effect
   City Girls   on the schools
   Great Salterns

2. As numbers contract in the sixth forms, there would be fewer courses offered and students would be likely to continue to leave the city, probably in growing numbers.
3. As the Portsmouth staffing component disappears there would be growing difficulty in supplementing reasonable sixth-form provision in other secondary schools.

   City Boys/Springfield   In order of possible effect
   Priory   on the schools
   Mayfield

4. The opportunities for post-16 pupils in schools managing to retain their sixth forms would not increase. From experience elsewhere in the County it would not be very likely that many pupils from the 12-16 schools

would join the sixth forms in the 12-18 schools. The present comparatively limited choice is likely to become more marked.
5. By 1988 the total numbers in secondary schools will have reduced by one-third. We shall be obliged for the sake of educational opportunities to be offered to the pupils to close at least one secondary school otherwise the schools will be too small to offer comprehensive education.
6. The morale of staff within schools with the most rapidly declining numbers would deteriorate.
7. Teachers in the city have expressed their preference to maintain the status quo, but in view of the serious reduction in numbers of pupils they realise that this is not a possible solution. They realise that in a fairly short time the city would have reached Solution 2 below.

Solution 2

Retain sixth forms in some secondary schools: designate some schools 12-16: some 12-18

Advantage
1. Certain schools will not be affected by the necessity to change staff and pupils will be allowed to continue as they are.

    Mayfield
    Priory
    City Boys - query
    Springfield - query

Disadvantages
1. Post-16 pupils in the schools without sixth forms will be handicapped. They will be offered sixth forms in 12-18 schools or F.E. College or sixth-form college outside the city. From Gosport experience they are unlikely to transfer·to 12-18 schools. The number leaving for sixth forms outside the city would probably grow.
2. There is a general feeling that this solution would result in first and second class schools and that parents would

wish to choose 12-18 schools at 12+ thus emphasising the differences between the schools.
3. There would be a need in the future to close one or two secondary schools as numbers in the main schools will decline by one-third. Closure would probably be required by 1987, but would not be possible much before that time. This would not solve the sixth-form problem.
4. The Combined Teachers' Association have expressed themselves against this solution.

Solution 3

Create a sixth-form college in an existing school and designate the remaining schools 12-16

Advantages
1. A sixth-form college would be a strong institution which experience elsewhere shows would attract post 16 pupils and offer a wide variety of courses.
2. The closure of one school for 12-16 pupils would increase the numbers in the remaining schools.
3. This is the solution that the main body of teachers would support. The majority would prefer no change but recognise that falling numbers will force some kind of change.
4. The overwhelming number of Governors of existing schools and colleges prefer this solution.

Disadvantages
1. One school would have to lose its 12-16 provision and the parents of the pupils who had expected to go to that school are likely to be deeply concerned.
2. Pupils who would be unable to go to the school, which was closed for the 12-16 age group, might be required to travel long distances while they were in the main school.
3. There would have to be more transfers of teaching staff round the city than would result from redeployment under solutions 1 and 2.
4. Fears have been expressed that main schools would suffer if sixth forms were removed, mainly because of the transfer of staff, who have taught in main school and sixth forms, to the sixth-form colleges.

Consulting for Change

5. Some teachers have expressed the view that their opportunities to teach in main school and sixth form would disappear.

Solution 4

Tertiary college in conjunction with the College of Art, Design and Further Education using an existing Secondary School: re-designate schools 12-16 and use one as a base for the tertiary college

Advantages
1. A strong institution which would attract post-16 pupils and offer a wide variety of courses of all kinds.
2. The closure of one school for 12-16 pupils would increase the numbers in the remaining schools.

Disadvantages
1. A split site would remove the advantage of a Tertiary College which is to mix pupils studying all kinds of course and allow students to study some academic/some practical subjects.
2. A split site institution is less likely to have the sense of identification with the College which helps student/teacher morale. The sense of organisational unity could be so much diminished as to offer no real advantage over two separate institutions.
3. The Governors and teachers of existing schools are not in favour of this solution.
4. There would have to be transfers of teaching staff round the city and some possible amalgamation with staff from the College of Art.
5. Fears have been expressed that main schools would suffer if sixth forms were removed, mainly because of the transfer of staff, who have taught in main school and sixth forms, to the sixth-form colleges.
6. Less need. Duplication of choice.
7. Limit parental choice. No institution based on School Regulations.

Chapter Two

DELEGATION AND COMMUNITY PARTICIPATION: AN ALTERNATIVE APPROACH TO THE PROBLEMS CREATED BY FALLING PRIMARY SCHOOL ROLLS

Michael Adler and Liz Bondi

INTRODUCTION

For the past 10-15 years, education authorities have been faced with a very substantial decline in the size of the school-age population. As a result of a drop in the birthrate, primary school rolls have been falling steadily since the early 1970s and, by the early 1980s, there were about 30 per cent fewer primary school pupils than there had been ten years previously (see Central Policy Review Staff, 1977). Although primary school enrolments are expected to pick up somewhat during the rest of this decade and into the 1990s, the projected increase in numbers will only partially offset the previous decline. Secondary school rolls began to fall in the late 1970s with the transfer of smaller cohorts from primary schools. This decline is expected to continue until the early 1990s, by which time secondary school numbers will be some 30 per cent lower than they were at their peak in the late 1970s. The increase in numbers thereafter is expected to be very gradual. (1)

The decline in the size of the school-age population has created a number of problems for the organisation and structure of educational provision. Among these problems are whether staffing levels should be reduced (to bring about financial savings) or maintained at current levels (to improve pupil-staff ratios and to protect the curriculum); whether surplus school places should be taken out of use by, for example, closing annexes, removing temporary accommodation, and amalgamating or closing schools (in order to 'rationalise' provision and achieve financial savings) or kept open (to allow for parental choice, sustain local

Delegation and Community Participation

communities or provide a residue of capacity to cater for the eventual upturn in pupil numbers); and whether to canvass more or less radical alternatives to existing schemes of provision (for discussion of these issues, see Briault and Smith, 1980; Dennison, 1983, 1985; Forsythe, 1983; MacFadyen and McMillan, 1984; Audit Commission, 1986).

For most of the period in question, decisions about how to respond to falling school rolls have been made against a background of financial constraint in the public sector and a squeeze on local authority expenditure (Hewton, 1986a). For the last few years, legislation to increase parental choice and to make schools more responsive to parental preferences has also been influential (on the English legislation see Stillman and Maychell, 1986; and on the Scottish legislation see Adler, Petch and Tweedie, 1987). These background factors have produced forces pulling in opposite directions and, at times, central government has appeared to be seeking mutually incompatible objectives. Certainly, the choices posed by falling school rolls are among the most controversial and far-reaching that confront educational policy-makers. This is, in part, because decisions (particularly to close schools) frequently generate a great deal of conflict in the short-term and because, at the same time, they necessarily have long-term consequences.

In this chapter, we examine how two education authorities, operating within different legislative frameworks, have responded to decreases in the number of primary-school pupils. One of these authorities (Manchester) is in England and the other (Tayside) is in Scotland, and we first describe the statutory positions and respective powers of central and local government north and south of the border. There are other contrasts between the two authorities we have selected for study. Manchester serves part of a major conurbation and is, essentially, an inner urban authority. Much of Tayside is rural and although this study focuses on the city of Dundee, there are clear differences of scale. What Dundee and Manchester have in common is a rapid decline in pupil numbers and our aim is to use these authorities to <u>illustrate</u> different strategies for dealing with this problem. Although very different, in both cases the strategies adopted generated much conflict. The last section of this chapter discussed how this conflict could be reduced. We argue that the roles of local communities, local government and central government must be reconsidered, and this leads us to advocate a set of procedures in which responsibility for making decisions about the provision of schooling is delegated to local communities. In doing so, we attempt to advance the current debate about local participation in decision-making, which is usually couched in general terms (see, for example, Fudge, 1984; Hambleton and Hoggett, 1984), by examining in depth one particular issue.

LEGISLATIVE FRAMEWORKS

The English system

(a) **The statutory position**
Prior to the Education Act 1980, local education authorities (LEAs) in England and Wales were obliged to submit to the Secretary of State for Education and Science any proposal to open, close or substantially alter a maintained school. Under the Education Act 1980 (Sections 12 to 16), LEAs were, for the first time, able to implement such proposals without central government approval. This possibility, however, remains subject to strict limitations. It applies only to proposals affecting non-denominational schools in connection with which no formal objections (see below) are raised. Moreover, the Secretary of State retains the power to 'call in' any proposal for approval even in the absence of local objections. In practice, the great majority of cases are still submitted to the Secretary of State: between 1980 and 1985 only 14 per cent of school closures were determined locally (Audit Commission, 1986).

The English system has attracted a number of criticisms. First, it has been argued that because the statutory procedures deal with individual institutions rather than plans for areas, the system militates against the development by LEAs of comprehensive strategies for the reorganisation of provision. Secondly, decisions running contrary to all that is implied by Department of Education and Science (DES) guidance on the closure of schools have led to the call for written explanations of the Secretary of State's decisions. Thirdly, disquiet has arisen not merely because of differences of opinion regarding the fate of particular proposals but also over the manner in which the Secretary of State has used his powers. In particular, lengthy delays in coming to a decision have prompted demands that the Secretary of State be required to respond to submissions from LEAs within a specified period (Meredith, 1984; Sallis, 1986).

(b) **Requirements for consultation**
The procedures governing the closure, alteration and establishment of schools require LEAs to publish statutory notices setting out their proposals, to which formal objections may be raised. These objections must be signed by ten or more local government electors and must be submitted to the LEA within two months of the issue of the statutory notice concerned. Objections are then forwarded to the Secretary of State, together with any observations the LEA wishes to make. Whilst there are no statutory requirements for LEAs to consult directly with local people before the formal publication of proposals, DES Circular 2/80 strongly exhorts LEAs to do so. The recommendation is repeated in DES Circular 2/81, which also urges LEAs to consult with diocesan authorities and teacher interests.

Existing consultation procedures and practices have not prevented the issue of school closures becoming one of intense conflict. It is widely assumed that LEAs have been slow to contract provision for this reason:

> In the face of what is often strenuous and well-organised opposition, councillors and officials have sought alternatives to closure. (Taylor, 1981, p. 25)

Ruffett and Chreseson (1984) suggest that the outcome of such conflict is not always to the benefit of the local education service:

> Battles for the survival of individual schools are often based on and won by local or out-dated myths concerning their supposed quality; on efficient self-advertisement, often carried out at the expense of the real work of the school; on the political clout of one or other party; or on more or less rationalised self interest. (p. 34)

However, Meredith (1984) argues that objectors are in a very weak position legally:

> individual or pressure group interests at local level are rarely able to make serious inroads into LEA policy by use of the statutory machinery ... (which offers) ... little opportunity to the objector to present an effective case. (p. 221)

The general point to be made is that neither non-statutory nor statutory consultation over school closures serves to promote constructive public debate about falling enrolments. Local communities almost invariably adopt defensive postures in relation to individual schools proposed for closure and, indeed are rarely invited to comment upon more general issues regarding the organisation of provision.

(c) **DES guidance to local authorities on the issue of falling school rolls**

Alongside the powers of intervention enjoyed by the Secretary of State, the DES has issued guidance to LEAs on falling school rolls and school closures. DES Circulars 5/77 and 2/81 give expression to the policies of both Labour and Conservative governments to secure savings in the education budget as the school-age population declines. Circular 5/77 exhorted LEAs to:

> make the most realistic assessments possible of future population trends ... and to ... examine systematically the educational opportunities offered to children in their schools and to consider how the premises, both buildings and sites, might best be used. (para. 3)

The closing of under-utilised schools was explicitly encouraged:

> the general policy of the Secretary of State will be to approve proposals to cease to maintain under-used schools. (para. 7)

The Circular went on to set out the factors to be considered by the Secretary of State in connection with proposals for closure.

Four years later, rather fewer places had been removed from use than envisaged by the DES and Circular 2/81 pressed LEAs to make more concerted efforts to reduce surplus capacity, employing what Meredith (1984) describes as:

> interventionist terms reminiscent of the then Labour government's 'request' to LEAs to submit plans for comprehensive reorganisation in 1965. (p. 211)

In this instance, LEAs were requested to:

> inform the Department by 31 December 1981 ... about the expected number of surplus places up to 1986, and their plans for taking places out of use. (para. 27)

(d) **Financial controls**
Turning to financial arrangements, the revenue available to LEAs is influenced, but not determined, by the distribution of central government grants. The new grant system introduced in 1981/2 is based on 'grant-related expenditure assessments' (GREAs) for each service. In education, client groups are identified for each part of the service (such as primary school pupils), together with a national average unit cost. In the assessments for each LEA, certain adjustments are made in respect of physical features of the area (for example, allowance may be made for sparsity of population) and the incidence of social disadvantage. Some allowance is also made for the effects of enrolment decline by basing assessments on enrolments for the preceding rather than current year.

The relationship between GREAs and grant allocation is extremely complex because of arrangements for equalisation and because of the application of penalties for high spending (see Bramley and Evans, 1981; Boddy, 1984). What is indisputable, however, is that the total level of central government finance available has been reduced over the last few years. Nevertheless, since rate support grant is a general rather than specific grant, and since local authorities retain (within limits) the power to raise rates, education budgets continue to be determined locally. Thus, central government cannot determine how many teachers an LEA employs or how individual schools are staffed.

LEAs also retain control over the provision of school accommodation, except that borrowing consent is required for major capital projects. In periods of expansion, this requirement gives central government an important means of influencing both local expenditure and the character of the school system. When numbers fall, borrowing consent may be granted subject to conditions, such as the closure of another school. However, since little new building is now required by LEAs, loan sanctions are only rarely brought into play.

The Scottish system

(a) **The statutory position**

Prior to the Education (Scotland) Act 1981, the approval of the Secretary of State for Scotland was required before an education authority could close a school or implement other major changes in educational provision. However, this requirement was repealed by the 1981 Act, in line with what Scottish Education Department (SED) Circular 1074 describes as:

> the Government's policy of relaxing, wherever possible, detailed controls over local authorities and enabling local decisions to be taken locally. (para. 19)

Instead, under Section 6 of the 1981 Act (inserted into the Education (Scotland) Act 1980 as Section 22A), education authorities were required to carry out consultations with prescribed persons and to 'have regard to' any representations they make. The Secretary of State's approval is still needed for proposals that require pupils to travel considerable distances (Section 22B), or that adversely affect the position of denominational schools compared with non-denominational schools (Section 22C and 22D). However, in all other cases, decisions about closing schools are wholly devolved to the education authorities (the Regions). The only exception to this is a reserve power retained by the Secretary of State under Section 70 of the Education (Scotland) Act 1980 to declare an education authority to be in default of any statutory duty placed upon it (in particular, to consult as prescribed) and to order the authority to discharge that duty. However, the Secretary of State has no other powers of intervention. Thus, the SED has rather more limited statutory powers than the DES and there are correspondingly fewer statutory controls over local authorities in Scotland than in England and Wales.

(b) Requirements for consultation

In Scotland, the procedures governing the closure of schools and other changes in educational provision require the education authority to advertise any proposal in brief in a local newspaper and to make available full details on request. For each kind of proposal, regulations prescribe precisely which local people must be consulted (Education (Publication and Consultation Etc.) (Scotland) Regulations 1981). However, the legislation does not specify what form the consultation should take and does not give objectors the right to refer the matter to the Secretary of State, unless an authority in some way defaults on its statutory obligations to consult. Beyond this, the authority must 'have regard to any representations' on its proposals that it receives from persons it is required to consult. This requirement is so vague that, electoral considerations apart, there is nothing to stop a local authority from proceeding with proposals in the face of widespread local opposition.

(c) SED guidance to local authorities on the issue of falling school rolls

Even before the passage of the 1981 Act, the SED had taken a less interventionist approach to the problem of falling school rolls than the DES. Thus, the SED did not issue any circulars analagous to DES Circulars 5/77 and 2/81. From time to time, particularly in the last year or two, ministers have drawn attention to the fact that spending on schools has not fallen as fast as pupil numbers, and have criticised education authorities for 'wasting' resources by maintaining more schools than are required for the reduced number of pupils. However, these ministerial statements have never been translated into more formal guidance and, other than by relaxing the requirement to consult, it is not clear how this could be done.

(d) Financial controls

Although there are substantial differences in the political control exercised by central government in regard to school closures north and south of the border, the financial controls are very similar. In Scotland the position is as follows: each year the SED calculates the number of teachers required to meet minimum staff complements (for primary schools), or 'Red Book' standards (for secondary schools). To these totals the government adds a 'flexibility factor' (primary schools) or an 'additional margin' (secondary schools), both of which are specified in the government's public expenditure forecasts. In recent years, as pupil numbers have fallen, staff complements and 'Red Book' standards have fallen. The 'flexibility factor' and the 'additional margin' have also been reduced, the net result being a cut in the resources allocated to local authorities for the employment of teachers through the rate support grant.

Financial controls enable the SED to influence how many teachers are employed by the Regions. However, the provision of accommodation is left entirely to the regional authorities (except that capital borrowing consent is required for projects over £1 million involving premises for a new school or new premises for an existing school). Although the number of primary school pupils has fallen since 1974, the number of primary schools increased slightly during the 1970s, generating a substantial decrease in the number of large primary schools and a corresponding increase in the number of small or medium-sized primary schools. Since 1980, the number of primary schools has decreased slightly as has the average primary school roll.

The financial controls outlined above are not, in themselves, designed to either encourage or discourage the closure, amalgamation or 'rationalisation' of school provision. As in England and Wales, education authorities may spend more on staffing than the amount allocated in the rate support grant. Borrowing consent may be conditional on the closure or 'rationalisation' of other schools, but this form of control is again of little significance because of the paucity of new capital projects.

Summary

Local authority responses to falling school rolls have been more closely regulated by central government in England than in Scotland. However, in neither case have the statutory mechanisms resulted in the degree of contraction apparently intended by central government. At the same time, the procedures adopted by local authorities have often generated a great deal of conflict. This is illustrated by the two case studies which are summarised below. Although the approaches adopted by the two authorities (Manchester and Tayside) were very different, and each was subject to a different set of statutory controls, the two authorities were alike in that both imposed unpopular decisions on local communities in the face of strenuous opposition.

THE CASE STUDIES

The Manchester example

Manchester is a sizeable metropolitan district with a population of about 400,000. Under continuous Labour control since well before local government reorganisation, by the early 1980s the City Council had become a stage upon which the conflict between the left and right wings of the Labour Party was played out with particular ferocity. Until 1984, the Labour Group remained under the control of the right-wing and, between 1980 and 1984, many left-wing councillors were expelled from the Group for voting against the Party Whip. On a council where Labour held at least two-thirds of the seats, this group of left-wing councillors formed the effective opposition to the ruling group, Conservative and Alliance members often voting with the latter. Both county secondary school provision and the entire maintained primary sector were reorganised during this period. The general viewpoint of the controlling group was informed by egalitarian principles and the administration can, perhaps, best be described as 'paternalistic'.

(a) **Background**
The reorganisation of county secondary school provision attracted much attention because the original plan, which involved the replacement of all existing school sixth-forms by a system of separate sixth-form colleges, was rejected by the Secretary of State, Sir Keith Joseph, on the grounds that three of the school sixth-forms had 'proved their worth' and should not, therefore, be discontinued. But, despite the conflict generated by the plan, both between local parents and the local authority and between the LEA and central government, the reorganisation was praised by the Audit Commission (1986) because it involved a strategic (rather than piecemeal) response to falling enrolments leading to the eventual relinquishment of about 75 per cent of the potential surplus accommodation.

The development of plans to reorganise primary school provision is less well known but, in terms of the broad strategy eventually adopted by the LEA, was similar (for a full discussion, see Bondi, 1986). Primary school numbers in Manchester began to fall in the late 1960s as a result of population out-migration and this decline was intensified as the effects of the downturn in the birthrate began to be felt. The primary school population fell by about 45 per cent by the time numbers stabilised in 1986. No more than a very modest increase in numbers is expected in the foreseeable future.

Some consolidation of provision occurred during the 1970s as the LEA took the opportunity to close 15 primary schools, most of which were small, inner-city schools in Victorian premises. However, by 1982 about 30 per cent of primary school places remained vacant. Only in 1979 did Manchester education committee institute a systematic procedure for reviewing primary school provision. Initially, this took the form of a series of local area reviews, conducted by education officers and education committee members, each dealing with five to ten primary schools. These reviews set out a number of options for contracting provision as numbers fell, but the usual response elicited from the public in the course of consultation was that no changes should be made. Consequently, the contraction of provision implemented as a result of these reviews was very limited. Thus, between September 1979 and April 1981, reviews were completed for only twelve of the 33 local areas in the city. The closure of six schools and the amalgamation of six pairs of infant and junior schools to form single primary schools resulted. These took place between July 1980 and December 1982 and led to the eventual removal of about 1,500 places. However, at this time, enrolments were falling by an average of 2,700 per year. In the early 1980s financial circumstances also became extremely difficult. The city faced recurrent budgetary crises as central government imposed severe penalties on 'overspending' authorities. The rapid contraction of primary school provision came to be seen as a vital means of securing savings. To this end, the local area reviews were abandoned in 1981 in favour of a city-wide approach aimed at securing a reduction of at least 15 per cent in the number of places available.

(b) The 1982 plan for rationalisation

To meet this goal, the education department drew up, and the education committee accepted, a plan to rationalise county and voluntary primary school provision. This plan set out the LEA's arguments for rationalisation, specified the criteria informing the selection of schools for closure or amalgamation (including surplus capacity, local housing developments, quality of accommodation and accessibility of alternative schools), and put forward proposals to close or amalgamate 45 of the city's 162 schools. If fully implemented, these proposals would have reduced primary school capacity by 20 per cent. Thus, Manchester became one of the few LEAs to develop a comprehensive strategy for dealing with falling rolls in primary schools.

(c) The consultation process

In June 1982, this plan was sent out for consultation and the LEA arranged a series of public meetings in different parts of the city to explain the plan and to elicit the views of those affected. Many of the proposals aroused vehement opposition: public meetings were noisy and heated, the local education department was inundated with objections, councillors were lobbied intensively and the local press printed many letters on the subject as well as reporting several colourful demonstrations. Consultations were also held with the denominational authorities (28 per cent of primary schools in Manchester are Roman Catholic and 21 per cent are Church of England) and the teachers' associations. The Roman Catholic Schools Commission raised some objections and negotiated an extended period of implementation for several of the proposals affecting its schools. However, the Church of England and all the teachers' associations gave their full support to the LEA's plan.

For most of the areas covered by the LEA, Manchester education committee put forward a single solution to the problem of enrolment decline. This tended to encourage defensive responses from local people, simply expressing the view that the school concerned should not be closed. However, in a few localities the public were presented with two options. Unfortunately, this did little to broaden discussion about the organisation of provision because the terms of the consultation undertaken by the LEA invited comments only as they related to individual schools.

Nevertheless, opponents questioned all aspects of the plan and raised issues of general relevance. For example, they challenged the LEA's demographic data; they argued that adequate allowance had not been made for the effects of new housing developments; they accused the LEA of imposing cuts; they stressed the vital role of primary schools within local communities; they drew attention to problems of access and to hazards facing children travelling to different schools.

Parents and other local people, however, found few allies. A small number of teachers and headteachers supported local campaigns against school closures, but most heeded the advice of their representatives in the teachers' associations and on the education committee and accepted the LEA's plan (which included arrangements for redeployment and explicitly excluded compulsory redundancies). Among elected members, the four Liberals opposed the plan and rallied in support of the one school proposed for closure in the wards they represented. However, the Conservatives supported the ruling group leaving only dissident left-wing Labour members as potential allies for local protestors. Several of these councillors supported local campaigns in their wards but they failed to develop any unified counter position to that of the ruling group. Consequently, opposition remained fragmented. Turning to MPs representing the constituencies concerned, four of the five were Labour and refrained from conflict with a Labour council despite approaches from their constituents. However, the fifth, Conservative, MP representing a Manchester constituency was very active in support of St Andrew's Church of England Primary School. Although this failed to impress the education committee, his efforts to arrange a deputation to the Secretary of State for Education did eventually yield the desired result.

After the three month period allowed by the LEA for consultation had elapsed, the plan was revised. Ten schools were reprieved at this stage and one not included in the original list became the subject of a closure proposal. However, the overall thrust of the plan remained intact, implying the removal from use of approximately 15 per cent of existing primary school accommodation. The revision of the plan suggests that the LEA was responsive to the views of local people. However, not only were the majority of objections ignored, or at least not met, but the LEA also conceded to the demands of middle-class communities in south Manchester rather than those of working-class communities in the inner-city. This was, perhaps, ironic for a Labour council but illustrates the more general observation that attempts to involve the public in decision-making frequently operate to the advantage of middle-class groups (Boaden, Goldsmith, Hampton and Stringer, 1982). Further, in spite of the presentation by the LEA of criteria for selecting schools for closure or amalgamation, for both practical and political reasons it proved impossible to apply these systematically.

(d) **Intervention from the centre**
Some of the proposals, for example those involving the amalgamation of infant and junior schools to form all-through primary schools under one headteacher, did not require approval from central government. In respect of the remainder, the statutory procedures were then brought into effect with the publication of notices in November and December 1982. Local action groups continued their protests and the LEA duly sent a substantial dossier of formal objections to the Secretary of State who relayed his approval of all but two proposals in April 1983. This permitted the implementation of the plan to commence in time for the school year commencing in September 1983.

The rejection by the Secretary of State of plans for county secondary school reorganisation a year earlier is described by Meredith (1984) as an example of: 'the evident readiness of the central department to use its powers in a highly interventionist manner' (p. 217). Consequently, Manchester LEA was only too well aware of the veto power of the Secretary of State when the plans for primary school reorganisation were drawn up. In the event, the rejection by the Secretary of State of two proposals (affecting St Andrew's Church of England primary school and Victoria Avenue infant and junior schools) did not jeopardise the overall plan. However, these rejections were regarded by some as a purely partisan move designed to irritate the local education committee and support likely Conservative voters. There is also some evidence to suggest that the education committee was extremely wary of rekindling the middle-class opposition which the Secretary of State had effectively supported in the secondary school reorganisation and therefore refrained from proposing any contraction of provision in the localities concerned. This suggests that the division of powers between central and local tiers of government became a mechanism for pursuing partisan disputes rather than ensuring that local educational provision was reorganised in the most appropriate manner for the area concerned.

The Dundee example

Tayside is a medium-sized Regional Authority with a population of about 400,000. Much of the Region is rural, containing a large number of small rural schools. However, it also contains a number of small towns, for example, Arbroath, Brechin and Forfar, a large town (Perth) and a city (Dundee). Administratively, the education department was, until very recently, split into three geographical divisions with across-the-board responsibility for educational provision in Angus, Dundee and its hinterland, and Perth and Kinross. From regionalisation in 1975 until the local elections of May 1986, Tayside had a Conservative administration and in the Regional election of May 1982, the Conservatives gained an absolute majority (the party breakdown was Conservatives 27, Independents 2, Labour 12, Scottish Nationalists 5).

(a) **Background**
In common with other education authorities in Scotland, Tayside Region had experienced an overall decline in primary school rolls from 1973 onwards, with a decline in secondary school rolls following some five years later. Although the Director of Education produced a report on falling school rolls in Tayside in 1979, which outlined some of the problems to be addressed, the Region did not attempt to formulate a general policy on the issue. Instead, the Director was instructed to bring forward for discussion proposals for making the most effective and efficient use of scarce resources for school education. However, because of the absence of a general policy and because of the internal structure of the education department, what this meant in practice was that the three divisions continued to tackle the problem in an ad hoc way.

Attempts to review primary school provision in Dundee Division were made in 1977/8 and in 1981. On the first occasion, attention focused on five schools in the West End of Dundee, all of which had surplus accommodation and two of which were in a very bad state of repair. Several alternatives for future provision in the area were canvassed and the issue provoked a great deal of concern within the local community. The Region finally agreed (after 18 months of deliberation) to close Blackness primary school with effect from the summer of 1981. (2)

In August 1981, primary school provision in another area of the city was reviewed. The area chosen contained three non-denominational and two Catholic schools, all within a few hundred yards of each other. The director of education wished to explore the possibility of reducing the number of non-denominational schools from three to two (with the closure of Balerno primary school) and the number of Catholic schools from two to one (with the closure of St Andrew's Roman Catholic primary school), and consultation took place on this basis. Both closures were opposed by parents; in addition the closure of Balerno was opposed by Dundee Labour Party and the closure of St Andrew's was opposed by the Roman Catholic hierarchy. In the case of the former, the Conservative administration used its majority to force the closure decision through. In the case of the latter, the Roman Catholic establishment invoked its statutory right of appeal to the Secretary of State to prevent the closure of St Andrew's.

Despite this setback, the Region's record on school closures during the period 1977 to 1983 was, in its own terms, rather successful. It picked its targets with some care, going for small and arguably non-viable rural primary schools (in Angus and Perth and Kinross Divisions), or schools in urban areas, which were in very bad physical condition located close to others serving the same community. However, the Region neither evolved a general policy nor even a general set of guidelines. Nevertheless, until this point, it had been pretty successful at 'muddling through' (for a more detailed discussion of this case, see Adler, 1985).

(b) **The 1983 school closure programme**
In October 1983, Tayside Region education committee considered and approved a report from the director of education, which proposed the closure of another seven primary schools. Six of these were in Dundee Division and they included three non-denominational and one Catholic primary school within the city itself. In the case of the city

schools, the proposals to begin the statutory consultations were approved by 16 votes to 12, with Conservatives on one side, and Labour, the Scottish Nationalists and the five co-opted members on the other.

The report itself was an extremely brief document comprising one and a half pages of text, to which were attached maps showing the delineated areas of the schools concerned; data on existing school rolls and estimates of future rolls based on the number of pre-school children and anticipated housing developments; a description of the existing buildings and an estimate of the savings likely to accrue from the closure of each of the seven schools. Apart from a brief reference to the fact that

> falling school rolls and public expenditure constraints make it important to monitor provision to ensure that it is sound and cost effective,

neither the report itself nor the discussion papers which were prepared for the parents of the children affected by the proposals outlined the case for closures in general or sought to justify the particular closures advocated.

Meetings were planned to take place over the November/December 1983 period although, in the event, the meetings relating to two of the proposed closures (of one non-denominational and one Catholic school) were subject to Interim Interdicts granted to parents in the Sheriff Court, on the grounds that estimates of the savings that would result from closing the schools were misleading and inaccurate. Although the Interim Interdicts were subsequently recalled, consultations in relation to the future of the Catholic school were substantially delayed.

(c) The consultation process

Well-attended public meetings were eventually held at each of the schools threatened with closure. At each of the four city schools, parents' action groups were set up and called further public meetings. Meetings were also held for parents of other named schools which would be affected by the proposals and the matter was discussed by each of the relevant Schools Councils and Community Councils and, in the case of the Catholic school, by the Roman Catholic hierarchy. Petitions were circulated, write-in campaigns were organised and deputations appeared before the

Delegation and Community Participation

education committee. Ernie Ross MP (Dundee West, Labour) played a very active role, using his position to raise the matter in the House of Commons. School closures became a major political issue in Tayside and, for several months, hardly a day passed without some new allegation or counter-allegation being reported in the local press.

Although several of the objections were specific to the schools concerned, there were a number of general responses which applied to all, or nearly all, the proposals. Thus, parents complained that they were not asked to consider any alternatives to the authority's choice of schools to close and that the only options they were asked to consider related to the school to which their children would be sent, and the speed with which the proposals would be effected. They wanted to know why 'their' school had been chosen and, at least in Dundee, complained that they had not been given information on all the city's schools. They criticised the Region for placing too much emphasis on financial factors and insufficient on educational and social factors. At the same time, they claimed that the financial data were misleading and inaccurate, particularly the alleged revenue savings. Many of the parents expressed considerable satisfaction with the schools their children attended and were concerned that the closures would bring about a serious diminution in educational standards. Population forecasts were often criticised, particularly for not taking proper account of the effects of new housing, and concerns were frequently expressed about road safety, particularly where children would have to cross an additional main road.

In spite of the strength of feeling generated by the proposals, the director of education recommended that five of the six non-denominational schools should close and, in February 1984, after five hours of discussion, the education committee accepted the director's recommendations by margins of 16 to 12 or thereabouts, Labour, Scottish Nationalist and co-opted members opposing the closures. The one school to escape the axe was a small but nonetheless viable school serving a rural community on the northern fringe of Dundee, where 'powerful social reasons' (largely concerned with arguments against sending children from a rural area to school in the city) persuaded the director to withdraw the proposal for closure.

(d) **Forms of redress**

Rather than accepting defeat, opponents of the closures stepped up their campaign by invoking all the available legal remedies: 750 parents submitted placing requests for the schools threatened with closure; an action was raised in the Court of Session as a result of which the Regional Council was served with an Interdict prohibiting it from reaching a final decision on the future of Invertay primary school; an allegation of maladministration was prepared for submission to the Local Government Ombudsman; and a complaint was lodged with the Secretary of State under Section 70 of the 1981 Act. These actions were all based, at least in part, on alleged irregularities in the consultation process.

A formal complaint about the consultation procedures adopted by the Region was sent to the Secretary of State at the end of March and the Region was subsequently asked for its comments on the allegations. In his reply to the complainants, the Secretary of State made it clear that the Region should not take any steps to close any of the schools until he had decided whether or not the consultative procedures complied with the regulations. However, the Secretary of State's timetable made it virtually impossible for the Region to complete the necessary procedures, even if fully exonerated, in time for the new session. At the end of May, the chairman of the education committee, accepted the inevitable and announced that all the schools under threat of closure would re-open in August 1984.

(e) **The power of the local authority prevails**

At the end of September, the Secretary of State dismissed complaints about the consultation procedures adopted by the Region, finding that they had 'complied substantially' with the duties placed upon them by the legislation. The education committee then instructed the chief executive to report on the legal options and the director of education to report on the educational factors that needed to be borne in mind in pursuing the closure programme. Thus, the stage was again set for a decision.

The education committee had already decided to take no action on the closure of St Margaret's Roman Catholic primary school, but decisions needed to be reached on the future of five remaining schools. After four and a half hours of debate, the committee decided that all five schools should close. Except in the case of one of the rural primary

Delegation and Community Participation

schools where the decision was unanimous, all the decisions were by margins of 15 to 10 or 11. The battle lines were still the same. The action groups all committed themselves to continue their opposition although it was by now clear that support had waned.

The Region decided against holding another set of public meetings and objectors were instead given 28 days to make written submissions. In January 1985, the education committee confirmed that four of the five schools would close at the end of the session, the fifth school being given a temporary stay pending further discussions.

Although it looked as though the end was near, the Labour Group urged parents to take further legal action. Another action of Interdict was raised in the Court of Session, but no procedural improprieties were found and the action was dismissed. One of the remaining action groups then gave up, on the grounds that: 'there was no point in continuing the struggle when there was no way of changing the authority's mind.' In a final act of resistance, another action group submitted a complaint of maladministration to the Local Government Ombudsman.

Turning to the fifth school, accommodation at the nearby non-denominational school was not sufficient to cater for all the children who would be displaced by its closure. However, the Catholic hierarchy agreed that part of a neighbouring Roman Catholic primary school could be used as an annexe, despite the disapproval of a large majority of the parents concerned. On the basis of a survey it had conducted, the Region was confident that the future intake of this school would correspond to a two class entry but, to make sure, it now proposed to impose a limit of 66 on the primary 1 entry and the director of education was asked to set the consultative process in train. Serious doubts about the validity and accuracy of the survey had been raised by the Labour Group and one of the remaining action groups submitted another complaint to the Secretary of State arguing that the survey had been defective. The complaint was submitted in April 1985 but, within ten days, the Region had, on its own initiative responded to the complaints. There were to be no more delays this time and, in spite of both this complaint and the Secretary of State's comments a year before, the Region announced its intention of closing this school. The action group tried and failed to obtain another Interdict preventing the Region from closing the school pending the Secretary of State's decision but were given leave to appeal. However, this subsequently lapsed when the Secretary of State dismissed the complaint. All five primary schools closed at the end of the session and the only crumb of comfort for the action groups was a statement that no more primary school closures would be brought forward until the regional elections of May 1986.

Manchester and Dundee compared

It is clear that the problem of falling enrolments in primary schools provoked rather different responses from the two authorities examined. Manchester adopted a comprehensive, authority-wide approach to the issue and formulated a set of general criteria, which were to be applied in individual cases. Tayside, on the other hand, adopted a piecemeal approach to the problem, proposing the closure of individual schools on an ad hoc basis. Thus, compared with Tayside, Manchester was able to provide stronger justification for its proposals, although it remained unable to apply its stated criteria systematically. By and large, both authorities put forward single rather than multiple solutions, and invited comments only as they related to individual schools. Although Tayside called a halt to further school closures, the authority remained unmoved by the substantial opposition prompted by the 1983 closure programme and used its majority on the council to force the proposals through. The outcome might have been different had central government been in a position to intervene not merely over procedural issues but, as in England, over the proposals themselves. By contrast, in the Manchester case, the Secretary of State drew upon the statutory powers available to him to sustain objections to proposals affecting two (predominantly middle-class) primary schools. Similar objections from working-class communities in other parts of Manchester were not sustained and there is clearly considerable force to the assertion that the Secretary of State used his powers in a partisan way.

LEARNING FROM THE PAST AND LOOKING TO THE FUTURE

In spite of the many differences between the two cases discussed above, they also exhibit some important features

Delegation and Community Participation

in common. In both cases, the proposals provoked a great deal of opposition from parents of children at schools that were threatened with closure and from the communities in which these schools were located. Likewise, in both cases, schools were closed in spite of this opposition. Although both authorities were eventually able to enact their proposals without making any major concessions, the price of their 'success' was a high degree of conflict between themselves and the local community. It is also apparent that existing arrangements in England frequently generate conflict between local and central government. Within the institutional arrangements that exist in England and Scotland today, such conflicts are probably inevitable. However, these institutional arrangements are not immutable and, within a different set of arrangements, it might be possible to substantially reduce (although probably not fully exclude) conflict.

Existing arrangements suffer from further shortcomings. Whether, as in the case of Tayside, education authorities approach the issue of falling rolls on a piecemeal basis or whether, as in the case of Manchester, comprehensive plans are developed, there is mounting evidence of a widespread failure by education authorities to implement rational procedures for deciding which schools to close (Audit Commission, 1986). This is chiefly because the 'experts' in local education departments are enjoined to devise disinterested and cost-effective proposals, while parents (and others in the community) usually respond in self-interested ways, with little regard to overall efficiency. Consequently, even where (as in Manchester) the education authority puts forward and attempts to justify criteria for retaining or closing schools, local opposition is likely to prevent their systematic application.

Turning to the role of central government, the existing statutory frameworks in England and Scotland attempt, in different ways, to balance the interests of central and local government. Whether either framework does so satisfactorily is debatable but certainly neither deals adequately with the interests of the local community. In England, although local community interests are, in theory, protected by the veto power of the Secretary of State, this power can be exercised in a highly partisan manner, as the Manchester case illustrates. In Scotland, the situation is no better since the preferences of local communities, as expressed through consultation, can be ignored (as was the case in Dundee) by a determined local authority. Moreover, recent government proposals to amend the regulations to give local authorities more discretion over school closures by reducing the requirements for consultation to merely 'making available' to parents and others the reports that go to the education committees are likely to worsen rather than improve the position (Munro, 1986).

The failure to arrive at rational decisions, together with the conflict generated by the issue of school closures, undermines the legitimacy of local government. Thus, in seeking alternatives to the existing procedures, we should look for ways in which to further the objectives of rationality, legitimacy and consensus.

1. Rationality. The objective of rationality would be met by arrangements that ensure schools are not kept open when there are good arguments for closing them and that schools are not closed when there are good arguments for keeping them open. Clearly, what constitutes a 'good argument' may be contested. Under existing arrangements local authorities are often insufficiently sensitive to the arguments for keeping individual schools open, while local communities frequently fail to appreciate the general case for closing schools. Promoting rationality calls for institutional arrangements that will reduce both types of 'error'.

2. Legitimacy. The objective of legitimacy would be met by ensuring that national, local and community interests are all brought to bear on the decision-making process. This would involve the identification of these interests and the design of an institutional framework that would allow each of them to be expressed.

3. Consensus. As far as possible, consensus should be maximised and conflict minimised. School closures will always be contentious. However, a framework sensitive to the different interests of different parties would reduce much of the conflict that the existing procedures encourage.

Designing a framework for making decisions about the provision of schooling that meet, or at least advance, these objectives requires consideration of the roles of three parties: central government, local government and the local community. Calls have emerged from various quarters to clarify and revise the way in which functions and responsibilities are divided between local and central government (Rhodes, 1981; Jones and Stewart, 1983; School for Advanced Urban Studies, 1983). We endorse such calls but wish to pursue the issue further by suggesting an expanded role for local communities in making decisions about educational provision. Boaden et al. (1982) note that opportunities for the public to influence education policy-making are limited to council elections and pressure group activities. Both methods are indirect: by voting, the public express a generalised preference for one particular political party and the package of policies with which it is associated; and by engaging in pressure group activities, they attempt to achieve particular policy objectives. However, neither method allows the public to participate, in any meaningful sense, in the process of decision-making and, as the examples discussed here demonstrate, arrangements for 'consulting' the public do not qualitatively alter this. To change the basis upon which the public are involved would require the delegation of appropriate decisions from the local authority to the local community. This would not only increase the influence of local opinion and enhance the legitimacy of local government, but would also strengthen the responsibility of the local community for the efficient organisation of local schooling, and increase the rationality of decisions. Lastly, conflict between the local authority and local communities would be reduced.

Some of the implications of such a system of delegation have been discussed by Hambleton (1978). In the context of area-based approaches in local government, he differentiates between decentralisation, delegation and devolution. Decentralisation is essentially administrative and refers to the physical dispersal of decisions to local offices, delegation implies entrusting certain decisions to a body other than the local council, whereas devolution refers to a more general transfer of political authority to a body other than the council. There are overlaps between these three, delegation occupying the central position and straddling the administrative and political aspects of area-based approaches. Thus, delegation implies (a) decentralising aspects of administration from departments responsible for the authority as a whole (or large divisions thereof) to bodies dealing with small areas within the authority, and (b) devolving responsibility for particular, well-specified, political decisions from the council to these bodies.

Returning to the broad division of functions and responsibilities between central government, local authority and local community, the following would appear to reflect the respective interests of each tier.

1. The role of central government should be to balance the competing expenditure claims of education and other public expenditure programmes; to lay down a statutory framework within which the education authorities actually responsible for the provision of primary and secondary education can operate; to allocate resources to education authorities; and to suggest priorities and promote good practice.
2. The role of local government should be to decide, within the broad financial constraints laid down by central government, what priority should be given to education at a local level; to formulate, within the statutory framework, general policies for local educational provision; and, where appropriate, to allocate resources to local communities.
3. The role of local communities should be to decide, within the broad financial constraints imposed by the local authority and, in accordance with more general policies, what pattern of schooling would be best suited to the needs of the local community.

In relation to primary school provision, this framework requires local government to assume two new tasks: first, that of allocating resources to local communities and, second, that of identifying and explaining the implications of alternative ways in which these resources could be spent. The choice between these options could then be delegated to people at the local level. The division of resources between local communities could be achieved in a number of ways. Education authorities might wish to allocate a fixed sum for each school-age child in the community. However, they would be free to adjust this to take into account the age of the child, the density of population, the extent of social deprivation in the area, or the age and size of the existing school buildings. Although we have suggested that resources would be allocated to local communities, it does not follow that money would actually change hands: there would really be no good reason for this, since it would be sufficient for the local community to have control of a notional budget. The authority would, of course, have to determine what would count as a local community. Where school catchment areas are in operation it would probably make most sense to use groups of contiguous catchment areas. In many cases,

Delegation and Community Participation

these might comprise the primary school catchment areas associated with a given secondary school. For example, where there are, say, five feeder primaries for a particular secondary school, the local authority would decide the total resources available, suggest alternative uses for these resources (for example, retaining all five schools, closing one and keeping four open, or merging two or more of them in some way), suggest criteria for evaluating the various options, and identify the pros and cons of each option. However, the choice between these options (and any others the local community wishes to consider) would be made by interested parties at the local level.

The local authority would have to determine the procedures local communities would be required to follow in reaching these decisions. Subject to certain minimum standards designed to ensure the participation of all interested parties, there could be considerable variation between the procedures adopted by different authorities. Some might opt for representative procedures while others might wish to prescribe local referenda. However, whatever procedures were laid down, the effect would be to ensure, on the one hand, that the local authority's expenditure targets are not exceeded and, on the other, that decisions reflect the preferences of those most directly affected. Local communities would acquire greater control over their own destinies, since their wishes could no longer be ignored by the local authority, and they would no longer be dependent on the vagaries of an appeal to the Secretary of State.

Such an arrangement would enhance the rationality and legitimacy of decision-making as well as reducing the conflict inherent in existing arrangements. At present, it is too easy for those directly affected by school closures to object, and for local authorities and/or central government to ignore these objections. If local people were given appropriate responsibilities and forced to make hard choices, it is likely that fewer 'errors' would be made and that the level of conflict would be reduced. Moreover, by clarifying the division of powers between tiers of government and by delegating certain powers to local communities, the intervention of central government in the detail of local decisions would be rendered unnecessary. This, in turn, would reduce conflict between central and local government.

Our proposed framework for delegating decision-making

would not be unproblematic. As we have pointed out, local authorities would have to formulate procedures designed to further democratic decision-making at the (local) community level, and to devise some means of ensuring that local opinion is properly canvassed. Existing opportunities for the participation of the public in the running of local services have been criticised for favouring middle-class interests (Boaden et al., 1982). This tendency should not be underestimated, but the proposals advanced here would be likely to alleviate rather than aggravate the problem: by bringing the locus of decision-making away from the Town Hall into the community, by delegating clearly specified decisions to the local community and by creating opportunities for direct participation in decision-making rather than the more remote methods implied by 'consultation', middle-class advantage is likely to be lessened. Some means would also have to be found for dealing with boundary problems since the provision of schooling in one community often has implications for adjoining communities. In order to ensure that the procedures work efficiently, it would also be necessary for the authority to service the new decision-making machinery and to outpost staff to local communities. British, European and North American examples of decentralisation highlight these problems and illustrate how they might be addressed (see Hambleton, 1978; Kjellberg, 1979; Magnusson, 1979; Fudge, 1984; Hambleton and Hoggett, 1984).

Alongside this framework for delegating decision-making, education authorities would still be expected to determine broad educational policies. We have outlined ways in which choice and diversity could be encouraged, but we would expect education authorities to retain control over other educational issues, such as the organisation and structure of educational provision, for example, whether there should be middle schools, sixth-form colleges, tertiary colleges or special schools for handicapped children. In addition, education authorities might wish to set limits on local choices. Thus, for example, in urban areas they might want to exclude arrangements that would result in composite (mixed age-group) classes in primary schools or to set minimum intakes for secondary schools in order to ensure an acceptable degree of curricular choice.

The proposals put forward in this chapter differ from the existing arrangements in many ways and run directly counter to the new proposals (outlined above) which are currently under consideration in Scotland. However, there are also clear affinities with policies of decentralisation and area management being pursued by a number of local authorities in Great Britain (see Hadley and Hatch, 1981; Hadley and McGrath, 1980; Fudge, 1984; Hadley, Dale and Sills, 1984; Hambleton and Hoggett, 1984; Seabrook, 1984) and elsewhere (see Sharpe, 1979). Most of these initiatives incorporate similar objectives to those we have outlined, although ambiguities regarding their scope remain (Fudge, 1984). However, while most have the long-term aim of multi-service decentralisation, several of the authorities involved have no remit for education (for example, the inner London Boroughs of Islington and Hackney), some have expressly excluded education (for example, Stockport) and others have given priority to other services, especially housing (for example, Walsall) and the social services (for example, East Sussex).

However, as the issue of falling school rolls becomes increasingly pressing, some education authorities are submitting their own policies and procedures to critical scrutiny and arriving at conclusions not dissimilar from our own. In particular, Strathclyde Regional Council has recently published the report of a working group examining the implications of falling school rolls that presents proposals designed to be responsive to local circumstances and opinions (Strathclyde Regional Council, 1986). The report accepts that rationalisation of educational provision is essential given the present financial pressures on local services. However, it rejects narrow, financial criteria for identifying schools for closure, considering 'such an approach ... too mechanistic and seriously deficient because it omits important social and educational factors' (ibid., p. 23). The report recognises that a programme of rationalisation can have a major influence on the lives of local communities' and argues that 'full account should be taken of local views before decisions are taken about changing the pattern of educational provision in a local community' (ibid., p. 24). To this end, it proposes the establishment of 'local review groups, based on identifiable local communities, which would evaluate school-based educational provision against clearly identified and widely-based criteria' (ibid., p. 24) (comprising population trends, the range and quality of educational provision, the role of the school in the community, as well as financial considerations) on the basis of statistical information provided by the education authority. The local review groups, made up of local elected members, primary and secondary headteachers, parents and the divisional educational officer, would 'be instructed to review local educational provision and would also be free to recommend how resources released through the rationalisation might be redistributed' (ibid., p. 25). (3)

The parallels with our suggested framework are clear. However, the Strathclyde proposals stop short of full delegation: the final decisions about school closures and resource implications would still remain with the council. The scheme, therefore, is similar to those discussed by Hambleton (1978) and Sharpe (1979) in which local authorities in Britain and elsewhere have attempted to decentralise the exercise of influence without delegating political authority. Moreover, the Strathclyde proposals are only one step beyond the unsuccessful local area reviews conducted in Manchester prior to the 1982 plan. In contrast to these initiatives, we have argued that it would be both possible and desirable to delegate decisions regarding the organisation of primary schooling. At the same time we recognise that the scope for such delegation is limited to particular kinds of decisions concerning particular issues. Thus, for example, it is not clear that it would be appropriate to deal with the provision of secondary schooling in this way.

As Blunkett and Green (1983) have remarked:

> To go beyond better communication or consultation to real delegation of both management and political decision-making brings its own problems. Clear lines have to be drawn between those decisions which affect overall policy resource distribution and political priorities, which must remain a collective and to some extent central process; and the decisions which can and should be taken by neighbourhoods, tenants, community groups, or service recipients. (p. 23)

We agree with them on both counts. As far as the provision of primary schooling and the question of possible school closures are concerned, we have attempted to distinguish between decisions that can only be made by central and local government, and those which it would make sense to delegate to local communities. We have not attempted to put forward a detailed blueprint for reform and accept that

Delegation and Community Participation

the delegation of responsibility for certain decisions from education authorities to local communities is bound to bring its own problems. Nevertheless, we believe that the framework we have outlined not only deserves serious consideration but also offers a more hopeful way forward than either existing procedures or the proposals currently under consideration in Scotland.

Acknowledgement

The Manchester fieldwork was carried out while Liz Bondi was in receipt of an ESRC postgraduate studentship; the Tayside fieldwork was carried out by Michael Adler in the course of an ESRC-funded programme of research on parental choice in education. We are both grateful to the ESRC for financial support.

NOTES

1. For details of the decline in pupil numbers and for official projections, see Central Policy Review Staff (1977), DES Statistics of Education (annual), DES Reports on Education (numbers 92, 96 and 97) and SED Statistical Bulletin (numbers 7/B2/1981, 2/B2/1984 and 2/B2/1986).

2. Initially, instead of deciding upon one of the alternatives canvassed, the director of education had been instructed by the education committee to seek guidance from the SED on the approach authorities ought to adopt (especially in large urban areas) in dealing with declining school rolls, ageing and deteriorating buildings and parental antipathy towards rationalising the use of accommodation, particularly in a period of constraint on public expenditure. The approach was made in early 1979, when the Secretary of State's approval was still required for any proposal to close a school. The SED's reply was not very helpful: on the grounds that the Secretary of State would eventually have to consider a formal proposal from the Region, the SED took the view that he should not commit himself in advance.

3. These proposals were accepted by Strathclyde Regional Council in May 1987. In the period between the publication of the report and its acceptance, there had been considerable debate on arrangements for 'ring fencing' the education budget. In the end it was agreed to retain 50 per

Delegation and Community Participation

cent of any savings realised for the education service. Suggestions that savings be retained within the local areas or for the sectors concerned were rejected.

Chapter Three

REZONING: AN EXERCISE IN COMPROMISE

Alison Petch

INTRODUCTION

In March 1984, Fife Education Department presented to its School subcommittee proposals for the rezoning of secondary catchment areas in Dunfermline. In August 1984, following a period of consultation with parents in the affected areas, it was decided that the majority of the proposals should not, at least for the present, be implemented. This chapter charts the development of these proposals and presents the different perspectives of the various parties involved, drawing extensively on official minutes and reports, on press accounts and on interviews with key individuals. It aims in particular to highlight, first, the precipitating factors which led to the proposal for boundary changes and the considerations which constrained the education department in formulating its proposals, and, secondly, to examine the strategies which were adopted by the pressure groups that emerged in particular areas. The case study explores the general context of accountability to the parental lobby and represents a more subtle response to the impact of falling rolls than the proposals for closure reported by Burnett and by Adler and Bondi. Also, it characterises much of the debate surrounding bureaucratic response to pressure group politics and illustrates the dilemmas inherent in 'community action' initiatives.

THE POLICY CONTEXT

Before detailing this case study of rezoning, comment is

83

required on the various different contexts within which the account can be read. There is no attempt in this presentation to argue the logic of a particular approach to the analysis of educational policy-making. The preference is to locate the case study and to explore the extent to which the example may provide illustration for a variety of different approaches. Nonetheless it is hoped to avoid the dangers inherent in the isolated case study whereby, in the absence of a more general framework, what is provided is 'at best an interesting contribution to historical scholarship and at worst an uninteresting episodic narrative' (Heclo, 1972, p. 93).

Although a considerable number of case studies of educational policy-making have been pursued, these have been concerned almost exclusively with the issue of secondary school reorganisation rather than rezoning per se. Ribbins and Brown (1979) attempt to remedy the observed lack of analytical discussion within such studies by detailing a threefold framework within which they can be located. First, the local authority is seen as the focus of a local political system, signified by local parties and interest groups. Secondly, the main function of this system is to process policy demands from the local population on specific issues such as education or housing. Thirdly, such policy demands vary in generality, policy-making emerging as the provision of increasingly specific decisions. Ribbins and Brown illustrate this process of policy-making, generalising from the various examples of reorganisation according to these increasingly specific states: the initial call for reorganisation, the debate over the type of organisation to be adopted, and the fitting of individual schools to the chosen reform. A fourth stage, internal reorganisation within each school, was beyond the scope of the specific studies under review.

Analysis of the process of policy-making within the local authority is of course a much pursued and debated activity and the aim is not to compete with that by, for example, Regan (1979), Dearlove (1973) or Donnison, Chapman, Meacher, Sears and Urwin (1975). Even to reproduce a detailed assessment for a single area such as that assembled for Cardiff by Geen (1981) or for 'Townley' by Saran (1973) would require consideration of a wider range of policy issues than the single item pursued here. Nonetheless, the single issue examined here can usefully be informed by the findings of the studies cited regarding both the components and the process of the policy debate. In their original study on innovation in different areas of social policy, for example, Donnison et al. (1975) concluded that initiation of change primarily lay with the providers of the service. Subsequently, however, and in response to the work of Saran (1973), they acknowledged the important, sometimes leading, role of politicians and other informed opinion. Likewise, Dearlove (1973) concludes from his analysis of the policy process in Kensington and Chelsea that the major concern of the authority is less with innovation or with policy decisions but with policy maintenance.

One study of particular relevance to the present context is that of Jennings (1977) who, from analysis in a variety of different local authorities, presents a six stage model of the policy process, concerned 'to explore the mix of politics and policy-making for education within local government' (p. 8). He teases out the complex web of interaction between officials and members and demonstrates the distribution of power between the two. Jennings' model identifies six overlapping stages of the policy process. An element of dissatisfaction leads to initiation of the process, and as opinion begins to gather reformulation takes place. As potential solutions are put forward alternatives emerge and during the fourth stage, discussion and debate, these are shaped into policy proposals. A specific policy is selected from the competing alternatives, legitimisation, and then finally the chosen policy reaches implementation. In reality of course much of the policy process is cyclical and indeed some would challenge this sequential notion of policy development. Nonetheless such a model is useful as an analytical tool, allowing in a specific example for the identification of the role of the different parties.

> The unique advantage of the individual case study is that it throws light on how policy decisions are actually made and on the role various participants play. (Saran, 1973, p. 2)

In the case study outlined here, the focus will be on a party often dismissed in the analysis of educational policy-making, the parent. The typical response of the local authority to the participatory process has been summarised by Hill (1974, p. 156):

> ... local councils are secretive, content to consult only when required to by statute or ministerial direction. They have not gone out of their way to promote citizen involvement,

an assessment that is endorsed by Ribbins and Brown (1979) in their review of studies specifically concerned with reorganisation:

> Certainly the usual pattern of consultation where it has existed has been for the authority to decide what it is going to do first and to ask for comments afterwards. (p. 193)

The limitations to participatory democracy have been well documented (for example Richardson, 1983). Parents are disadvantaged in their contribution to the policy process in that they rarely have a direct entry. Moreover, issues may come to their attention only when the process is at an advanced stage, for example, the discussion and debate phase (the fourth) of Jennings' model. By this date the generation of alternatives is very often foreclosed and the parent can only respond to a limited agenda. The details of even this limited agenda may be difficult to obtain and the strategy for organisation amongst a dispersed population on a limited time budget may be defeating.

> The real difficulty is perhaps that parental participation is unlikely to arise spontaneously and few authorities are likely to work hard to stimulate it. (Ribbins and Brown, 1979, p. 195)

There are, nonetheless, a few examples of parental initiative in the policy process. Ribbins and Brown cite the campaign in Liverpool which contributed to a parental rejection of the reorganisation proposals, and the tradition of consultation in Bath which ensured that discussion extended over lengthy periods. The major analysis by Saran (1973) examines in detail two examples of parental involvement in the policy process. In one area, parental pressure contributed to the defeat of a scheme for comprehensive reorganisation; in a second a newly established comprehensive was successfully defended. Saran concludes on the parental role,

All organised parental pressure was in favour of conservation. Thus vocal or potentially vocal pressures exerted by parents were directed against change, were usually connected with access to grammar schools and prevented those comprehensive schools which were established from getting a balanced intake. (Saran, 1973, p. 263)

Whilst of particular interest because of its concern with an educational issue, Saran's painstaking analysis also devotes considerable attention to the mechanics of the participatory process available to the public, in this case parents. Similar evidence of participatory strategy is provided by a different group of studies, those concerned with housing and predominantly with the threats from redevelopment proposals (Dennis, 1970; Davies, 1974; Jacobs, 1976). An alternative perspective therefore would be to align the case study with the general literature on community initiatives exemplified by these studies, to acknowledge the primary focus on the role of parents and to ground the study less in an analysis of the policy process than in the sociology of community action.

BACKGROUND TO THE PROPOSALS

The town of Dunfermline is served by three non-denominational secondary schools, Dunfermline High School (HS), Queen Anne High School and Woodmill High School, with a further secondary school at Inverkeithing, approximately three miles south of the town. Dunfermline HS was historically the selective Senior Secondary, whilst Queen Anne and Woodmill were originally Junior Secondary schools. As in the rest of Fife, secondary school catchments are composed of feeder primary schools. Dunfermline HS receives from seven feeder primaries and Woodmill from six. In the case of Queen Anne HS the number of feeder primaries extends to 14, drawing geographically from a large area of West Fife. All three schools, however, involve the provision of special school buses and none of the catchment areas, as can be seen in Figure 3.1, form a wholly contiguous area. Dunfermline HS, for example, whilst primarily serving primary schools in the town, also provides for children brought in from Tulliallan School in Kincardine. Transport arrangements, particularly outwith the town, are

Figure 3.1: Secondary School Catchments in West Fife

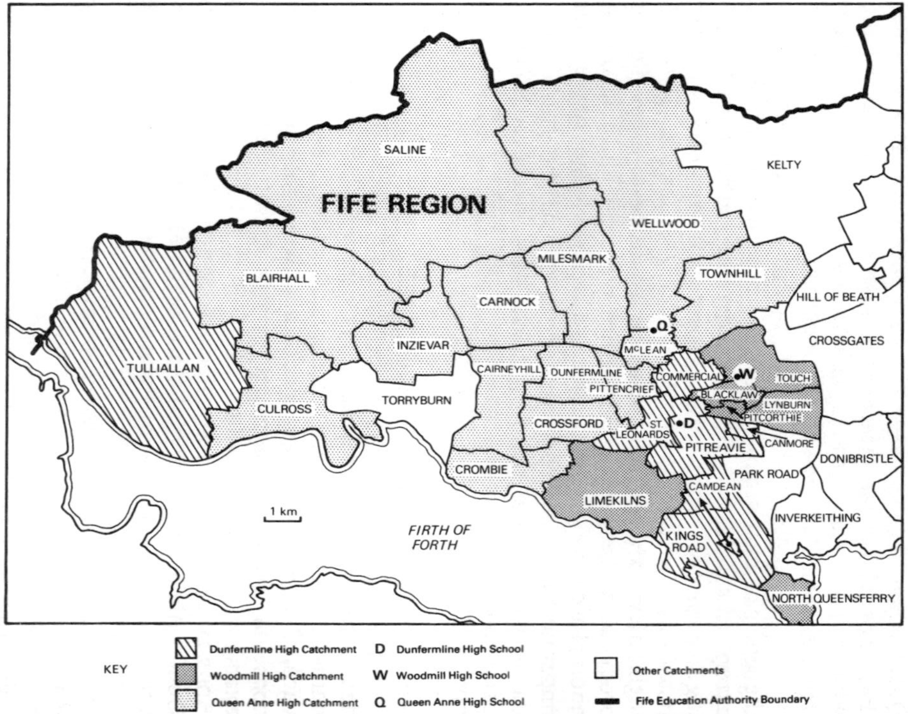

Table 3.1: Number of First Year Pupils Opting out of and into Local Secondary School Catchments in West Fife

	August 1982 Lost	August 1982 Gained	August 1983 Lost	August 1983 Gained	August 1984 Lost	August 1984 Gained
Dunfermline High School	8	23	16	39	19	25
Queen Anne High School	3	14	13	28	12	27
Woodmill High School	15	5	29	4	18	12

therefore likely to exert considerable influence upon the extent to which parents can make use of the parental choice legislation to select an alternative school. The authority itself, having anticipated by a year the parental choice legislation of the Education (Scotland) Act 1981, through provision of their own scheme at entry to primary school, do not regard the parental choice provisions to be of major importance. For secondary entry throughout Fife as a whole, the number of first year (S1) pupils opting out of their local catchment area in August 1984 was 272 or 5.27 per cent. For Dunfermline itself at that date, the figures are shown in Table 3.1. Politically, the region has a comfortable and longstanding Labour majority.

The catalyst which led to the rezoning proposals was a desire to reduce the number of temporary accommodation units at Queen Anne HS. This in turn reflected a need to fill vacancies at the other two schools before any building consents would be granted by the Scottish Office, for example, for improvements to the main fabric of Queen Anne HS. Debate over the distribution of pupils amongst the Dunfermline secondary schools extends back over several years and has hinged primarily upon the difficulties of predicting accurately the school rolls. The sophisticated models detailed by Maxfield (1972) and by Thomas and Robson (1984), which make use of linear programming techniques are far removed from the 'back-of-the-envelope' calculations of the educational administrator. The Dunfermline area has, until recently, been characterised by net inward migration, a factor that has offset the fall in enrolment with which the majority of areas are concerned and which are the focus of the paper by Thomas and Robson.

From the mid-seventies, the education authority had felt that the accommodation provided at Queen Anne HS was unsatisfactory and that action would have to be taken both to reduce the reliance upon temporary accommodation (extending in 1984 to 36 temporary classrooms, approximately one-third of the total accommodation) and to upgrade and extend the facilities available in the main buildings. Until 1981, reflecting the projected increase in the area's population, there had been provision in the Capital Building Programme for a new school (West Fife High School) to be built. Located on the west side of the town, this would have served the hinterland to Kincardine and would have reduced much of the pressure on Queen Anne HS, maintaining Queen Anne HS at the 1,300 capacity that equated with the permanent accommodation. It would, moreover, have reduced the reliance on piecemeal improvement to a building that was already less than satisfactory.

Until the early eighties, therefore, the expectation had been that inward migration would be sufficient to support the construction of a new school. Regional planning documents identified Dunfermline district as a growth point and there was pressure from the Region for the district to release additional land for housing. A complicating factor in the Dunfermline area is the presence of the naval base at Rosyth, a highly mobile population with associated problems of predicting the child product. At one stage in the early eighties, there was speculation that there would be a considerable increase in the numbers of personnel at the base and this again suggested that the need for secondary school places would be high.

The prediction of school rolls is always a highly complex exercise, but in Dunfermline this is compounded by the availability of housing land, the planning intentions for this land, and by the existence of a naval population. Until the early eighties the authority worked on the assumption that the declining rolls of the national population would be offset by the inward migration associated with housing development. It became apparent, however, that inward migration was not being sustained, house building had slowed down and that much of the projected growth was not occurring. Land for public housing was sold off for private building and this in turn brought new problems of prediction, both in the highly volatile nature of completion plans dependent on market forces, and in the different types and sizes of house with different implications for the child product. To exemplify, new housing in the St Leonards area

Rezoning

adjacent to Dunfermline HS had in practice yielded very few children: the houses were large and were purchased either by those whose children were beyond school or whose children travelled to private schools in Edinburgh. With the considerable reduction in projected rolls, the West Fife HS was removed from the Capital Building Programme and attention was focused on redistribution amongst the existing schools. There remains, however, the difficulty of predicting with any certainty the product of the private building land. In the case of Commercial primary school this has been of particular significance. For entry in August 1984, placing requests from outwith the catchment area exceeded the capacity of the school (the only school in Fife at which this occurred). It was therefore necessary to refuse certain of these placing requests (a number of which subsequently went to appeal). But in order to do this, given Fife's commitment to accommodate all pupils from within the catchment area, a prediction had to be made of the number of children likely to originate from the private house completions. Space had to be reserved therefore for a potential (but uncertain) client population whilst an actual population was clamouring for access.

In 1982 therefore the authority began to consider various options for the utilisation of the existing accommodation, with the declared objective of reducing the roll at Queen Anne HS and of providing the three High schools 'with balanced catchment areas, as far as practicable, in accordance with Regional Council Policy of comprehensive education'. (1) This second objective is of major significance for it represents a commitment to the achievement of social balance within a school's catchment area, balancing the different socio-economic areas in order to produce a heterogeneous child population. It is this principle, for example, that underlies the visually somewhat bizarre instance of the Torryburn and Valleyfield areas (areas of high deprivation) being separated from the rest of West Fife and feeding to Inverkeithing HS, where they offset the predominantly middle-class population for the Dalgety Bay area (east of the area shown in Figure 3.1). Retention of this objective was a major constraint on the reorganisation proposals.

Other constraints also became evident. There was a desire that the two primary schools which were serving the naval base at Rosyth, Camdean and Kings Road, should feed to the same secondary school and therefore the option of transferring one of these to enhance the roll at Woodmill HS was foreclosed. Similarly, there was sensitivity about large numbers of children travelling by bus to a school and a consequent desire to reduce the amount of bussing as much as possible. At Woodmill HS this desire was enhanced by the inadequacy of the surrounding road to cope with the congestion resultant from a large number of buses at the school. One argument was that children who were being bussed anyway from the West of Fife could simply be transported to an alternative school. The danger here, however, was that the principle of social balance would be breached. If, for example, Crossford and Cairneyhill were to be redirected from Queen Anne HS to Dunfermline HS there was the danger that Queen Anne would be left with a catchment skewed towards areas of lower socio-economic status. The authority would be particularly sensitive, in the case of Queen Anne HS, of being seen to threaten the character of a school which had successfully evolved from its original status as a Junior Secondary school to a comprehensive school with a good reputation in terms of academic achievement.

A further constraint was the extent to which different areas of Dunfermline were traditionally committed to long established patterns of educational provision. For example, it was felt that parents in the central area of Dunfermline, those for example with children at Commercial primary school, were likely to exhibit historical allegiances towards certain schools, particularly to the originally selective school (Dunfermline HS) and therefore to be more vigorous (and vociferous) in their opposition to change than residents on the recently established estates. For example parents with children at Canmore primary school were more likely to be incomers with consequently less of a heritage based on historical precedent. Whilst acknowledging the constraints imposed by traditional allegiance, there was nevertheless past experience within the authority to suggest that initial opposition to any proposal for change was likely to be shortlived, and that over a period of a few years implementation of change was achieved without lasting detriment. For example, when Limekilns primary school had been transferred to the catchment of Woodmill there had initially been considerable opposition but over time this had dissipated. Officials were therefore able to view perhaps with some complacency potential dissent. Experience of this kind also influenced the attitude which the authority

Rezoning

adopted to the possibility that enforced implementation of boundary changes would result in large-scale utilisation of the placing request legislation by parents anxious to maintain the earlier boundaries. The authority was willing to weather an increase in placing requests in the short-term, confident that within a few years the new boundaries would become established. If excessive placing requests were to persist this would suggest more serious problems at the exporting school, calling for more radical action within the school.

A more immediate concern that constrained in particular the timing of the proposals was that, as a consequence of ill health, Woodmill HS had had a succession of three Rectors (headmasters) over a very short period of time. There was therefore a reluctance to introduce too immediately upon the arrival of the new Rector rezoning proposals likely to result in pressure and disruption.

Working with a knowledge of the constraints outlined above, the authority therefore experimented with 'the various options ... trying to pin numbers to them' (educational department official). They were aware that 'whichever way you looked at this one, there was no answer that was going to be readily acceptable to everybody - some particular pressure group would be disappointed.' Over this period officials maintained a dialogue with the chairman of the education committee and the proposals that emerged in the paper of March 1984, consisting of a distillation from the various permutations available of a proposal that would not breach basic principles, were judged acceptable to the majority of councillors on the committee.

> I think in this business you more or less have to know each other's thinking - we outlined the problem with the councillors so hence you rule out, for example, transporting a large number of children. (education department official)

THE PROPOSALS

The suggested rezoning was (see Figure 3.1)

(a) Crombie primary school from Queen Anne HS to Woodmill HS
(b) Culross primary school from Queen Anne HS to

Rezoning

      Woodmill HS
(c) Canmore primary school from Dunfermline HS to Woodmill HS
(d) Commercial primary school totally to Dunfermline HS (at present catchment split with Queen Anne HS)
(e) Townhill primary school from Queen Anne HS to Dunfermline HS

The proposals, it should be noted, formed a single option rather than a set of alternatives. In accordance with the requirements for consultation introduced by section 6 of the Education (Scotland) Act 1981, the Schools subcommittee accepted that affected parents be consulted on the basis of the outline proposals and the consultative process was set in motion.

THE PUBLIC RESPONSE

The first that many parents learnt of the intention of the education authority was in the Dunfermline Press of 6 April, 1984, the result of a 'leak' of the confidential report prior to the meeting of the full education committee. This press report was in part inaccurate in that it listed Townhill as transferring to Woodmill HS and 'provoked a blistering attack' from the education committee chairman, Councillor Dair, the following week:

> The resultant situation is that, before parents, who have a right to be consulted, can be consulted, they are advised by newspaper story. It makes me wonder about issuing reports in advance in future. (Dunfermline Press, 13 April 1984)

Dair's opinion that the 'leak' destroyed the opportunity for effective debate was not, however, shared by all. A response from Councillor Moyes, regional councillor for the Canmore area, argued that public awareness of the proposals could only be beneficial.

> Far from destroying the chance of proper debate we have ensured that, at least as far as Canmore Primary is concerned, full debate and consultation will take place. It is our contention that this consultation should have been made before the matter went to the

Rezoning

Education Committee and the recommendation was there accepted. (Dunfermline Press, 20 April 1984)

From the beginning of the public debate therefore there was already suspicion that Councillor Dair was reluctant to participate in debate. A group of Townhill parents wrote:

> We wonder why Councillor Dair, in a so-called democratic society, is so afraid of the subcommittee's proposals being known. Perhaps because they might be opposed before they were taken any further. (Dunfermline Press, 27 April 1984)

And Councillor Davison, critic over a long period of most of the education authority practice, and himself previously involved in an extended and public battle over parental choice for his own children argued that parents were being presented with a fait accompli. Councillor Dair was compelled to assure the public that no decision had yet been taken and that full discussion would be held.

Central to the consultative process was to be a series of public meetings held in each of the affected primary schools. Several weeks before these meetings, however, there was already evidence of strong opposition to the proposals, with two areas in particular forming parent-initiated action groups. These action groups together with other individuals, notably Councillor Davison, were to ensure that the proposals maintained a high profile, particularly in the local press, during the ensuing weeks. The emergence of the two action groups and the formulation of their arguments and strategies for opposition will be traced in some detail.

TOWNHILL

In the Townhill area, the first intimation of the rezoning was from the Press Report, which inaccurately stated that Townhill children were to be redirected to Woodmill HS, an error which was corrected the following week. From within the community, a couple of parents clarified the situation with Queen Anne HS and then, two or three weeks after the announcement, approached the headmaster at Townhill. His stance was neutral but he co-operated in the distribution through the school of a letter to all parents inviting them to a public meeting in the local community centre to discuss the proposals. It is important to stress that none of the parents initiating this action had been involved in any similar campaign in the past. In the period prior to this meeting, advice was sought from a former councillor who was a candidate in the local election and he directed the parents to Councillor Davison. Councillor Davison furnished advice on procedures and clarified the rights under parental choice legislation. Councillor Davison himself argued that

> School zoning and creation of social mixes are means Fife has used for decades to socially engineer the education of our children, and to frustrate parents who choose to live near schools in which they believe. (Dunfermline Press, 7 June 1984)

The district councillor for the area took no part in the debate; the Regional councillor, Mrs Mackie, was chairperson of the Schools subcommittee and expressed her intention of endorsing local wishes but without active participation. Her position was inevitably uncomfortable and she was no doubt conscious of the fact that she had lost her seat for a while some years previously following the closure of the primary school at Halbeath. She declared publicly

> I feel a bit like Tweedledum and Tweedledee - I am right in the middle of it, but there is no way that I am going to dodge the issue ... I can see the Director's point of view in bringing forward these proposals, but I can also see the point of view of the parents and it would be foolish of me, as their elected representative, not to back up their cause. (Dunfermline Press, 11 May 1984)

Advice was also obtained in this initial period from those who had formed the action group in the Canmore area.

The public meeting called by the parents was attended by about 80 people. It was chaired by Dorothy Thomson, one of the original parents to show concern, and initially a range of fairly noisy disparate views were expressed. A few parents accepted the proposed transfer to Dunfermline HS and one spoke in favour of Woodmill HS. The fact that Queen Anne HS was to be removed as an option was sufficient, however, to provoke widespread unified opposition to the proposals, and on a show of hands it was agreed to proceed with a campaign of resistance. A committee was formed, composed of five parents from Townhill itself, two from the village of Kingseat and two from the 'bottom end' of the catchment area towards Dunfermline; Dorothy Thomson was confirmed as chairwoman.

A significant argument was presented by one member of the committee who initially had been uncertain (himself having been to Dunfermline HS) of his stance towards the proposals. His co-operation was ensured, however, by what he saw as the dictatorial nature of the reorganisation, interpreted as a demand to 'fall in line with this missive from Kirkcaldy'. The rest of the committee volunteered, only half in jest, that he had been so argumentative at the public meeting that they had thought it best to co-opt him.

From the public meeting the decision was taken to proceed with the collection of signatures to a petition (400 signatures achieved) and individuals were encouraged to write to the education department in Kirkcaldy. The committee meanwhile met weekly and pursued a campaign of letters to the Press and to the education department, following up on non-response by phone calls. They collected statistics and other information through Councillors Mackie and Davison and had a meeting with their MP, Dick Douglas. They were particularly annoyed at this stage by the lack of response to their communications with the education department. Thus, the committee member mentioned above who was initially wary, became increasingly incensed by what he saw as the closed nature of the organisation. The education department maintained however that the volume of correspondence was such that initially personal replies had to be replaced by a standard response.

By the time it became known that the education authority was to organise a series of public meetings the Townhill Action Group had developed its arguments against the proposal as it affected them. At the top of their list were factors of distance and of weather, many from Townhill primary school being able to walk to Queen Anne HS, whereas transfer to Dunfermline HS would entail bus travel. Townhill was notorious for being cut off in snow: 'if our children are going to miss exams, etc. and our children's education is put at risk because the buses can't get up, you haven't seen us begin to fight.' A second argument was that Townhill would be deprived of its local community school, a base within walking distance of the majority, where parents also took part in activities. The majority of the committee also argued that Queen Anne HS was the best school educationally, although attempts by the action group to obtain what they termed 'reports' in order to make a detailed comparison of results had met with what they considered to be prevarication. At first their request was interpreted to be for Inspectors' Reports of which there were none; on being referred to the school prospectus, they found results only available for one year.

The action group consider that they learnt much from attending the education authority public meetings held prior to their own, and that they were as a consequence more assured of the strategy which they wished to adopt in presentation of their own case. At the first meeting (at Crombie) they had considered that the presentation of slides on the Queen Anne HS building had been biased and prejudiced; an example of the extent to which the education authority was willing to distort. Arguments were presented, for example, of the dangers from traffic, but all the cars shown belonged to teachers and therefore remained stationary. This view was also shared by the headmaster of Queen Anne HS who had spoken out at the Crombie meeting and was later quoted as saying

> I find it difficult to sit quiet and watch an unfair presentation - a denigration - of a school I love by what are misrepresentations and untruths. (Dunfermline Press, 1 June 1984)

The education authority, however, found his attitude ambivalent in that in the past complaints had been received from the school on these very issues.

> This doesn't seem to tie up with his complaint, but perhaps he didn't think about that when he made his remarks. (Director of Education, Dunfermline Press, 7 June 1984)

There was a feeling moreover that the Rector had timed his remarks to ensure maximum impact, capitalising on bringing before the public issues that could easily have been resolved at departmental level.

Townhill parents had also been taken aback by what they considered the unruly nature of the meeting held in Canmore, and were determined that their own should not get out of hand.

> We had a public meeting at Canmore that was something of a fracas, I think that a lot of people regretted that with hindsight. (Education department official)

They had also been shocked by the strategy of the Canmore Action Group, previously considered allies, who in their eyes had turned traitor by suggesting to the authority that Canmore could be left alone if Townhill were redirected to Woodmill HS. This did serve the purpose, however, of reviving parents' opposition immediately prior to the public meeting at Townhill in that many considered Woodmill HS to be unacceptable on educational grounds. The action group ensured that there were people willing to speak out at their own meeting and agreed points of strategy. For example, while generally agreeing that they could see no objection to transferring those who were already on a bus, for example, from Cairneyhill and Crossford to Dunfermline HS, they did not wish to adopt the Canmore attitude and to redirect others in public. They were willing to allow the authority to make its case, confident in the knowledge that they had arguments prepared.

The action group felt satisfied after the public meeting that they had got their case across and that the meeting had not got out of hand. Certainly to the outside observer, the conduct of the meeting was more orderly than that at Canmore, where an estimated 350 parents had reacted angrily to much that they heard. Nonetheless both meetings failed to impress the observer in terms of the quality of presentation and the argument offered by the local authority. Officials appeared unable to respond to the details of local layout or transport routes and often appeared contradictory in the arguments which they pursued. Responses were given in statutory terms, for example, by reading the priorities for considering placing requests, rather than engaging in the debate over the reality of limited places. The strategy for implementation of the repairs programme appeared uncertain and hazily costed. Indeed to the independent observer, the professionals appeared singularly ill-prepared and offered little in the way of persuasion. Their performance did little to impress a well-prepared and highly vocal action campaign. After witnessing an earlier presentation at Culross, Councillor

Davison had declared

> I have rarely been so ashamed of highly paid officials. I have often criticised the Fife Education Directorate for overstaffing and incompetence but this was the most inept and overpowered performance I have seen. (Dunfermline Press, 7 June 1984)

After the complete cycle of meetings Councillor Davison considered that the authority's case over the temporary accommodation had been destroyed by the detailed questioning of the informed parents: heating and maintenance costs had been refuted and inconsistent arguments had been exposed. Moreover,

> In my view, the standard of misleading information at those meetings and the insufferable arrogance behind the Authority's actions was completely intolerable. (Dunfermline Press, 10 July 1984)

It should be noted however that given the history of his involvement with Fife Region, Councillor Davison was unlikely to miss any opportunity for challenging the educational administration. Moreover he was using the process of consultation as a platform for highlighting his views on the folly of a new secondary school currently under construction at Lochgelly. Nonetheless a surprisingly detailed editorial in the local press endorsed his view:

> They seem strangely inept in 'feeling the pulse' of public opinion. Their public relations expertise seems to be non-existent and their verbal communication seriously wanting and unconvincing. (Dunfermline Press, 8 June 1984)

This editorial went on to argue that much of the conflict stemmed from leaving the consultative process until too late a stage.

> What should have happened is that the education committee should have been frank and open. They should have conveyed to parents, from the outset, that they had a problem in seeking to rezone the catchment area and they should have sought out the parents' feelings in the matter. (Dunfermline Press, 8 June 1984)

One of the officials involved in the public meetings confessed that he had been surprised both at the strength of reaction and at the organisation of the parents.

> I had not experienced the sort of organised disruption and the heckling - I mean we were subjected to sustained, organised pressure. The purpose of consultation was to get the views of individual parents in particular. What you had was the involvement of, not political groups, but of what could be conceived as a minority of articulate and committed parents who knew all about - I'm not saying disruptive practices - there are certain techniques that are followed - I'm aware of these now. I hadn't the slightest idea before I went to the meetings. (Education department official)

A number of specific points contributed perhaps unjustly to the impression of ineptitude conveyed by the authority. The authority had anticipated in its arguments the granting of planning permission for a housing development which members of the public erroneously believed to have been refused. Similarly, members of the public disputed bus routes from outdated information. The action groups capitalised on arithmetical errors that the authority had allowed to slip through, gaining maximum impact from what were in effect errors of only single figures and in projection terms of minimal significance. And the interventions of the Queen Anne HS headteacher outlined earlier were tactically crucial in helping to raise the temperature of the debate and in further undermining the presentation by the local authority official.

CANMORE

In the Pitcorthie area (served by Canmore school rather than Pitcorthie school), parents of children at Canmore primary school had also become aware of the proposed rezoning through the leaked report that appeared in the Dunfermline Press. As in Townhill, a public meeting was called in the school hall, primarily at the instigation of the headteacher who was receiving many 'phone calls from concerned parents. Letters were distributed through the school, and approximately 200 parents attended, representative of virtually every child in the school. The headteacher presented what he knew of the situation (little more than had appeared in the press), general opposition to the proposal was evident, and the headteacher suggested that if parents were sufficiently concerned they should form some sort of committee to present their objections to the statutory meeting. Ten individuals, again all without previous experience of such campaigns, volunteered to form a committee (later reduced to eight active members) and they developed the campaign over the subsequent weeks, although at this stage there was

> a lot of dubiety I think in our minds as to whether in fact at that statutory meeting there would be an opportunity to present our opposition or whether it would be a fait accompli by them. (Canmore Action Group (CAG) Committee member)

Another of those who joined the committee explained his own involvement:

> I went along to that first meeting with a very, very open mind. I had, and have, no objection to Woodmill as a school and I was not going into that meeting with a preconceived idea that I am going to be so much against it that I'm going to be on the committee and fight it tooth and nail but really by the end of the evening and having heard the arguments for and against, it was quite clear to me in my own mind. (CAG Committee Member)

None of the committee felt at this stage that they could win the argument: they were concerned rather to cause maximum impact and embarrassment.

The main arguments that emerged from this first meeting centred on the effect the proposal would have of splitting the Pitcorthie estate (geographically well-defined) and on the inadequate transport provisions serving Woodmill. In the weeks prior to the statutory meeting, these and other arguments were developed in great detail, with many hours spent checking housing and pupil projections, studying timetables, visiting the planning department, devising alternatives. For, unlike the Townhill group, committee members in Canmore felt it was essential that they were not only able to challenge the logic of the authority's proposal, but had also developed detailed alternatives.

Rezoning

Indeed, one of their main objections to the proposal was that it presented no options or alternative strategies. In contrast therefore the group worked on the detailed figures and constraints and devised a total of four options that could be compared with the proposal of the authority. (2) These included:

(i) rezone Crossford and Cairneyhill from Queen Anne HS to Woodmill
(ii) rezone Townhill and Commercial (part) from Queen Anne HS to Woodmill
(iii) rezone Townhill and Commercial (all) to Woodmill
(iv) rezone Commercial (all) to Woodmill and rezone Townhill to Dunfermline.

Committee members were also concerned to maintain contact with the body of parents they represented and therefore a further two public meetings were convened in the period prior to the local authority meeting. Attendance remained high and parents were given for example a detailed presentation, with slides, of the options which had been devised.

Meanwhile, other strategies similar to those of the Townhill parents were being pursued. A petition was circulated amongst all Canmore parents, followed by a second petition that sought to tap the support of the wider community. Indeed the community argument was developed to incorporate the eight years it had taken to get an appropriate bus route for the community and the fight that had developed over the provision of a community centre.

> We saw it as a community issue, that Pitcorthie as a community, with one community centre, with one identity, one Regional councillor and up until then one High School, could be split into two. (CAG committee member)

Similarly, a campaign of letter writing to Kirkcaldy and of a high profile in the local press was pursued. The local SDP regional councillor and the SDP candidate in the imminent district election offered their services and were drawn on for information and advice. The committee were anxious, however, to avoid any political involvement. Although they felt that the SDP interest was offered without thought of political gain, they were more wary of the approaches from

Councillor Davison, anxious about associating with a campaigner who aroused such antipathy within the education committee.

There was much reflection within the committee on the strategies they should pursue. For example there was general agreement within the committee that they should make clear that they had no objection to Woodmill as a school.

> Our case that we were making for and on behalf of the majority of parents was that we had nothing against Woodmill school as a school or as an educational institute in itself, it was more what they were doing to us, to get us to go to Woodmill, that we were against. (CAG committee member)

They were conscious that such a presentation was necessary if they were to avoid accusations of elitism.

> It was a genuine feeling on our part but it was also ... our belief that the education department would use this as a dirty weapon against us, that this was a group of middle class, Pitcorthie, snobbish approach, basically that they didn't want their children to go to a predominantly working class school. (CAG committee member)

> If we had gone down the line of Woodmill is a crummy school and we don't want our children to go there our case would have collapsed because we didn't have the evidence. (CAG committee member)

Nonetheless one objection to emerge was the fear of parents that house prices would be affected if the area was rezoned.

> For right or wrong reasons some people did not want their children to go to Woodmill and therefore some parents rightly or wrongly believed that the houses at this end of the scheme would become less attractive. (CAG committee member)

But this, they argued, was because of the nature of the area in which Woodmill was situated, particularly the characteristics of Abbey View, a local authority housing area that suffers from considerable deprivation, rather than

Rezoning

the actual standard of educational provision at the school itself. However, the reasoning on this issue appeared to remain somewhat ambivalent. As a matter of strategy, therefore, at the statutory meeting there was no discussion of the educational quality of the different schools, indeed an anxiety to stress that this was not an issue, and only veiled hints on the reputation of Abbey View. There was considerable consternation, however, when a lone individual attempted to pursue the logic of the parents' presentation by challenging that the only objection he had heard during the evening was over transport and asking if adequate buses were provided, would the proposal be acceptable?

The committee had called a public meeting ten days prior to the statutory meeting and had told parents exactly what they should do if they wanted their case to be carried through. They detailed a list of questions they wanted directed to the officials and explained the arguments they would be using. At the same time, they were careful to ensure that details of these arguments were not publicised, not wishing to alert the education department to their tactics in advance. Further the committee forearmed itself with knowledge of the education department's strategy by attending the meeting at Culross. They found it 'quite amazing' that the officials were unable to respond to public questioning and were exposed as totally inept as soon as they departed from their predetermined script. At their own statutory meeting, the Canmore Group were intent that they should be allowed to present their arguments and that the agenda should not be determined by the authority. After presenting their petition, the chair of the meeting asked that the official should be allowed to present his case but 'needless to say we didn't let him finish'. Their first intervention was a strategy to throw the officials off balance by exposing the arithmetical errors in the projection figures. The body of parents then took over, capitalising on the official's lack of detailed knowledge, on their inability to provide detailed costings or, in the course of two and a half hours, to answer a single question.

> I think what annoyed a lot of parents and really got them going was the inability of the education representatives to answer a straight question. (CAG committee member)

Committee members found this particularly surprising

105

because they had been warned by the headmaster when they initiated their campaign that 'Mr Flett and the education department were really sharp cookies'.

> Having been warned that these people were the professionals and that we were definitely the amateurs going against them ... from the very start it became obvious that they hadn't even done elementary homework far less gone into it in the depth that we as a committee had gone into it. (CAG committee member)

The officials had not even excluded from their script errors exposed at previous meetings and these continued to be presented at the Townhill meeting and at the presentation to the School Council.

The action groups had asked that the minutes reporting the consultation meetings should be made publicly available. When these were eventually secured they were found to be wholly inadequate, consisting of a one-sided summary which totally failed, they considered, to convey the strength of parental opposition. The Canmore committee therefore decided to produce their own closely argued document, which they delivered by hand to every member of the School Council prior to its meeting on the issue. The public were allowed to observe, but not to participate at this meeting; again 'the real depth of feeling was not conveyed by any stretch of the imagination'. Dorothy Thomson of the Townhill Action Committee wrote a lengthy letter to the press detailing the discrepancy:

> In failing to convey this total rejection by the parents of the Director's proposals to the members of the Council, the committee has not served the community well and we fear is continuing, however unintentionally, the policy of disinformation and misrepresentation initiated by the Education Authority in presenting their proposals. (Dunfermline Press, 21 June 1984)

Nonetheless, the School Council, whilst endorsing the general principle of rezoning, called for alternative options to be considered. It would appear, however, that the arguments voiced by parents at the public meetings were only part of the problem. The letters received by the education authority over the period of consultation elaborated on parents' disquiet. Parents at Culross, for

Rezoning

example, were concerned that in the short term at least, the new arrangements would require that the children travel on the same bus as children attending the denominational secondary school. Parents in the Canmore area wrote at length about their fears of children walking through the Abbey View area. The education authority went to considerable lengths to meet certain of the objections, negotiating, for example, plans to provide a new service route from the Canmore area to Woodmill HS which would provide transport in the morning and evening. But not every cost could be offset: for some Townhill children, for example, there would be additional travel; Dunfermline HS would experience increased pedestrian and bus traffic.

> Somewhere along the line we had to trade off these sort of objections against the long-term property implications of keeping the status quo. (Education department official)

A number of objections, however, particularly those from Canmore parents relating to their fears about children crossing the Abbey View area, were considered by the authority to be 'irrational':

> good law abiding citizens live in Abbey View, the totality of the environment is something that leaves a lot to be desired but the problem here is to improve the environment, not for the benefit of the people who are occasionally walking to and fro, but for the benefit of the people who are living there. (Education department official)

Counter-arguments were presented and alternative suggestions made, but not all objections could be endorsed:

> we think we went as far as was reasonable to meeting objections ... the transport one for instance ... and that the balance of views expressed were not rationally grounded ... they were based on this attitude towards this area called Abbey View rather than on the actual needs of their children. (Education department official)

The argument from homeowners in Canmore that the estate would develop differential house prices according to the secondary catchment was also declared to be without substance: Limekilns had exhibited no such tendency after rezoning.

OUTCOME

The outcome of the process outlined in this paper was that in August 1984 Fife education committee agreed to the necessity of rezoning in principle, but with the exception of the small school at Crombie where, encouraged by the headteacher, there had been general agreement to the plan to rezone to Woodmill, the proposals under discussion would not be implemented. It was stressed in the report to committee that from the public meetings 'the Schools subcommittee can be left in no doubt that the proposals were not acceptable to the communities concerned'. (3) The presentation of the report on public consultation demonstrates a desire to illustrate that public opinion has indeed been heard; a desire to quash those who at public meetings had anticipated that their views would not be reported, or were sceptical that they would be heeded. Indeed, so many parents speculated on what would have been the outcome if there had been no leak and therefore no time to prepare their detailed opposition. This strategy of presenting the authority as responsive and flexible is further demonstrated by the tone of the press statement released by the chair of the committee. He acknowledged the necessity to protect standards of educational provision in the three schools, but argued that with possible housing developments rezoning would be premature.

> I trust that this statement will confirm in the clearest possible fashion that we do consider the views expressed by those who are consulted and that in the final analysis these views either collectively or individually are taken in account before any decision or recommendation is proposed. (Press release, July 1984)

The local press comment was less conciliatory.

> Education Committee Convenor, Regional Councillor Tom Dair, as a long-in-the-tooth local authority politician, recognised when he and his committee were on a 'loser'. And as gracefully as he could, and making

the usual specious noises relative to the exercise of the democratic process by 'listening to the parents' views' he, last week, publicly indicated that the current rezoning proposals were to be shelved. Protocol demands that he should not publicly scourge his officials for having so monumentally misjudged the mood and intelligence of parents in the area. (Dunfermline Press, 20 July 1984)

The initial reaction of the two action groups to the abandonment of the proposals was, of course, one of delight. Neither group had initially thought there was any prospect of success: they were concerned rather to register maximum parental opposition to what they considered to be mere 'tokenism' (Arnstein, 1969). Dorothy Thomson, chairwoman of Townhill, gave her analysis of the situation:

I really think they were unprepared for what they got. I think they thought we were a lot of women with nothing to do with our time but sit and take what they threw at us. It was the power of the people and the fact that parents did their homework before these meetings. I don't think the Education Department did their homework. They didn't have any other options, but now they are going to have to find some. (Dunfermline Press, 13 July 1984)

After the initial celebration of victory, however, the relief of both groups was tempered by an awareness that a revised plan might emerge at a later date. Canmore parents considered that the issue would resurface after the next elections and quoted a headline from Councillor Dair in the Dunfermline Press of 14 September 1984 to the effect that 'rezoning is the ultimate solution'. Townhill believed that their school was being run down in anticipation of a new school at Bellyeoman as that housing area develops, a school that would feed to Woodmill HS. Members of the action group were determined that the impetus developed over this proposal should be sustained and that any option produced in the future should be submitted to equal scrutiny. More significantly, however, there was evidence of a wider process of politicisation. Group members who had previously been ignorant of the operation of the local authority (that, for example, teachers were appointed by council members) had now had a glimpse of the authority in action and, displeased at what they saw, particularly at what they perceived as a lack of openness, a lack of will to consult or even to inform, were interested in pursuing the debate further. At the most immediate level, for example, members began to ask why there was no parent-teacher association at Townhill primary school. More generally, the Townhill group member who was initially wary of the campaign has now become interested in the issue of parental representation as a whole and has attended, as have individuals from Canmore, discussions on the future organisation of school councils in the area. It is too early to assess whether the response was limited to the single issue or whether a longer term demand for accountability has been initiated. However, there are at least suggestions of the latter.

The professionals who produced the rezoning plan consider that 'the committee has simply shelved it'. Guided by political expediency, the authority felt compelled to respond to the strength of public objection and to abandon, at least for the present, its objective of rationalising accommodation and educational provision.

> You're in a politically sensitive environment, you are in an area where the committee are saying we have to be aware of political realities, if we go ahead with this as a proposal it might be in political terms you could lose out at the next election. (Education department official)

With this particular problem, however, the authority appear to have little prospect of success, if they are going to be constrained by the extent of public reaction.

> If you're going to go by the yardstick of public reaction, your only means of reducing the catchment area is to go to the areas such as perhaps Inzievar where you have largely working class areas, where you would not have vociferous reaction. (Education department official)

To organise on such a basis would, however, be to breach the basic commitment to a socially varied catchment population.

CONCLUSION

This case study has provided a good example both of the detailed negotiations which underlie the first four stages of Jennings' policy-making process and of the operation of a small section of the participatory process. It illustrates the tensions between professionals concerned to promote consistent policy development and politicians responding to unanticipated local outcry. In this respect it is of course unusual in that the parental response was heeded and the reorganisation proposals were set aside. Participation exercises are increasingly viewed with suspicion:

> Participation is ... a process of cooling-in people to decisions which have in fact been taken in advance, and which, apart from small, even derisory points, will not be changed. (Rose and Hanmer, 1975, p. 33)

In this instance, although the consultation process was set in train as little more than a formality, probably not even with overtones of manipulation, it quickly gathered a momentum to which officials appeared unable to respond. Although anxious to hold to their convictions 'that in the fullness of time the situation would have evened itself out' and that what they were witnessing was 'in part anyway a simple hysteria, a hysterical reaction to proposals for perhaps socio-political motives', the use in particular of the public meetings as a ventilating mechanism became too disordered for the members to contain and it was felt necessary to respond to that vocal section of the community who were able to express their opposition to the proposals.

The education authority emerges from this exercise with the problem unresolved and with uncertainty over how they should proceed. The dilemma would appear to highlight, critically, questions central to any consultative process, namely the weights attached to the interests of different groups within society and the extent to which the exigencies of the democratic process dictate that the voice of certain of these groups should dominate. The fear of several officials, based not only on this exercise but on their experience of other attempts at reorganisation within and between primary schools, is that to take heed of public outcry may be to hear only a section of public opinion. This would be further endorsed by their awareness that when they have been successful in overcoming the initial threshold of resistance plans have proceeded with minimum objection, generally they would argue, to the greater benefit of the population as a whole. For the conflict, as in so much of policy-making, is in the relationship between individual choice and collective gain: a distribution of pupils more optimal in terms of the authority's objectives or the short-term disquiet of those most immediately affected.

NOTES

The research on which this chapter is based forms part of an ESRC-funded programme of research on parental choice in education, carried out at the University of Edinburgh. I am grateful to the ESRC for financial support and to the parents, officials and councillors who discussed the proposals with me.

1. Rezoning of the Catchment of Secondary Schools in the Dunfermline Area. Report for meeting of the Schools subcommittee, Fife Regional Council, March 1984.
2. Paper on Proposed Rezoning of Catchment Areas of Secondary Schools in Dunfermline, Canmore Parents Action Group, June 1984.
3. Rezoning of Catchment Areas of Secondary Schools in the Dunfermline Area. Report on Public Consultation. Report for meeting of the Schools subcommittee, Fife Regional Council, August 1984.
4. Townhill parents did object that one of their major points, that children did not reach school at all in bad weather, had been minuted incorrectly. The distortion of minutes is a device chronicled by Dennis (in Leonard, (ed.) 1975).

Chapter Four

A TALE OF TWO CITIES: THE IMPACT OF PARENTAL CHOICE ON ADMISSIONS TO PRIMARY SCHOOLS IN EDINBURGH AND DUNDEE

Gillian Raab and Michael Adler

INTRODUCTION

Section 28A of the Education (Scotland) Act 1980 gives parents in Scotland the right to choose the schools which they wish their children to attend. As of 1982, parents can make a 'placing request' for a school other than the school to which their child is allocated by the local authority, and the request must be granted unless one of a small number of statutory grounds for refusal applies. Before this date local authorities were free to operate whatever allocation policies they wished, and while some were very flexible, others were not. A larger proportion of parents have made placing requests in the cities than in rural areas, and the majority of requests have been at the start of primary (P1) or secondary (S1) schooling. We have therefore focused on P1 and S1 requests in two Scottish cities, Dundee and Edinburgh. We report on the P1 requests here.

Edinburgh is the larger and more middle-class of the two cities, yet the proportion of parents making requests in Edinburgh has been lower than in Dundee. Placing requests at P1 rose from 13 per cent of pupils in 1982 to 19 per cent in 1985. The corresponding figures for Dundee were 15 per cent and 22 per cent. Before the 'Parents' Charter' legislation, Edinburgh operated a more rigid allocation policy than Dundee.

The proportion of placing requests was much lower in the Catholic sector, probably because of the larger area served by each school. In both cities there was substantial movement between non-denominational schools in all parts of the city, with some schools making substantial gains and others suffering substantial losses. In seven out of 38 schools in Dundee more than half the P1 pupils came from outside the catchment area, while in Edinburgh this was true for only three out of 82 schools.

Most of the movement between schools involved a move to an adjacent school (83 per cent of all requests in Edinburgh and 85 per cent in Dundee). There are extreme differences in social composition between school catchment areas in both cities. However similar schools tend to be grouped together in certain areas of the city. Because of the local nature of the P1 requests, movement was predominantly within areas which are homogeneous with respect to social composition and housing tenure. In both cities there is evidence of a set of sub-systems of movement, usually within these defined areas.

The main factors which influenced moves between adjacent schools were similar in the two cities. Movement tended to be towards larger schools and away from schools in areas of economic and social deprivation (measured by unemployment, single parents and lack of car ownership). In Dundee there was no tendency for requests to be made away from schools in council housing schemes, but in Edinburgh there was some evidence of this. However, in both cities, there was considerable local movement which could not be explained by any of these factors.

In both cities, the moves to non-adjacent schools were rather different. They tended to be away from local authority housing schemes, towards schools in middle-class areas and areas where a high proportion of adults have been through higher education.

Thus the impact of the placing request legislation on the primary school intake has resulted in sharp gains and losses for individual schools. However, these aggregate analyses suggest that the gains and losses are unlikely to have resulted in major changes to the social composition of the schools. This comes about from the local nature of the movement between schools and the social geography of the two cities where the existing school catchment areas seem to follow social as well as physical boundaries.

BACKGROUND TO THE 1981 ACT

Prior to the passage of the Education (Scotland) Act 1981, education authorities in Scotland, like their counterparts in

A Tale of Two Cities

England and Wales, enjoyed considerable freedom in determining which school children should attend. Under Section 1(1) of the Education (Scotland) Act 1946, a statutory duty was placed on education authorities 'to secure that adequate and efficient provision is made throughout their area of all forms of primary, secondary and further education'. The 1946 Act imposed a further duty on authorities 'to prepare and submit for the approval of the Secretary of State a scheme or schemes of their powers and duties' and the Secretary of State could either approve or ask the authority to modify its scheme. The Secretary of State was also given powers to declare an education authority in default of its statutory duties and to order it to discharge its duty.

It was, of course, the case that, under Section 29(1), the Secretary of State and education authorities were

> to have regard to the general principle that, as far as is compatible with the provision of suitable instruction and training and the avoidance of unreasonable public expenditure, pupils are to be educated in accordance with the wishes of their parents.

However, this did not mean, nor was it intended to mean, that individual pupils were necessarily and in all cases to be educated in accordance with the wishes of their parents. This provision, which was modelled on the analogous provisions of Section 76 of the Education Act 1944, was part of the historic compromise between Church and State which brought the majority of church schools into the state education system. As a result of this compromise, education authorities were free to operate denominational schools, to which pupils could be allocated 'in accordance with the wishes of their parents'. But, 'having regard to the general principle' did not impose an absolute duty on authorities to respect parental wishes (Meredith, 1981). Thus, it did not confer strong or enforceable rights on individual parents. As Lord Justice Denning said of the analogous provisions in the 1944 Act in Watt v Kesteven C C (1955) 1 QB 408, one of the leading English cases,

> Section 76 does not say that pupils must in all cases be educated in accordance with the wishes of their parents. It only lays down a general principle to which the (authority) must have regard. This leaves it open to

115

A Tale of Two Cities

the (authority) to have regard to other things as well and also to make exceptions to the general principle if it thinks fit to do so. It cannot be said that an (authority) is simply at fault because it does not see fit to comply with parents' wishes.

A number of Scottish decisions likewise made it clear that Section 29(1) of the Scottish Act placed Scottish education authorities under a duty to take parents' wishes into account but did not require an authority to give effect to the wishes of an individual parent (Himsworth, 1980).

As far as initial allocation to primary school was concerned, most education authorities in Scotland adopted the catchment area principle under which all the children living in a designated area were allocated to their district school. Some authorities were more rigid than others and were reluctant to make exceptions while others were more flexible and could be persuaded to do so without difficulty if space was available at the requested school. Transfer from primary school to secondary school was, at least in urban areas, initially based on the principle of selection. However, with the advent of comprehensive reorganisation, selection was replaced - either by a system of 'feeder' primary schools or through the use of catchment areas analogous to those used for primary schools. As with allocation to primary school, some education authorities operated rather rigid transfer schemes and countenanced few exceptions, while others were much more flexible. However, the Secretary of State could, and in one celebrated case (described below), did use his powers to force an education authority to admit pupils to secondary schools where places were available.

Parents who were unable to secure the admission of their child to the school of their choice could refuse to send their child to school. They would then be served with an attendance order, ordering them to discharge their statutory duty to provide education for their child by sending him or her to the school named in the order. However, they also had a right of appeal to the sheriff, who could substitute another school for the one named by the authority. A few parents used this procedure and were able in this way to secure the admission of their child to the school of their choice (Himsworth, 1980). The comparable procedures in England and Wales involved an appeal to the Secretary of State rather than an appeal to the courts. However, while

A Tale of Two Cities

Scottish parents had to keep their children off school before they could exercise their right to appeal, English parents did not have to do so and could, in addition, appeal to the Secretary of State on the grounds that the decision of the authority to refuse their child a place had not been reasonable. By the late 1970s, the DES was receiving over 1,000 such appeals per year (Meredith, 1981). Although few of them were upheld, the DES did get involved in disputes between parents and a fair number of authorities which operated fairly rigid allocation and transfer policies. This was not the case in Scotland where, with one or two exceptions, education authorities operated their allocation and transfer policies in a reasonably flexible manner. As a result, although the Scottish Office was under some pressure to confront the more restrictive authorities, this pressure was local rather than national and there was no very audible clamour for legislation in Scotland.

This was in stark contrast to the situation in England and Wales (Stillman and Maychell, 1986; Tweedie, 1986). There the issue of parental choice had been on the political agenda for several years. Norman St John Stevas launched the 'Parents' Charter' in 1974 and a Charter of Parents' Rights was included in the Conservative Manifesto for the October 1974 election. A Conservative back-bencher put forward a Private Member's Bill in 1974 and in 1976, the Conservatives introduced a series of amendments to Labour's Education Bill in an attempt to publicise their concern with parental choice. Although neither of these parliamentary initiatives met with any success, they did help to put pressure on the Labour government to propose some form of parental choice legislation of its own. A number of parental choice provisions were included in the 1978 Education Bill, which lapsed when the 1979 general election was called.

While the Conservative opposition and the Labour government both attempted to legislate for parental choice in England and Wales, there was no comparable attempts to legislate for Scotland. However, the 1979 Conservative election manifesto included a commitment to legislate for parental choice and it was clear that this commitment was intended to apply to Scotland as well as to England and Wales. Soon after being returned to office, the Thatcher government introduced legislation for England and Wales, and this was followed, a short while later, by legislation for Scotland.

COMPARISONS BETWEEN SCOTTISH AND ENGLISH LEGISLATION

The general structure of the parental choice provisions introduced by Sections 28A to 28F of the Education (Scotland) Act 1980 (inserted by Section 1 of the Education (Scotland) Act 1981) resembles quite clearly the parental choice provisions introduced by Section 6 of the Education Act 1980. In Scotland, as in England, parents were given the right to request that their children are admitted to a particular school or schools; education authorities are required to comply with parental requests unless a statutory exception to this general duty applies; dissatisfied parents have the right to appeal to a statutory appeal committee and, if the latter finds in favour of the parent, its decision is binding on the authority; and the authority is required to provide the parent with information about the school to which their child is allocated and about any other school if requested by the parents. However, there are also some important differences between the two pieces of legislation. First, the statutory exceptions to the authorities' general duty to comply with parents' requests are broad and general in England but much more specific in Scotland. In England, the crucial exception, which applies when compliance with the parents' requests would 'prejudice the provision of efficient education or the efficient use of resources', enables an authority to justify a refusal by referring to conditions at schools other than the one requested by the parents, including the effects of granting requests on the intakes to under-subscribed schools. By contrast, in Scotland, where the primary exceptions apply when compliance would entail the employment of an additional teacher by the authority or significant extensions or alterations to the school or 'be likely to be seriously detrimental to order and discipline at the school or the educational well-being of the pupils there', the authority can only refer to conditions at the school requested by the parents. Secondly, parents in Scotland can appeal an adverse decision of an appeal committee to a sheriff (whose standing and jurisdiction approximates to that of a County Court judge) while parents in England have no further right of appeal. Thirdly, where an appeal committee or a sheriff upholds an appeal in Scotland, the authority must review the cases of all parents in similar circumstances who have not appealed and, if it does not alter its decisions, it must grant

A Tale of Two Cities

the parents a further right of appeal. There are no comparable provisions in the English legislation.
From the above, it should be clear that Scottish parents have rather stronger rights to choose schools for their children than their English counterparts. This is somewhat ironic, since, as we have shown, the primary impetus for parental choice legislation came from England. It is not known whether Kenneth Baker was aware of these differences when he made his pre-election pledge to strengthen parental choice in England. However, if his proposal to prevent authorities from turning down requests for popular schools which could accommodate the children in question was enacted into legislation, it would have the effect of bringing the English legislation into line with legislation which is already in place in Scotland (Boseley, 1987; Judd, 1987). For this reason, the operational consequences of the Scottish legislation should be of considerable interest to an English as well as a Scottish audience.

THE TAKE-UP OF PLACING REQUESTS (1)

In the first four years following the implementation of the Scottish legislation, the number of placing requests doubled from 10,456 in 1982 to 20,795 in 1985 (see Table 4.1). Of these placing requests 96.3 per cent were for children of school age and 3.7 per cent for under-age children, the number of such requests increasing from 251 (1.5 per cent of the total) in 1983 (no statistics are available for 1982) to 1,844 (8.8 per cent of the total) in 1985. Among children of school age, more than half the requests (56.5 per cent) were for primary school while less than half (43.5 per cent) were for secondary school. After increasing steadily from 1982-84, the number of placing requests for primary schools levelled off in 1985 while the number for secondary schools actually declined somewhat. Although these figures should be interpreted in the context of falling school rolls, they suggest that a plateau may now have been reached.
Over the four years 1982-85, 97.4 per cent of requests for primary school and 93.8 per cent of requests for secondary school were granted, either at the initial stage or at appeal committee or on appeal to the sheriff (see Table 4.2). However, there was a downward trend between 1983 (when 98.5 per cent of primary school requests and 97.3 per

A Tale of Two Cities

Table 4.1: Number of Placing Requests received by Stage of Schooling, 1982-5

	1982	1983	1984	1985	Total	
Under-age	-	261	513	1,844	2,618	3.7%
Primary	5,746	9,440	11,272	11,561	38,019	54.4%
Secondary	4,710	7,432	8,758	8,390	29,290	41.9%
	10,456	17,133	20,543	21,795	69,927	(100%)

Source: Scottish Education Department (1986)

Table 4.2: Proportion of Placing Requests Granted (initially or on appeal) by Stage of Schooling, 1982-85

	1982	1983	1984	1985	Overall
Under-age	-	47.0%	63.0%	63.4%	61.2%
Primary	96.9%	98.5%	97.7%	95.7%	97.4%
Secondary	96.3%	97.3%	92.8%	90.3%	93.8%

Source: Scottish Education Department (1986)

Table 4.3: First-year Placing Requests as a Proportion of Total for Primary and Secondary Schools, 1982-85

	1982	1983	1984	1985	Total
Primaries					
% P1	n.a.	48.2%	50.9%	55.3%	51.7%
% P2-P7	n.a.	51.8%	49.1%	44.7%	48.3%
Secondaries					
% S1	n.a.	62.9%	66.9%	68.7%	66.3%
% S2-S6	n.a.	37.1%	33.1%	31.3%	33.7%

Source: Scottish Education Department (1986)

cent of secondary school requests were granted) and 1985 (when the corresponding figures were 95.7 per cent and 90.3 per cent), reflecting the growing practice of a number of authorities to restrict admissions to schools which would otherwise have been over-subscribed. In contrast to these very high success rates, the success rates for under-age placing requests were substantially lower.

At both primary and secondary levels, the majority of requests have been for children entering the first year of school (see Table 4.3). In 1985, 55.3 per cent of primary requests were for Primary 1 (P1) while 68.7 per cent of secondary requests were for Secondary 1 (S1). It follows that 9.6 per cent of pupils entering the first year of primary school and 8.7 per cent of pupils entering the first year of secondary school had made placing requests, compared with an average of 1.4 per cent for pupils entering P2-P7 and 0.9 per cent for pupils entering S2-S6.

National figures, such as those mentioned above, mask considerable regional and local variations. The more urbanised education authorities, where many schools are situated relatively near one another and several schools are within reasonable travelling distance for many pupils, have higher placing request rates than the largely rural authorities (see Table 4.4).

Within regions, the same relationships are to be found and placing request rates are highest in the cities and lowest in the rural areas surrounding them. Thus, for example, in 1984, 21.1 per cent of pupils entering the first year of primary school and 19.8 per cent of pupils entering the first year of secondary school in Dundee had made placing requests, compared with rates of 15.4 per cent and 13.1 per cent for Tayside Region. Likewise, in Edinburgh, 16.1 per cent of pupils entering P1 and 16.9 per cent of pupils entering S1 had made placing requests compared with rates of 11.0 per cent and 11.8 per cent in Lothian Region.

BACKGROUND TO THE STUDY

In the course of a wide-ranging programme of research on the origins and impact of the Parents' Charter in Scotland, we have examined the impact of parental choice on admissions to primary and secondary schools in the education authorities (Adler, Petch and Tweedie, 1987). The two authorities, Tayside and Lothian, rank first and second in the proportion of placing requests received at both primary and secondary level. However, in other respects, they embody some important historical and contextual differences. Prior to the implementation of the 1981 Act,

Table 4.4: Placing Request Rates by Region, 1984

Under-age		Primary 1 (P1)		Secondary 1 (S1)	
Highlands	3.4%	Tayside	15.4%	Tayside	13.3%
Borders	2.1%	Lothian	11.0%	Lothian	11.8%
Shetland	1.8%	Grampian	10.0%	Grampian	11.0%
Western Isles	1.8%	Strathclyde	9.1%	Strathclyde	7.8%
Strathclyde	0.8%	(Glasgow)	(12.7%)	(Glasgow)	(10.3%)
(Renfrew)	1.7%				
Lothian	0.3%	Highland	1.6%	Highland	1.9%
Grampian	0.2%	Western Isles	1.3%	Shetland	1.3%
Dumfries and Galloway	0.0	Orkney	0.8%	Orkney	0.7%
Orkney	0.0	Shetland	0.0	Borders	0.7%

Source: Scottish Education Department (1986)

A Tale of Two Cities

Tayside Region had, for many years, been under Conservative control and had operated a very flexible allocation and transfer policy. As a result, the legislation made little immediate difference to regional policy. By contrast, Lothian Region, which was under Labour control until 1982, became strongly committed to the concept of the neighbourhood school. Children were allocated to their local (catchment area) school and, although they could request an alternative school, such requests were usually turned down unless the child in question already had a sibling at the school or there were documented medical reasons which made it appropriate that the child should be offered a place. When the Conservatives were returned to government in 1979, Lothian soon found itself in conflict with the government over its transfer policies. The government scored a partial victory when it called in and amended Lothian's transfer scheme but, with the passage of the 1981 Act, its victory became total and the region was forced to reverse its previous policy and to drop its strict adherence to neighbourhood schools.

Instead of examining flows between schools throughout these two Regions, we focused on moves between schools in Dundee and Edinburgh where the incidence of placing requests is highest. For similar reasons, we focused on admissions to the first year of primary and the first year of secondary school. In this chapter, we discuss the results of our primary school analysis; our analysis of moves between secondary schools is reported elsewhere (Adler and Raab, 1988).

In analysing our data, we have attempted to bear in mind some of the arguments which were advanced by supporters and opponents of the 1981 legislation. It was widely believed that the legislation was introduced specifically to deal with the situation in Lothian and, in particular with the situation in Edinburgh, and that it would have greatest impact there. Advocates of the legislation pointed to the fact that 'good' schools would grow while critics pointed to the fact that the loss of pupils would accentuate the problems faced by schools in 'poor' areas. Supporters of the legislation argued that it would provide a means for some children, at least, to escape from schools in deprived areas while opponents predicted that the main beneficiaries would be middle-class parents who would use it to obtain the schooling they wanted for their children. However, it is important to note that both these views

Table 4.5: Placing Requests at P1 Entry, 1982-85

| | Non-denominational schools |||| | Catholic schools ||||
| | Edinburgh || Dundee || | Edinburgh || Dundee ||
	Number	%	Number	%		Number	%	Number	%
1982	408	13.1	280	17.5		23	8.1	22	5.8
1983	443	14.4	377	24.7		25	8.6	42	11.4
1984	604	16.8	371	23.5		30	8.6	34	11.1
1985	688	19.2	402	24.6		51	17.4	34	10.0

Sources: Lothian Regional Council and Tayside Regional Council

A Tale of Two Cities

implied that the legislation could have quite a substantial effect on the social and educational composition of school intakes. The data used in this analysis comprise placing request data and other administrative data made available to us by the education authorities, and catchment area data derived from the 1981 census. The analysis is all based on aggregate data and considerable care must be taken in making inferences which apply to individual pupils (Borgatta and Jackson, 1980). Moreover, because we did not have any measures of the 'quality' of the schools concerned (neither Region makes any standardised measurements of pupil attainment or keeps any standardised record of teaching styles or school based activities) the analysis lacks certain key variables. Nevertheless, the results are not only of interest in themselves but also provide a context for interpreting data derived from a survey of 400 parents whose children entered the first year of primary school in 1984 (Petch, 1986).

THE TWO CITIES

Edinburgh is about twice the size of Dundee and has 82 non-denominational primary schools with more than 3,000 pupils entering P1 in each year. Dundee, by comparison, has 38 non-denominational primary schools and an annual intake of about 1,500 pupils into P1. In each city there is a small Catholic sector: this comprises 15 primary schools in Edinburgh and 14 in Dundee. In each of the four years since the legislation was introduced, the proportion of placing requests in Dundee was higher than in Edinburgh (Table 4.5). One plausible reason for this is that there are proportionately more P1 places at independent schools in Edinburgh than there are in Dundee. (2) Among the non-denominational schools in Edinburgh, the proportion of P1 pupils making placing requests increased steadily from 13 per cent in 1982 to 19 per cent in 1985. In Dundee, the proportion increased from 18 per cent in 1982 to about 25 per cent in 1983 and then levelled off. These increases are in line with trends for the rest of Scotland shown in Table 4.3. The proportion of placing requests for Catholic schools was much lower, probably because catchment areas for Catholic primary schools are much larger and the schools therefore further apart. The Catholic sector is, in any case,

125

Figure 4.1A: Placing Requests out of Edinburgh Primary Schools, 1982-5

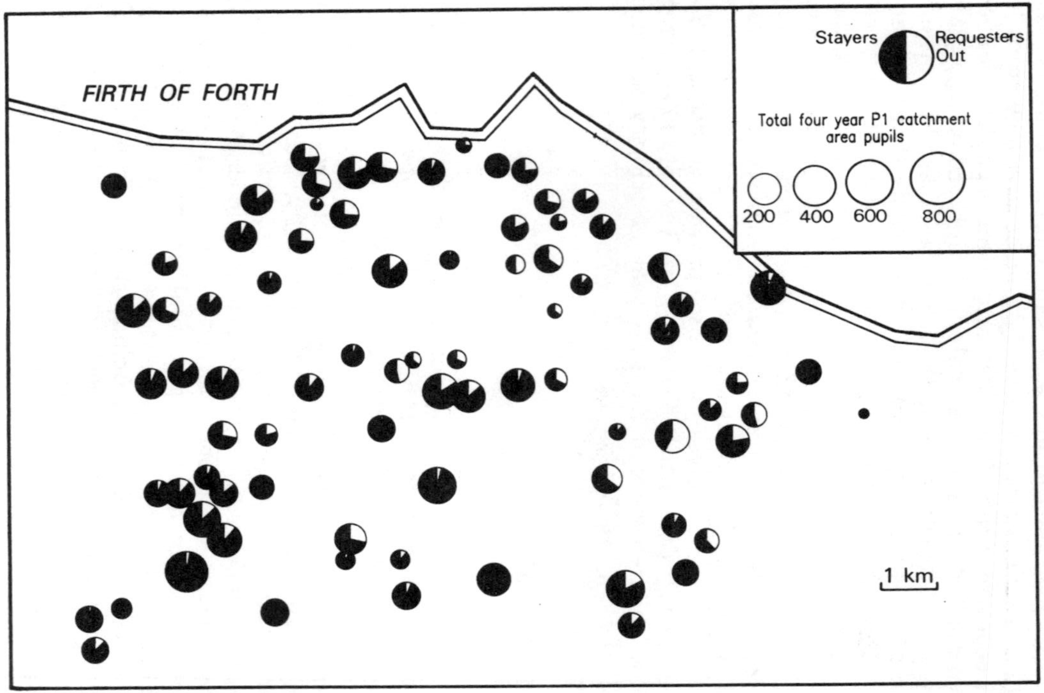

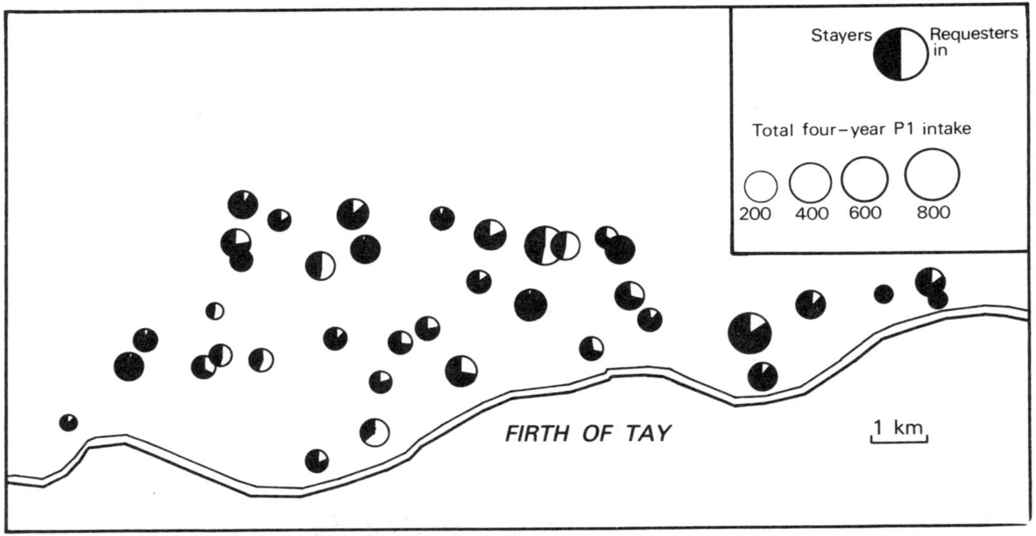

Figure 4.1B: Placing Requests into Dundee Primary Schools, 1982-5

quite small in both cities and will not be considered further. In Dundee, no P1 placing requests were refused over the period 1982-5, although some schools exceeded their nominal capacities. In Edinburgh, a total of 35 P1 placing requests (1.6 per cent of the total) were refused over the four-year period, and in addition nine children who registered late were refused admission to their catchment area school.

In both Edinburgh and Dundee schools that lost pupils and schools that gained pupils were to be found in all areas of the city. The Edinburgh map (Figure 4.1A) shows the proportion of catchment area pupils who made a placing request for another school. Each circle represents a school. The centre of each circle corresponds to the geographical location of the school, (3) while the area of each circle is proportional to the P1 catchment area population over the period 1982-5. The white segments represent the proportion of pupils who made a placing request for a school outside the catchment area during this period. The Dundee map (Figure 4.1B) shows the proportion of pupils at each school who had made a placing request from outside the catchment area. On this map, the area of each circle now is proportional to the number of P1 pupils starting school. Thus, the white segments show the proportion of the pupils who entered the school by making a placing request over the four-year period. Thus, the Edinburgh map represents movements out of catchment areas while the Dundee map represents movements into schools over the four-year period.

In both cities, some schools made substantial gains while others made substantial losses. However, substantial losses and gains were more common in Dundee than in Edinburgh. Figure 4.1A shows that one primary school out of the 82 primary schools in Edinburgh lost more than half its catchment area population. The figure for Dundee was two out of 38 (map not shown). More strikingly, Figure 4.1B shows that seven out of the 38 primary schools in Dundee gained more than half their first year pupils from outside their catchment areas. This compares with three out of 82 primary schools in Edinburgh (map not shown). Both sets of figures are in line with the relative numbers of placing requests in the two cities noted above.

A Tale of Two Cities

MOVEMENT BETWEEN SCHOOLS

Complete data for movements between schools in the two cities were available for 1984 only. Preliminary analyses showed that most of the P1 requests were for a school close to the catchment area school. To capture this, every pair of adjacent schools was identified (without reference to placing request data) by the following operational definition: two schools were defined as 'adjacent' if their catchment areas had a common boundary running through a residential area. Thus, schools with contiguous catchment areas which were separated, for example, by a park or a golf course were not held to be adjacent. In Edinburgh, 83 per cent of placing requests and, in Dundee, 85 per cent were to an adjacent school, so defined. Thus, it made a good deal of sense initially to focus on moves between adjacent schools. This made it possible to examine the influences on choice of school by calculating the probability of moving from each school to every adjacent school and relating this probability to the characteristics of the schools concerned and their catchment areas.

First, network diagrams showing every possible adjacent boundary and the movements in both directions across each boundary were prepared (see Figure 4.2A for Edinburgh and Figure 4.2B for Dundee). The positions of several schools in each city had to be adjusted to make it possible to plot all the movements (cf. Figures 4.1A and 4.1B). Several features are immediately apparent for both cities. There are very few pairs of schools between which pupils moved in both directions. The movement between schools took place among subsystems or groups of schools, which appear to correspond to neighbourhoods within the city. For Edinburgh, in particular, which has more natural barriers (for example, Edinburgh Castle and various parks) than Dundee, these neighbourhoods are partly determined by the physical geography of the city. We will see below that they also correspond to areas that are relatively homogeneous in their social composition.

EXPLAINING MOVEMENT

What differences between schools best predict movement between two adjacent schools? To answer this question, two sources of data for classifying schools were available. The

129

Figures 4.2A: Placing Requests across Adjacent Boundaries between Primary Schools in Edinburgh in 1984

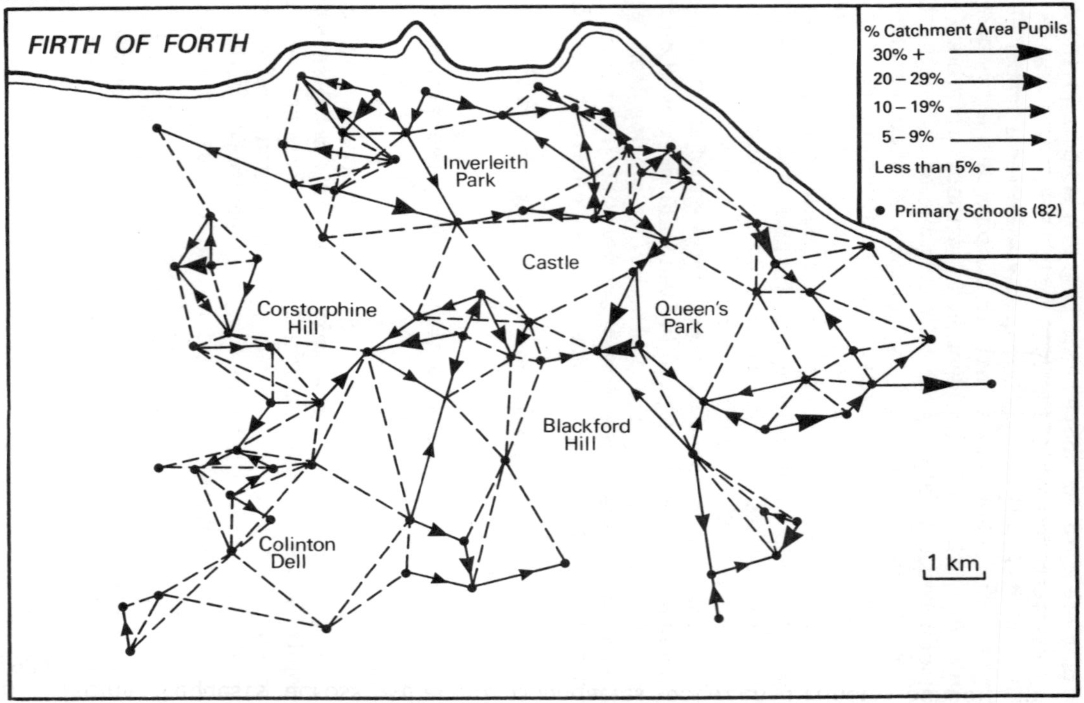

Figure 4.2B: Placing Requests across Adjacent Boundaries between Primary Schools in Dundee in 1984

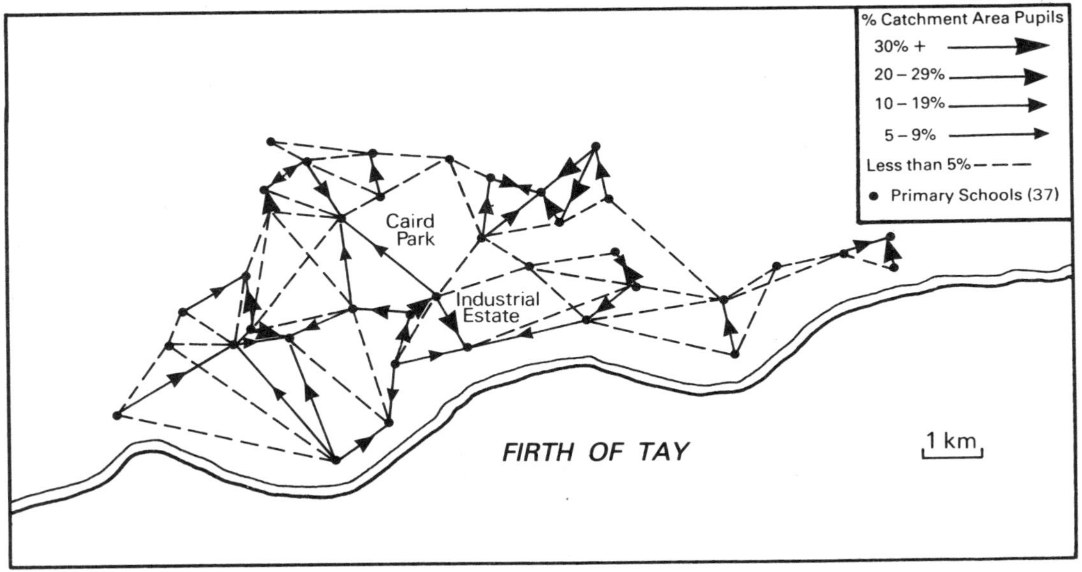

A Tale of Two Cities

Figure 4.3: Distributions of Six Variables derived from the 1981 Census for Primary School Catchment Areas (see Table 4.6 for mnemonics)

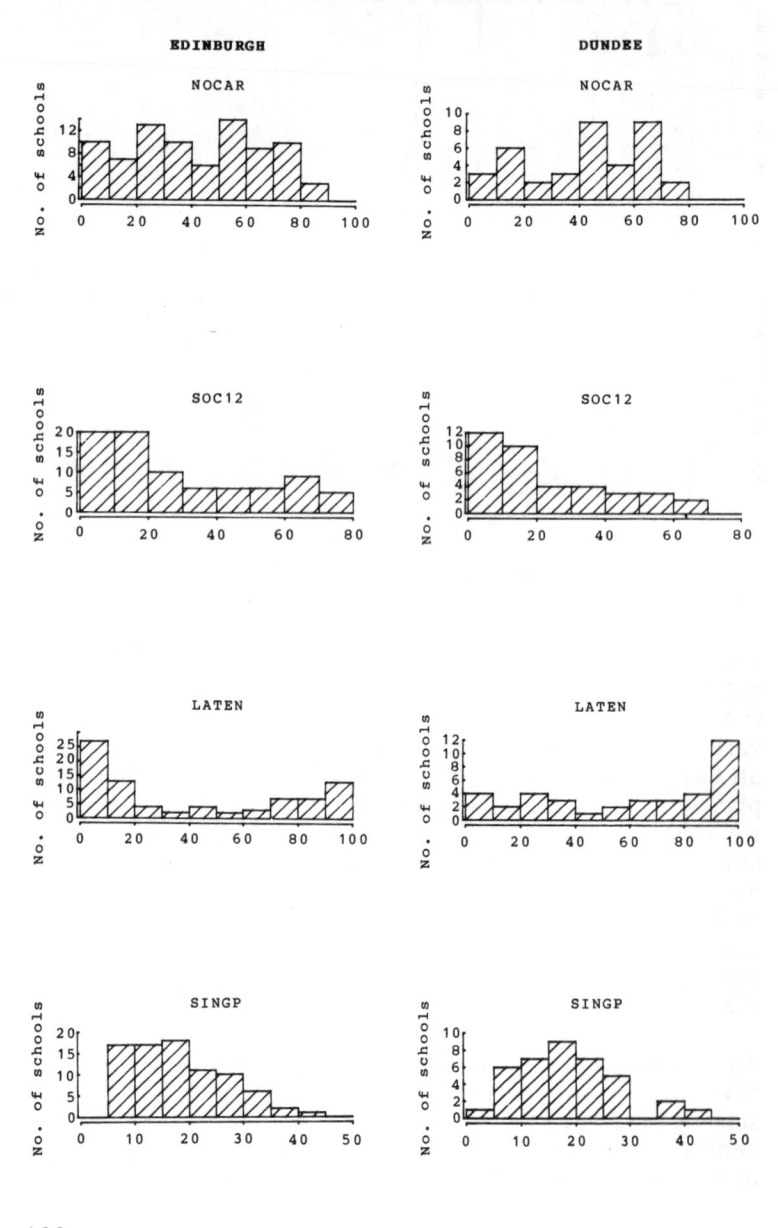

A Tale of Two Cities

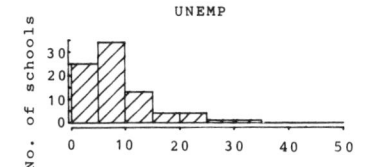

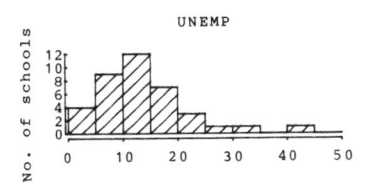

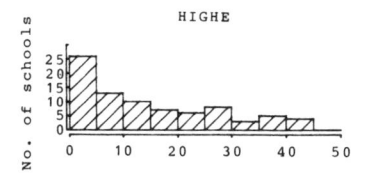

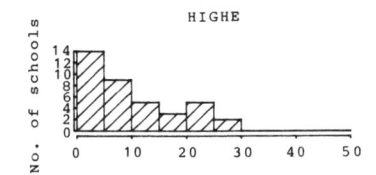

Source: 1981 Population Census

first was data from the 1981 census, aggregated to school catchment areas using the Small Area Statistics Package (SASPAC (SASPAC, 1983)). We selected a total of six variables from the 1981 census on the grounds that they had all been used in other pieces of social research and had some plausible relationship to parental choice. Wherever possible we obtained information from the census that related to children in the catchment area, for example the local authority tenure variable refers to the percentage of children aged 5-15 in the catchment area living in local authority housing. Details of the six variables derived from the census data are given in Table 4.6. The distributions of these census indicators are shown in Figure 4.3.

In both cities residential segregation resulted in distributions of the census variables that were skewed towards the two extremes. Thus, 16 of the 38 primary schools in Dundee have catchment areas in which 80-100 per cent of the children live in council housing. The same is true in Edinburgh where 24 out of the 82 primary schools have

133

Table 4.6: Variables derived from the 1981 Census Data

Mnemonic	Description	Census table	Sample (a)
NOCAR	Percentage of children aged 5-15 living in households with no car	31	(100%)
SOC12	Percentage of children aged 0-15 living in households with head in social class I and II	52	(10%)
LATEN	Percentage of children aged 5-15 living in local authority housing	29	(100%)
SINGP	Percentage of households with dependent children containing one-parent families	31	(100%)
UNEMP	Percentage of economically active residents seeking work	20	(100%)
HIGHE	Percentage of residents aged 18-59/64 with degrees etc	48 and 52	(10%)

(a) Some of the census data are only coded for a 10% random sample of households

Source: 1981 Population Census

catchment areas which consist almost entirely of local authority housing. In Edinburgh, which has a smaller percentage of local authority housing overall, there are also 40 schools whose catchment areas contain virtually no local authority housing. There is a smaller number of such schools in Dundee, but in neither city are there many schools whose catchment areas contain a roughly equal mix of public and private housing.

A similar picture emerges for social class I and II. In Edinburgh there are a number of schools with catchment areas containing 70-80 per cent social class I and II households (which, in terms of national figures, is a very high percentage), while 20 schools out of the 82 have catchment areas containing almost no social class I and II households. In Dundee there are also a very large number of

A Tale of Two Cities

schools with almost no social class I and II households and rather fewer at the other end of the spectrum, since Dundee is a more working-class city than Edinburgh. In each city the census variables are very highly correlated with one another. The correlations ranged from 0.60 to 0.92 in absolute value, with roughly half the correlations exceeding 0.80 for each city. Principal component analysis gave very similar results in the two cities identifying two principal components (after varimax rotation) with very similar weightings in the two cities. The first principal component had the highest weighting from the three variables unemployment (UNEMP), single parents (SINGP) and families with no car (NOCAR). The second one had the highest weightings for percentage of children in social class I and II households (SOC12) and for percentage with higher education (HIGHE). These two components explained 92 per cent and 95 per cent of the total variance in Edinburgh and Dundee respectively. Thus, in the analyses reported below we have replaced UNEMP, SINGP and NOCAR with a composite variable SEP (socio-economic problems) which combines these three variables with equal weight and was scaled to range from 0 to 100 in each city. Similarly SOC12 and HIGHE were replaced by a composite variable SOCED which again was scaled from 0 to 100 in each city.

In addition to census data, we collected data from the local authority on characteristics of the schools. In this respect we were much better served at the secondary level where considerably more data were available. However, at the primary school level, we were able to collect the following data: the date on which the school was built, the roll of the school, the percentage of pupils in composite classes, the percentage receiving free meals (which was similar to some of the census variables and had a correlation of 0.90 with the socio-economic deprivation component), pupil/staff ratio (which in Edinburgh also correlated very highly with socio-economic deprivation because the percentage of free meals is used to allocate extra teachers to deprived areas), the growth rate (calculated as the ratio of P1 pupils to P7 pupils) and the capacity of the building. The last item was found, on checking, to be inaccurate in many cases, and we have therefore not reported results for it below.

The census and school variables were used as predictors of movement between schools in a logistic regression of movement across adjacent boundaries. Using this model, the odds of moving between two schools with identical school and census variables are the same in both directions (say 1:30). However a difference in school and/or census variables will create different odds for each direction of movement. For example, if the differences increase the odds in one direction by a factor of 5 (say) to 1:6, then the odds of movement in the opposite direction will be reduced to 1:150. Using this model we can identify the variables that best predict movement in the two cities, by a regression in which the proportion of movement across every possible adjacent boundary is the dependent variable. There were 362 such directions of movement in Edinburgh and 162 in Dundee. The computations can be performed by standard statistical methods (for example, McCullagh and Nelder, 1983), although the accompanying significance levels will not be correct because decisions to move school are not taken by individuals independently of others. Thus the assumption of independent events implicit in the statistical model is not justified. This approach is very similar to one used by Flowerdew and Aitkin (1982) to predict migration patterns between areas, and they are likewise cautious about how to interpret the associated significance levels. Flowerdew and Aitkin use a Poisson model which is appropriate since their migration rates are small enough to have little impact on the population of the areas from which movement is taking place. Our logistic model is more suitable for larger percentage movements. The use of the logistic model, however, introduces a further complication. Should one consider the whole catchment area population as the denominator in the calculation of the percentage movement to one particular school, or should children who have moved to other schools be excluded from the calculations? The latter approach would be equivalent to the competing risk models which are employed in survival analysis. There are pros and cons for each choice, but we have selected the first option and have used the total catchment area population as the denominator. This might lead to inappropriate results were almost all the pupils in one school to select other schools, but this was not the case in either city.

The results of predicting movement by one variable at a time are given in Table 4.7 where they are expressed in terms of the maximum increase in odds of movement for each variable. For example, taking 'Roll' for Edinburgh, the

A Tale of Two Cities

Table 4.7: Logistic Regressions of Predictors on Placing Request Rates to Adjacent Schools

Each variable as a single predictor

Variable	Edinburgh Maximum odds ratio (a)	Direction (b)	Dundee Maximum odds ratio (a)	Direction (b)
Roll	5.0	+	7.7	+
Pupil/staff ratio	5.5	+	3.0	+
Growth	4.6	+	3.7	+
% in composite classes	4.0	+	1.3	+
SEP	4.3	−	2.5	−
Free meals	3.9	−	1.5	−
SOCED	3.1	+	1.1	+
LATEN	3.1	−	1.3	−
P1 catchment area pupils	1.5	+	1.4	+
Date built	1.4	−	1.2	−

Odds of making a request when schools do not differ   1:29   1:21

(a) this is the increase in the odds of movement across the adjacent boundary corresponding to the largest difference in the value of the variable between two schools.
(b) + indicates that the higher values of the variable are associated with more placing requests and - indicates the opposite.

pair of adjacent schools with the largest difference in their rolls differ by 293 pupils. The fitted model predicts that the odds of moving from the smaller of these two schools to the larger will increase by a factor of 5 compared to the odds of movement between schools with identical rolls (from 1:29 to 1:6). Similarly the odds of moving from the larger school to the smaller one are predicted to decrease from 1:29 to 1:145.

In both cities school roll, pupil/staff ratio and growth

rate are the best predictors of placing requests, with movement being towards larger, growing schools with high pupil/staff ratios. All three of these variables, and also the percentage of pupils in composite classes, may have been influenced by movement into the schools. Thus we may be, effectively, predicting movement in 1984 from movement in previous years. This interpretation is strengthened by the results of using the P1 catchment area population as a measure of size instead of school roll. In both cities (Table 4.7) the P1 catchment area size is only a very weak predictor of the rate of placing requests. The other non-growth related variables which influence movement show remarkably similar patterns in the two cities. The measure of socio-economic problems (SEP) is the best predictor of movement in both cities, followed by free meals which we noted above was highly correlated with SEP.

There were also some differences between the cities. In Edinburgh there was some tendency for pupils to move away from areas of local authority housing and towards higher social class I and II/higher education (SOCED) areas, whereas in Dundee these two variables had almost no influence on movement. In general the social variables had a stronger influence on movement in Edinburgh than in Dundee. In neither city, however, were the influences on movement particularly strong and examination of the data showed examples of movements between schools which could not be predicted from their differences in either the school size or the social variables. The shorter odds for Dundee (1:21) compared with Edinburgh (1:29) of movement between schools when there is no difference between them reflect the higher background level of movement in Dundee.

As well as looking at the predictors of movement individually, we examined their joint effect in a step-wise analysis. In both cities the best two predictors of movement were school roll and SEP. The third variable to enter the regression (SOCED) was also the same in the two cities. Its effect was much less than that of the first two and its direction of influence was different in the two cities. No other variable had much influence on movement once these three were included. In Edinburgh, once SEP was in the equation, the direction of movement was towards schools with higher SOCED. However in Dundee the additional influence of SOCED was in the opposite direction, away from areas with more social class I and II and higher education. A possible explanation of this is that at

A Tale of Two Cities

equivalent levels of SEP a school in a working-class area is gaining more pupils, i.e. it is the schools in the more advantaged working-class areas which receive most placing requests in Dundee. However, it should be noted that the interpretation of multivariate analysis is complicated by the correlations between the predictors and the influence of all the predictors on movement is fairly weak.

Given the polarisation of the school catchment areas by housing tenure and social class, it seems at first surprising that these variables do little to affect movement. To understand these results we must return to our network diagrams to consider the social geography of the two cities. Figures 4.4A and 4.4B display the six census variables for the Edinburgh and Dundee schools, using a star for each school. Each 'arm' represents a census variable. To take one example, the arm pointing upwards refers to the rate of unemployment. The school with the lowest unemployment rate in the city will be marked in the centre for unemployment; the school with the highest unemployment rate will be marked at the extremity. Notice that the social class and higher education variables have been reversed so as to be positively correlated with the other variables. The school with highest values on all six indicators (unemployment, single parents, no car, local authority tenure, social class III-V, no higher education) will be a 'closed' hexagon. The school that is lowest on all the indicators will be represented by a completely 'open' star. South and west Edinburgh, which are clearly middle-class areas, contain many such schools. From the maps, one can also pick out the housing estates and their characteristics. There are two very deprived housing estates in Edinburgh, one in the north-west and one to the east of the city. One can also pick out areas of council housing with fewer social and economic problems (represented by hexagons, squashed down on the top), where the three top variables (single parents, unemployment and no car) are less extreme. In Dundee, deprived areas of council housing are to be found to the north of the city, particularly in the north-east, in contrast with the more affluent suburbs along the eastern coastline.

A striking feature of both cities is the extent to which primary schools that are alike in terms of housing tenure and social class cluster together in neighbourhoods. This result accords with an analysis of the socio-economic status of secondary school pupils (Willms, 1986) which revealed

Figure 4.4A: Characteristics of Primary School Catchment Areas in Edinburgh

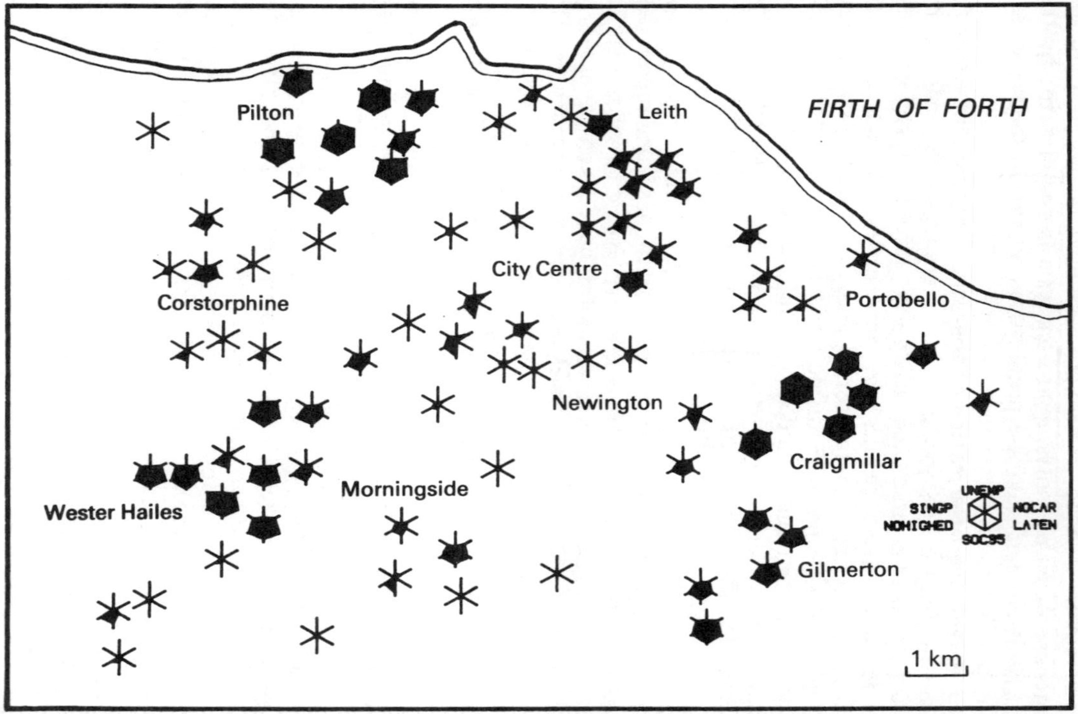

Figure 4.4B: Characteristics of Primary School Catchment Areas in Dundee

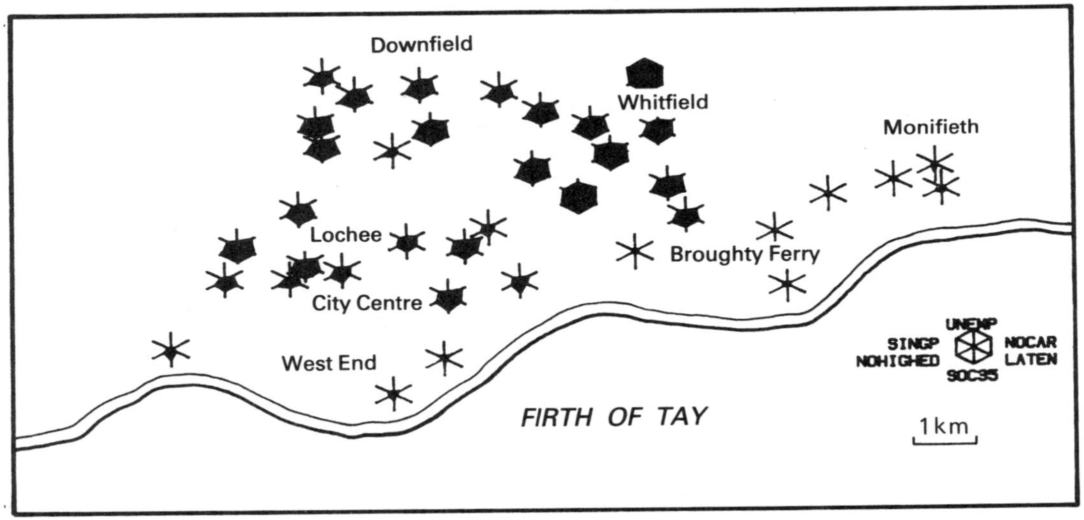

Figure 4.5A: Inter-school Movement between Primary Schools in North-west Edinburgh (percentage of catchment area pupils)

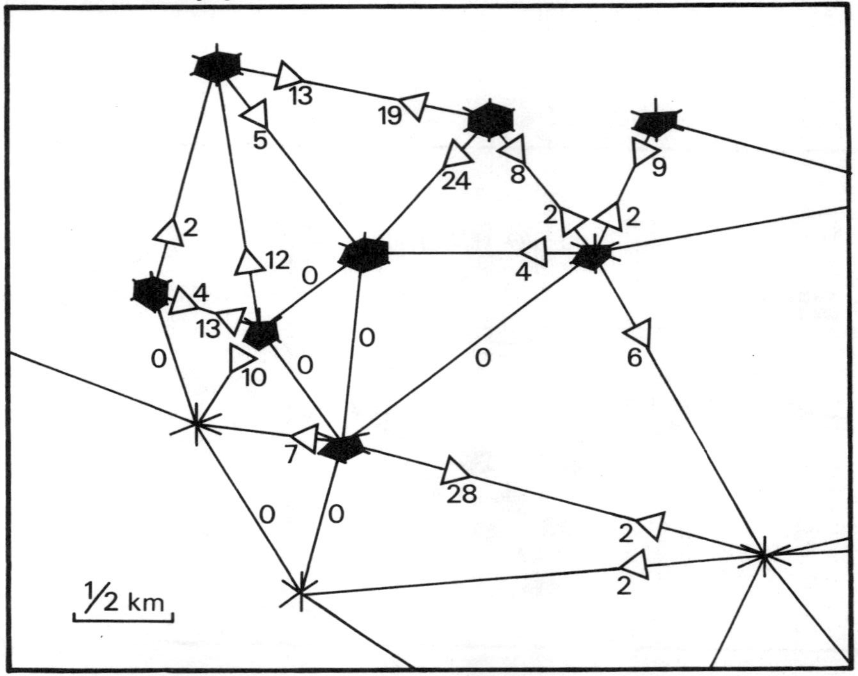

Figure 4.5B: Inter-school Movement between Primary Schools in North-east Dundee (percentage of catchment area pupils)

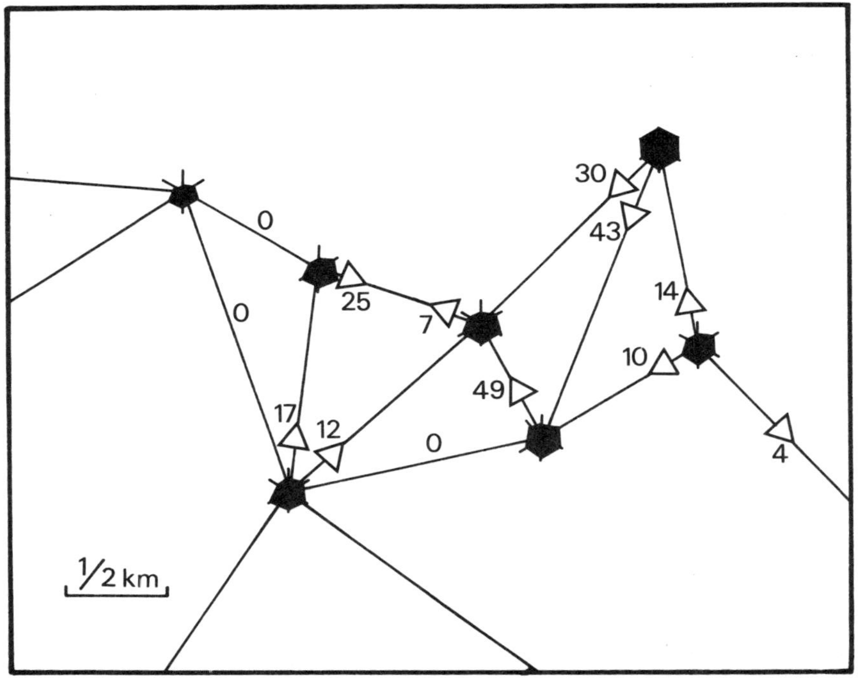

A Tale of Two Cities

that the degree of social segregation among secondary schools in Edinburgh and Dundee came second and third to that of Glasgow, which was the highest in Scotland. Taken together with the local nature of movement between schools, it explains why there is very little tendency to move between schools that differ in terms of housing tenure and social class. In Dundee, in particular, the pattern of movements is almost entirely within areas that are homogeneous with respect to housing tenure and social class. Within the neighbourhoods there is movement away from areas with more to areas with fewer socio-economic problems. Subsystems of movement occur both in middle-class and working-class areas in Dundee, but the system with the largest total movement is the area of council housing to the north-east of the city. This is illustrated in Figure 4.5B where it is clear that movement is taking place within the housing scheme, and not to the surrounding areas of private housing. The pattern in Edinburgh is somewhat different. Although there is movement within the housing schemes, and also within areas of private housing, we can also find examples of movement from areas of council housing to the surrounding areas of private housing. This is illustrated for the housing estates in the north-west of Edinburgh in Figure 4.5A.

NON-ADJACENT MOVES

In 1984, 15 per cent of all P1 placing requests in Dundee and 17 per cent in Edinburgh were to a non-adjacent school. The characteristics of these moves were very different from those of moves between adjacent schools. They frequently involved travel over considerable distances, and movement towards schools with very different catchment areas. In each city, a number of schools were involved. Moves were away from areas of council housing and areas with socio-economic problems towards areas containing more social class I and II households and more households with higher education housing. In Dundee 50 of the 55 moves between non-adjacent schools were towards schools with catchment areas containing less council housing. The corresponding figure for Edinburgh was 81 of 102 moves. Although these moves seem to fulfil the expectations of those drafting the legislation, that it would 'allow children to escape from deprived areas', they are very much a minority of placing requests. The considerable cost to parents involved in transporting such children suggests that the children may not be the 'disadvantaged' ones whom the legislation was purportedly intended to help. For this reason, their impact on school intakes, even in the most popular schools, was extremely small.

CONCLUSIONS

What conclusions can we draw from these aggregate results? First, proportionately more parents have used the legislation to select a primary school in Dundee than in Edinburgh. Although we have no direct evidence on the reasons for this, it may be due to the fact that the independent sector is much smaller in Dundee than in Edinburgh. Because of this, Dundee parents who are dissatisfied with their local primary school do not have the same opportunities to take up a place at an independent school and, as a result, more of them may make a placing request. However, it may also be a residue of the liberal allocation policy that existed in Tayside before the legislation was introduced. Second, there has been considerable movement between primary schools right across both cities and, as a result, some primary school rolls have altered substantially, albeit not as much as some secondary school rolls (Adler and Raab, 1988). By and large, schools have either gained or lost pupils and there were relatively few schools in which gains have been offset by losses. Third, those parents who have used the legislation cannot all have been middle-class since substantial inter-school movement has taken place in areas of Dundee and Edinburgh where no middle-class people live. This conclusion is consistent with the results of two surveys (Macbeth, Strachan and Macaulay, 1986; Petch, 1986) which make it clear that placing requests have been made by parents across the entire social class spectrum and not predominantly by a middle-class minority. Fourth, most of the moves have been to an adjacent school and have taken place between, rather than within, relatively homogeneous areas. In Edinburgh, but not in Dundee, there has been some movement from areas of council housing to more middle-class areas and, in both cities, parents have moved their children away from schools with catchment areas that contain more to schools with catchment areas that contain fewer socio-economic problems. These results are again consistent with survey data (Petch, 1986) which suggests that about 70 per cent of parents who make a placing request for their child to enter P1 are concerned to avoid sending their child to the local (catchment area) school. In doing so, they frequently referred to 'poor discipline' at the district school and to the 'rough and rowdy' children who went there and, in selecting another school, they most often referred to proximity and safety considerations.

The above results notwithstanding, the extent of unexplained movement is considerable and suggests that there are other factors that we have been unable to measure that affect the decision to make a placing request. Among the possible reasons for our relatively poor predictions of local movement are the following.

1. Merely considering adjacent boundaries may not be enough to explain geographical reasons for making placing requests, for example schools which don't involve crossing busy roads or are near shops and local facilities may be more attractive.
2. At primary school level, the available school variables are very limited and tell us little about the schools' characteristics or achievements. Better school variables, if they were available, might enable us to make better predictions.
3. Even if we had better school variables, the flows across adjacent boundaries might still not bear a simple relationship to any of the measurable aspects of the schools or their catchment areas. This would be the case if movement was influenced by (non-generalisable) local considerations.

Although we are not in a position to assess the impact of parental choice on schools which have gained or lost pupils, the extent of inter-school movement between primary schools in the two cities is substantial and may well have significant effects. It is thus, in our view, important to conduct further research to find out what, if any, have been the effects of parental choice on school morale, pupil/teacher ratios, the use of composite classes and the social composition of school intakes, and the educational and social experiences of primary school pupils.

A Tale of Two Cities

NOTES

The research on which this chapter is based forms part of a programme of research on parental choice in education, funded initially by the Economic and Social Research Council and latterly by the Scottish Education Department. We acknowledge our thanks to both these organisations for their financial support. We should also like to thank Lothian Regional Council and Tayside Regional Council for their co-operation, Howard Davis for assisting with the data collection, Helen Williams for assisting with the data analysis, Ann Carruthers for preparing two of the maps, Elizabeth Clark for producing the figures and Peter Burnhill for facilitating the research.

This chapter has already been published in Research Papers in Education Volume 2, Number 3, October 1987.

    1. The data in this section are based on official statistics, as reported in the SED's Statistical Bulletin (Scottish Education Department, 1986).
    2. According to the Independent Schools Information Services (ISIS), there is only one independent school with a primary department in Dundee compared with 13 in Edinburgh.
    3. Some slight adjustment was made to the position of a few schools which were located very close to one another.

Chapter Five

EDUCATIONAL POLICY INNOVATION: A CONCEPTUAL APPROACH

Frank Burdett

INTRODUCTION

The provision of education in England and Wales by more or less autonomous local education authorities (LEAs) has led inevitably to variations in the nature of that provision. The so-called 'outputs' approach (Pinch, 1985, p. 38) has shown that educational expenditure varies across LEAs (see for example Boaden, 1971; Pyle, 1976; Howick and Hassani 1979, 1980). An examination of recent statistics indicates that this variation still exists, as shown in Figure 5.1. Expenditure, however, is only a crude indicator of provision. The efficiency with which expenditure is used to provide educational resources affects the quantity of provision; and the effectiveness of the application of those resources means that high spending alone will not guarantee quality in educational provision (Chartered Institute of Public Finance and Accountancy (CIPFA), 1986; Department of Education and Science (DES), 1986).

One crucial link between expenditure and the nature of provision is LEA policy. Authority policy on the number and type of staff, buildings, and equipment affects the level of resource provision. Authority policy on the management of those resources, on in-service training for teachers (INSET) or on the monitoring and evaluation of classroom practice, for example, could affect the quality of provision. Such variations are not adequately captured by expenditure data.

There have been relatively few studies of variations in LEA policy. Those that exist have tended to focus on structural policy such as secondary school reorganisation (David, 1977; Ribbins and Brown, 1979; Pattison 1980;

Figure 5.1: Secondary Expenditure per Pupil

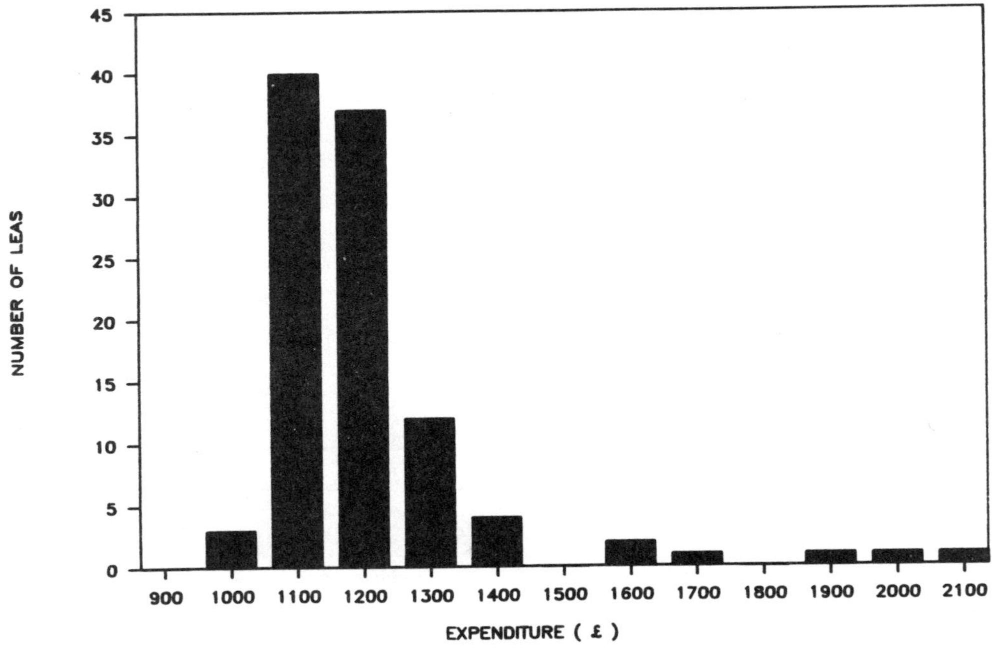

Source: CIPFA 1986 Estimates

Figure 5.2: Percentage of Schools in each LEA with at least one Microcomputer

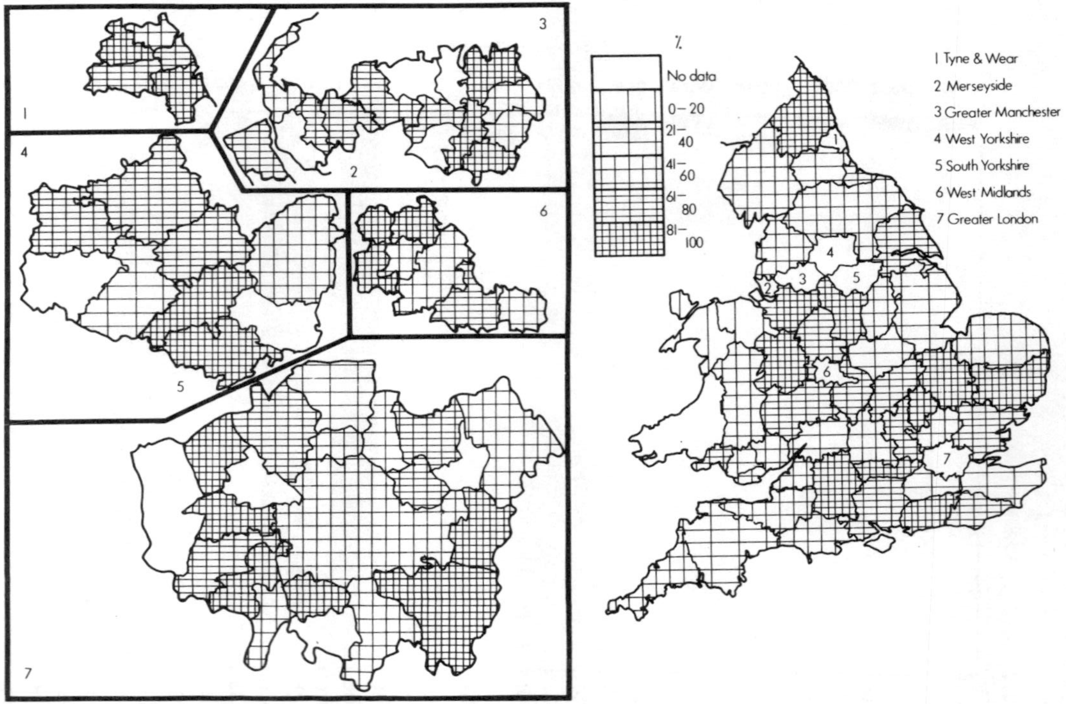

Howell and Brown, 1983). Policies concerned with the process of education have received rather less attention (Gatherer, 1981). The responses to DES Circular 14/77 provide the most comprehensive data available on LEA curricular policies (DES, 1979). This Circular sought information from each LEA about policies on, for example, staffing, staff development, assessment of performance and resourcing. The results showed that few LEAs made any 'policies' for the school curriculum. Where policy was claimed to exist, the concept of a 'policy' was interpreted widely, ranging from detailed written statements produced by the LEA, to less formal initiation or encouragement of practices already adopted. There was, however, a wide variation between LEAs. For example, the authorities were asked what procedures they used to oversee the curriculum of schools. Over 60 per cent of the authorities had, as one LEA put it, '... not established, and would not wish to develop, a formal system of detailed control over the curriculum of individual schools ...'. Most curriculum matters were left to the heads of schools. Only 20 per cent of LEAs involved education committees in policy-making on curricular provision. Only 10 per cent of LEAs formulated local policy in the context of national developments. Less than 40 per cent of LEAs had initiated any curriculum development in the previous three years.

Variations in LEA policy have particular importance for the part of the curriculum examined in this chapter, namely the use of microcomputers in secondary schools. The introduction of advanced educational technology into schools requires careful co-ordination and management in order to maximise educational benefits. The underlying assumption in this chapter is that those LEAs with a policy that co-ordinates the provision and use of hardware, software and in-service training, that employs suitably qualified personnel, and that commits sufficient financial resources, will be making provision of a superior quality to those LEAs that do not have such a policy. Further, it is assumed that the earlier there is a policy the more effective the development and use of computers in their schools will be. Unfortunately, there is little information on LEA policies on computers in education at a national level. Some idea of the extent of variation is given in Figure 5.2. The map shows the percentage of schools in each LEA with at least one computer in March 1981. Such differences in the level of provision in hardware give some indication of policy

Educational Policy Innovation

variation. These data represent the position in LEAs before the commencement of government schemes. The Microelectronics Education Programme (MEP) was announced by the Department of Education and Science in a Press Note on 4 March 1980. The MEP aimed to encourage the use of computers in the curriculum through teacher training and educational software development. The Department of Industry (DoI) launched its 'Micros for Schools' scheme in February 1981 (Times Educational Supplement 20 February 1981), this aimed to provide subsidised hardware for schools.

This chapter examines the rate of policy innovation by LEAs for the use of microcomputers in education. It seeks to describe how LEAs have varied in the speed with which they have produced policy and the type of policy they produced. It attempts to understand why LEAs varied in their rate of policy innovation by examining their organisational processes.

THE RATE OF POLICY INNOVATION

Any study of policy innovation must address the problem of how policy is defined. Certainly many of the types of policy described in response to DES Circular 14/77 would not appear to be sufficient to cope with the large-scale introduction of computer-based learning into schools. For the purposes of this study, policy is defined as a formal statement passed by an education committee that co-ordinates hardware, software and personnel, that creates some form of resource centre, that manages curriculum change and that allocates sufficient resources to carry these through.

Policy innovation has often been treated as a single act in studies that are essentially static (see for example Baldridge and Burnham, 1975; Danziger and Dutton, 1977; Davies and Ferlie, 1982). Such treatment stems from mechanistic views of organisations that see policy innovation as an uncontested process. This study draws on work in organisation theory that sees policy innovation as a process that involves individuals and groups, their relative levels of power and authority, and the conflicts that develop. Indeed, policy innovation is seen as a long-term activity that is both part of other organisational activity and is itself a continuing activity as policies evolve. The dynamics of policy innovation have led to attempts to identify various stages. Unfortunately, little agreement exists. For example, some authors distinguish policy-making from implementation but others include implementation within the policy-making process (Barrett and Fudge, 1981). In this study it is recognised that no stage is entirely separate from another but the notion of stages is retained as a descriptive device.

The three stage model of Yin (1979) has been adopted here. The first stage identified by Yin is initiation, defined as the period when an idea is first considered, preliminary experiments are carried out and the results lead to a decision on whether to continue. The second stage is implementation, defined as a period of gaining broader support, making plans, creating a formal policy and introducing change as widely as possible whilst monitoring the results. As this point it is still relatively easy to halt change but once the developments have become part of the established service with, for example, permanent staff and buildings, the process of policy innovation becomes increasingly hard to reverse and routinisation (the third stage) has occurred. Full routinisation is distinguished once the policy innovation is established in the various cycles of the organisation, such as becoming an annual fixed item on the budget and, in the longer term, surviving the turnover of key staff (Yin, 1979). This stage model, then, is based on levels of commitment. During the first stage the organisation, in this case the LEA, is testing and then committing itself to the idea of a policy, during implementation short term resources are committed, and during routinisation the structure of the organisation is altered.

It is useful to distinguish stages in educational policy innovation because they allow authorities to be compared over time. It is possible to establish not only when different LEAs formed a policy, but also the timing of critical points in the policy-making process and of periods of rapid change or periods without activity. These variations in the timing and duration of stages are the first steps towards an understanding of differential rates of policy innovation.

UNDERSTANDING THE RATE OF POLICY INNOVATION

In order to understand variations in the timing and duration of stages, the organisational processes that affect policy innovation have to be considered. Past studies have drawn attention to various factors. Unfortunately, these studies have tended to over-emphasise the structure of the organisation at the expense of the processes occurring within that structure, and have tended to ignore the nature of the innovations being analysed.

Many of the studies of innovation have focused on organisational attributes such as size, complexity, heterogeneity of staff and specialisation. Downs (1976) argues that the preponderance of such 'structural' characteristics arises from the impact of Weber on organisation theory, in particular his concern with bureaucracy as an efficient means of large-scale administration. Research on innovation has subsequently given disproportionate attention to factors that facilitate innovation rather than factors that motivate it. Motivation has, however, been considered in studies of innovation by individuals: research has found individual attributes such as educational status, social status and 'cosmopoliteness' are related to innovation (Rogers and Shoemaker, 1971). However, it is unlikely that the aggregation of these characteristics can capture the qualities important for innovation at the level of the organisation. It would seem likely that the interaction of individuals would be of greater importance than their characteristics. Research has also tended to seek universal attributes of organisations that foster any innovation. Distinctions have not been made, for example, between product innovations (some form of output) and process innovations (the means of achieving outputs). In short, past studies have focused on organisations as structures rather than on the processes within those structures, and in consequence, have not considered the nature of the innovation to be important (Downs, 1976).

Within organisation theory several perspectives have developed, each of which may help differential rates of policy innovation to be understood. These can be termed the psychological, political and ideological perspectives (cf. Burdett, 1985).

The psychological perspective stresses the role of individuals in organisations. A low level of individual satisfaction, for example, is seen as one of the key motivators of policy innovation in texts such as March and Simon (1958). The rate of change depends on the individual's creativity, depth of understanding and access to information. Criticisms of the psychological perspective have stressed the lack of attention paid to the organisation as a social unit. The psychological approach stresses the individual at the expense of groups or departments and assumes all individuals act in an altruisitic way. The political perspective focuses on organisational sub-units and how they use their power to bargain for particular outcomes. Innovation, because it is likely to threaten the existing distribution of status and power in the organisation, is particularly prone to internal political struggles (Pettigrew, 1973). The ideological perspective of organisations, however, argues that decisions may have little to do with decision-making. March and Olsen (1976) coined the phrase that decisions are '... the stage for many dramas'. The timing and duration of a policy innovation may be less dependent on its intrinsic merits and have more to do with problems in other parts of the organisation. Starbuck (1982) stresses that organisations are 'action-generators' not 'problem-solvers': they generate action to survive. Hence policy innovation can only be understood by recognising what else is happening in the organisation that may affect the 'rationality' or the 'legitimacy' of the policy innovation.

Drawing on this literature it is possible to identify three fundamental organisational processes that may affect the rate of innovation. The psychological approach leads to a concern with information. In particular, the processes of information handling. These include searching, collecting, evaluating and diagnosing activities, which can be collectively referred to as 'scrutiny'. The political perspective has drawn attention to the role of power in organisations. The rate of innovation has been shown, in particular, to depend on the degree and type of 'conflict', defined as a breakdown in the process of bargaining within power relations. The management of conflict has been seen as one possible cause of 'centralisation', the process by which the control over a decision moves up the hierarchy (or down if decentralisation occurs). More recent work from the ideological perspective has shown that the cause or effect of processes such as scrutiny, conflict and centralisation are not necessarily neutral in organisational terms. For example, Starbuck (1982) argues that centralisation is the primary way the hierarchy justifies and legitimates itself and preserves the myth of 'the' organisation. Organisational activity may not occur either for the reasons suggested by the organisation or for the reasons that appear most obvious.

Figure 5.3: Concepts for the Analysis of Policy Innovation

Stage 1	Aspect		Variation	Effect
Scrutiny	Origin		Internal	+
			External	−
	Cause		Satisfaction	−
			Slack resources	+
			Politics	−
			Crisis	+
Conflict	Initial perception of proposals		Incompatible	−
			Compatible	+
	Containment of conflict		Low	−
			High	+
Centralisation	Level of entry		High tier	+
			Low tier	−
	Level of impact	(a) support	High tier	+
			Low tier	−
		(b) opposition	High tier	+
			Low tier	−

Stage II

Scrutiny	Method	Individual	+
		Working party	−
		Programmed	+
		Bounded	+
	Quality	Higher	−
		Lower	+
	Quantity	Higher	−
		Lower	+
Conflict	Type	Individuals	+
		Groups/departments	−
	Relative power of opponents	Equal	−
		Unequal	+
	Cause	Vested interest	−
		Inability to cope	
		Rational	+
Centralisation	Cause	Negative	−
		Positive	+
	Mode	Induce rivals	−
		Buy off	
		Over-ride	+

An understanding of the timing and duration of educational policy innovation can be gained using the three fundamental concepts of scrutiny, conflict and centralisation (Burdett, 1987a; Burdett and Bradford, in press). In this chapter, particular aspects of these concepts are explored in relation to the timing and duration of two of the different stages of policy innovation: initiation and implementation. These are summarised in Figure 5.3.

Initiation

(a) Scrutiny

During the initiation stage two aspects of scrutiny affect the timing of policy innovation: the origin and the cause of the idea of a policy. The origin of the idea may be internal or external to the organisation. If the idea arises within the organisation it is more likely to be accepted than if outsiders try to impose their ideas (Mintzberg, 1985). One exception to this may arise if the organisation is dependent, either partially or wholly, on an external agent (Rhodes, 1979).

The cause of internal ideas depends on how the organisation is viewed. From the psychological perspective the cause must lie with individuals and their levels of satisfaction: low levels of satisfaction lead to pressure for change. From a political perspective access to resources and the potential shifts in power and status associated with the internal politics of the innovation are likely to be the cause. Alternatively, the ideological perspective would seek the cause of policy innovation deep in the sociology of the organisation, possibly a long running 'drama' not directly related to the policy itself (March and Olsen, 1976). There is no simple relationship between these causes of scrutiny and the timing of initiation. The duration of initiation will tend to increase with the complexity of the cause (Astley, Axelsson, Butler, Hickson and Wilson, 1982), with individual-level causes being simpler than political or ideological causes.

(b) Conflict

The timing and duration of initiation is also dependent on whether or not conflict develops. The initial perception of the compatability of the idea to the current work and priorities of the organisation can range from intense opposition through no reaction to strong support. An initial perception of high incompatibility can considerably delay the start of formal initiation and hence extend policy duration. If opposition can be contained, then the policy will progress more rapidly (Cyert and March, 1963). Intense opposition throughout the organisation, particularly in the early stages, can consume so much energy that the organisation itself may be threatened (Mintzberg, 1985).

(c) **Centralisation**
The level of entry is the tier in the hierarchy at which the idea is proposed. In general the higher the level of entry, the earlier initiation will be formalised because of the greater power of senior actors. In terms of education authorities five tiers can be identified ranging from the chief executive to advisory teachers (see Figure 5.4). The subsequent impact of the idea on the organisational hierarchy is also important. The higher the tier offering support, the sooner initiation will be complete, unless opposition is expressed at a comparable level in the hierarchy (Astley et al., 1982).

Figure 5.4: Tiers within a Local Education Authority Hierarchy

Tier	Actors
I	Chief Executive
II	Director (i.e. the CEO) and any Deputy Director(s)
III	Senior Assistant Education Officers; Chief and Senior Inspectors and Advisers
IV	Assistant Education Officers; Inspectors and Advisers
V	Advisory Teachers; Heads of Sub-Branches

(Based on Brooksbank and Ackstine, 1984, pp. 180-1)

Implementation

(a) **Scrutiny**
In the implementation stage, support for the innovation is sought throughout the organisation as the ideas are developed towards a formal policy. Besides the substantive value of the content of a proposed policy, the way in which

the ideas are evolved, and the way in which support is canvassed within the organisation, are all likely to affect the timing of creation of a formal policy. The method of scrutiny can affect the duration of the implementation stage. For example, a committee or a working party takes longer to conduct scrutiny than an individual (Astley et al., 1982). The method of scrutiny also covers the extent to which scrutiny can be 'programmed' so as to preclude the emergence of conflicting interests, or 'bounded' to prevent the generation of multiple or novel opportunities. The method of scrutiny is most likely to affect the duration of the implementation stage because this is when most scrutiny is conducted.

Related to the method are the quantity and quality of scrutiny. One of the reasons committees take longer is because they conduct a greater quantity of scrutiny: many actors with different perspectives leads to more extensive scrutiny. The greater the number of choices considered, the more scrutiny is generated, the larger and more 'fluid' the sphere of activity becomes and hence the longer the policy process (Astley et al., 1982). The quality of scrutiny similarly affects policy change. Higher quality scrutiny may even include formal research projects conducted over a long time period.

(b) **Conflict**

During the implementation stage different types of conflict may develop between individuals, groups or departments. Generally, if the conflict is limited to individual disagreements less delay will occur than if it becomes institutionalised in departmental relations (Pettigrew, 1973). However, the power of the conflicting units is also important: the more equal this is the longer any conflict is likely to persist (Mintzberg, 1985; Wilson and Kenny, 1985).

Different causes of conflict can create different effects on the policy process. Rational debate has the least delaying effect. Conflict arising from actors' inability to cope because of the complexity or uncertainty surrounding a decision can cause substantial delay. Conflict caused by the internal politics of vested interests can also cause major delays (Pettigrew, 1973, Mintzberg, 1985).

(c) Centralisation

Decision-making tends to move up the hierarchy during the implementation stage. The cause of this centralisation can either be positive, to support the policy by co-ordinating activity or resolve conflict, or negative, to oppose the policy. If it is supportive the duration will be decreased. If it is oppositional, duration will be increased, perhaps indefinitely (Astley et al., 1982). The mode of centralisation will affect how rapidly it takes place. If senior actors seek to induce rivals to compromise or to buy them off, duration will be longer than if the senior actors simply over-ride their subordinates (Mintzberg, 1985).

EMPIRICAL ANALYSIS

The concepts derived from organisation theory provide a range of tools with which to understand the dynamics of educational policy innovation. The complexity of the processes necessitated a case study methodology. Four authorities were selected to provide a range of potential situations and comparisons over a number of dimensions. LEAs were rated in terms of how innovative they had been in a number of fields including curriculum development, educational technology and organisational structure, but excluding the use of computers in education (Burdett, 1985). Of those LEAs rated as highly innovative one LEA with a high percentage of schools with computers (suggesting the authority had a policy on computers in education) and one LEA with a low percentage of schools with computers (suggesting the authority had no policy on computers) were selected. Of the LEAs rated as having a history of low levels of educational innovation, two authorities were chosen with a high percentage of schools with computers, suggesting the authorities had a policy. This research design aimed to produce one LEA that had a policy because it was an educational innovator, one LEA that did not have a policy despite being an innovator in the past, and two LEAs who defied their reputations as non-innovators, each having produced a policy. LEAs where policy innovation could simply be a result of high expenditure were eliminated: all the LEAs chosen had below-average rates of expenditure per pupil in secondary education.

In the four case studies a total of over 60 semi-structured interviews with key actors were conducted to

Figure 5.5: Details of Policies on Computers in the Four LEAs

LEA	1	2
Policy date	May 1981	–
Hardware	£42k (1981-82) £31k (1982-83)	Mainframe terminals
Software	£16k and secondments (report of Jan 1982)	(IBM packages)
New personnel	Adviser @ £17.5K and technician @ £8k (both from April 1982)	None
Centre(s)	£5k	None
Curriculum change	Computer awareness Computer-Assisted Learning Computer Studies (report of Jan 1982)	Computer science Computer Administration Information Processing Computer-Assisted Teaching

Figure 5.5: continued

LEA	3	4
Policy date	November 1980	December 1980
Hardware	£150k + £50k p.a.	£19k (1981-2) £40k (1982-3)
Software	Library @ £25k Staff @ 30K	Curriculum group
New personnel	Adviser @ £15k Tutor @ £15k Audio-Visual Aids @ £12k	In-service training teacher
Centre(s)	Resources software	Computer resource base @ £20k
Curriculum change	Computer appreciation Computer studies Computer-Assisted Learning Computer-Managed Learning	Computers in society Computer-Assisted Learning Control Technology Computer Studies

operationalise both the stages of policy innovation and the explanatory concepts. In the rest of this section a brief chronological summary of each case study is given followed by a comparative analysis of the four authorities.

In LEA 1 initiation began when a group of teachers, led by an advisory teacher, started to meet to discuss their use of microcomputers. There was also some early informal discussion among councillors and a liaison group of local employers produced a report on the need for computers in education. However, no formal policy was established owing, according to one local councillor, to the director's preference for the arts and music. In late 1979, however, the director of education produced a report for the education committee. This document discussed technological change and noted its importance for the education service, but no action was announced because of advice from the treasurer's department on '... the present economic climate...'. Subsequently, this was challenged by a Labour Party motion in the full council. When this motion fell, formal policy progress was halted. Even the announcement of the national government's Microelectronics Education Programme for software and teacher training did not revive the fortunes of a microcomputer policy. Advancement occurred only when the Department of Industry's scheme, which funded hardware purchases for schools was announced. Suddenly, a policy response on computers in education was 'imperative' and 'essential', as the director described it in May 1981. A policy was passed at the next education committee meeting committing the LEA to hardware and personnel (see Figure 5.5) and money was spent almost immediately.

In this authority a formal working party was only established after most of the decisions had been made. Hence, in one sense, implementation preceded initiation. The working party identified the need for a resource centre for computer education and for software co-ordination. It also recommended that attention should be paid in the early years of secondary education to developing computer awareness, to introducing computer assisted learning (CAL) and to provide an opportunity for children with a special aptitude for computing to develop their expertise through courses in computer studies. This report was accepted in March 1982. Routinisation can be identified in late 1982 when a resource centre was finally established (see Figure 5.5).

Educational Policy Innovation

In LEA 2 initiation came from an informal group of teachers led by the mathematics adviser. The attempts made by the adviser to gain formal recognition for the group failed because '... the real decisions were being made elsewhere ...': the issue had strayed outside the education division to the computer division. The computer division had proposed, in February 1979, supplying all schools with on-line mainframe workstations. It was argued (by the mainframe manufacturer) that computing in schools fell into four categories: computer science, administration, information processing/work experience and (experimental) computer-assisted training. The value of the mainframe was opposed by the mathematics adviser on educational grounds. He claimed that there was no educational software available, no training for teachers and that the mainframe was far from user-friendly. Nonetheless, the mainframe proposals were later accepted at a meeting of all headteachers. The subsequent use of mainframe terminals in schools did not represent a policy for computers in education as defined above. That is, in addition to the adviser's objections on the lack of software and training, the proposals included neither the employment of appropriately qualified personnel nor the necessary organisational changes such as providing a computer resource centre. Hence no policy for computers in education existed in this authority, at least until the end of the study period.

In LEA 3 a senior adviser initiated informal discussion by means of an ad hoc committee in late 1978. The discussions that followed met with widespread, if covert, support from senior actors, including the chief executive. This led to the purchase of hardware from funds for curriculum development for some experimental work. At this point the committee became an official working party of the authority. The start of implementation was marked by the overt interest of senior actors: the chief executive wanted to 'modernise' the authority, the director of education wanted to keep up with other education authorities, and the chair of education felt education should reflect the needs of employers and their changing technology.

Planning for a formal policy started in the summer of 1979 when the chair of the working party was taken over by the principal assistant director of education at the suggestion of the chief executive. A formal policy for a quarter of a million pounds was accepted by the education committee in November 1980. This provided hardware, software, in-service training and advisory support as well as a resources centre. The policy argued that computer appreciation was essential for all pupils, that developments in computer-assisted learning and computer-managed learning had implications throughout the curriculum and that the demand for courses in computer studies would increase considerably (see Figure 5.5). This commitment of resources was followed by routinisation in January 1981 when the running costs of the policy became an annual budget item and the resource centre was created.

In LEA 4 activity was initiated at the end of 1978 through the explorations of a research officer into the administrative uses of computers in schools and through an unconnected bid by the mathematics adviser for funds for computers in schools. Although this bid failed, discussions continued until the autumn of 1979 when a formal LEA survey of the use of computers in schools was conducted. The results of this study convinced the authority of the potential of the technology and the implementation stage was marked by a formal report in December 1979. However, this contained conflicting papers by the officer and the adviser, who emphasised the administrative and pedagogic uses respectively. The detailed planning discussions that followed broke down in early 1980 because of continuing disagreement, despite attempts by the director of education to reconcile their views. Implementation only recommenced when the chief executive and other senior actors put pressure on the education department to produce a policy, which led to the deputy director of education taking over the responsibility from the research officer and adviser. This act of co-ordination brought about a 'Proposed Development Programme' in July 1980 for £92,000 to be spent over three years for computers in both school administration and teaching. Continued opposition from the adviser led to further delays until the administrative dimension was dropped. A formal policy was passed by the education committee in December 1980. This identified four areas: computers in society, computer-assisted learning, control technology and computer studies. These were to be provided for with hardware in schools, by developing a staffed computer resource base, through in-service training and a curriculum development group (see Figure 5.5). Routinisation of this policy can be identified from early 1981 when the development programme was put into action.

Educational Policy Innovation

In summary, Figure 5.5 shows that three of the four LEAs produced policies that co-ordinated computing. Authorities 3 and 4 produced well-planned and resourced policies after considerable consultation. Authority 1 only produced a policy to take advantage of the national funds available and authority 2 did not produce a policy on microcomputers for schools.

Figure 5.6 summarises the histories of the four authorities in terms of stage theory. An exact time at which 'policy innovation' occurs cannot be identified in any of the authorities: in each case policy evolved over some considerable time. For example, delays of around two years between initiation and policy were experienced even in the leading LEAs. Indeed, the microcomputer policies themselves emerged from long term discussions in each LEA about the use of mainframe computers in education.

Figure 5.6 shows the differential rates of policy innovation: both the timing and duration of the stages varies across the authorities. The chronological 'stories' given above provide unique explanations, in one sense, of the policy history of each of the authorities. Further understanding can be gained by examining the roles of different types of actors across the LEAs (cf. Burdett, 1987b). The absolute and relative timing and duration of the policy process can best be understood, however, using the concepts derived from organisation theory.

Initiation

Figure 5.7 summarises the variations in scrutiny, conflict and centralisation between the LEAs in relation to the timing and duration of the initiation stage.

The origin of scrutiny was internal in all four cases, which therefore cannot account for any variations in timing. However, in LEA 1 there was also external pressure from local employers on the education-industry liaison group. This external pressure created some resistance within the authority and partially explains the relatively late initiation.

Dissatisfaction of individuals was a cause of scrutiny common to each of the authorities, but an understanding of the variation between the authorities is provided by other aspects of the cause of scrutiny. For example, the delayed timing of initiation in LEA 1 was caused, in part, by the suppression of informal search processes. As a result a crisis

Educational Policy Innovation

Figure 5.6: Stages of Policy Innovation in the Four Case Studies

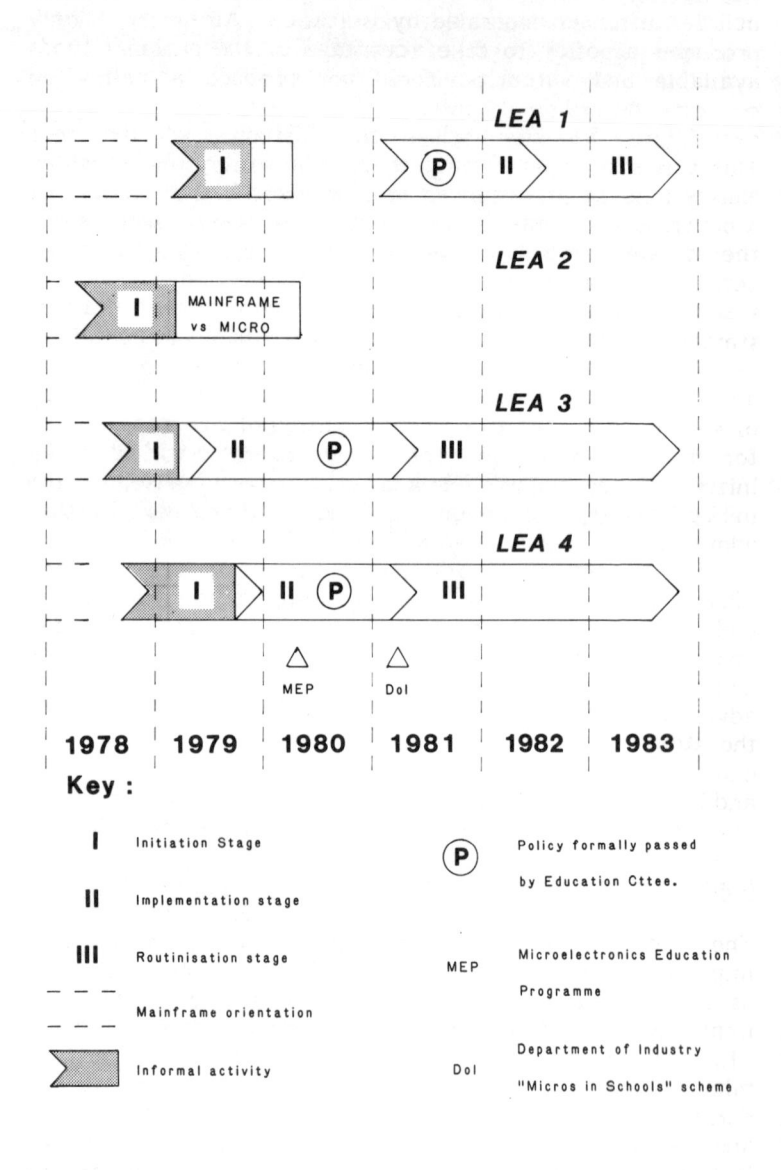

Key :

I	Initiation Stage
II	Implementation stage
III	Routinisation stage
– – –	Mainframe orientation
(shaded)	Informal activity
ⓟ	Policy formally passed by Education Cttee.
MEP	Microelectronics Education Programme
DoI	Department of Industry "Micros in Schools" scheme

arose in the authority when the DoI scheme was announced. It was this crisis that caused scrutiny and therefore started the initiation stage. The short duration of formal initiation in LEA 3 is also explained by the cause of scrutiny: slack resources, in the form of curriculum development funds available to the senior adviser, made for rapid progress.

The duration of the initiation stage proved to be particularly dependent on the level of entry of the idea. This was highest in LEA 3, where the senior adviser was a third tier actor. This helped bring about the early start and short duration to the initiation stage. By contrast, in LEA 1 the idea entered with the advisory teacher, a fifth tier actor. As a consequence of this low level of entry, scrutiny was ignored and much time elapsed before initiation was started formally.

A lack of conflict in LEA 3 also contributed to an early and rapid initiation stage. The initial perception of a number of senior actors was of compatibility of the idea of a policy for microcomputers. In the other three authorities the initial perception was of incompatibility: with art and music in LEA 1, with the mainframe in LEA 2 and between administrative and pedagogic uses in LEA 4.

Following these initial perceptions the impact on the ideas of the hierarchy generated varying degrees of support and opposition at different tiers in the four LEAs. In LEA 1 opposition from the chief education officer (CEO) and the county treasurer, and only low tier support (from an advisory teacher), ensured a long initiation stage. In LEA 3, the high tier support of the chief executive, CEO and the chair of the education committee met with no opposition and led to a short initiation stage.

Implementation

The timing and duration of the second stage, implementation, varied considerably between the authorities as shown in Figure 5.6. LEA 3 was the earliest to start implementation, followed by LEA 4 seven months later and LEA 1, 23 months later. LEA 2 did not begin to implement a microcomputer based policy during the study period. The duration of the period between the start of implementation and the formal statement of policy varied from zero months in LEA 1 to 14 months in LEA 3. The differences in timing of formal policy acceptance were markedly less than the

Figure 5.7: Timing and Duration of Initiation

Case	1	2	3	4
Informal start	March 1979	March 1978	December 1978	December 1978
Duration	9 months (long)	12 months (long)	5 months (short)	11 months (long)
Formal start	November 1979 (late)	None for micro-computer policy	April 1979 (early)	October 1979 (late)
Duration	18 months (long)		3 months (short)	3 months (short)
Scrutiny				
Origin	Internal / Teachers Councillors	Internal / Adviser	Internal / Senior Adviser	Internal / Officer Adviser Computer Dept.
	External / Employers			
Cause	Dissatisfaction / Teachers search suppressed	Dissatisfaction / Teacher and Adviser	Dissatisfaction / Senior Adviser	Dissatisfaction / Officer and Adviser
	Crisis / DoI initiative		Slack / Curriculum	

Conflict

Initial Perception	Incompatible CEO sees vs music/art	Incompatible vs mainframe	Compatible Broad support	Incompatible Administration vs education
Containment	Low CEO and Treasurer	Low Computer manager and Director	High None	High Senior Adviser

Centralisation

Level of entry	5th Tier Advisory teacher	4th Tier Adviser	3rd Tier Senior Adviser	4th Tier Adviser and officer
Impact (a) Support	Low Advisory teacher	Low Adviser	High Chief Executive CEO, Chair of Education	High Research department
(b) Opposition	High CEO and Treasurer	High Finance Director and Computer Manager	None	High Senior Adviser

Figure 5.8: Implementation: duration to policy

Case	1	2	3	4
Start of implementation	April 1981 (late)	(Mainframe policy)	June 1979 (early)	December 1979
Formal policy statement	May 1981 (late)		November 1980 (early)	December 1980
Duration to policy	1 month (short)		18 months (long)	13 months (long)
Scrutiny				
Method	Individual CEO		Individuals Chief Executive CEO, Senior Adviser, Chair then	Individuals Adviser Research officer then
			Working party	Working party
Quality	Low CEO's narrow report		High Extensive consultations and reports	High Several written reports

Quantity	Low CEO report	High Four sources of interest	High Evolved through several schemes
Conflict			
Type	None	None	Individual Adviser vs officer
Relative power			Equal
Cause			Rational/Vested interests
Centralisation			
Cause	Negative then Positive Co-ordination encourage change	Positive Co-ordination encourage change	Positive Resolution to support change
Mode	Over-ride CEO dominated	Induce Chief executive support	Induce In education failed then Over-ride at LA level

differences in timing of the inception of the implementation stage (Figure 5.6).

One of the reasons for the variation in duration between the start of implementation and the creation of formal policy lies in the method of scrutiny (Figure 5.8). The rapid formation of policy in LEA 1 was in part because the scrutiny was conducted on an individual basis by the CEO. This avoided the delays associated with scrutiny by a working party, such as experienced in LEAs 3 and 4. In the latter two authorities the delays arose from the wide ranging interests of working-party members: from pedagogic to industrial.

Owing to these differences in method, the quality and quantity of scrutiny was lower in LEA 1 and higher in LEAs 3 and 4. In LEA 1 the individual scrutiny of the director led to lower quality reports in terms of their depth of analysis. It also led to a lower quantity of scrutiny because the director's views were the only ones considered. In LEA 3 the quality and quantity of scrutiny was high since the senior adviser consulted widely, and in LEA 4 both the officer and the adviser produced a high quantity of scrutiny through several written reports. As a result of these differences the duration of implementation was longer in LEAs 3 and 4 than in LEA 1.

The absence of conflict during the implementation stage in LEA 1, clearly helped to bring about the rapid policy innovation. In LEA 3, the absence of conflict did not have such a dramatic effect on the timing of formal policy. In part, this was because of the scrutiny described above, for the attempts to avoid conflict through the working party itself produced delays. In part though, delay was caused by the illness of the senior adviser. In LEA 4 conflict was not prevented by scrutiny, and, though the type of conflict was between individuals rather than departments, the similarity in power of the officer and adviser was so great that conflict was protracted. The conflict in LEA 4 would have been less if the initial cause had not been founded on such deep-seated, vested interests, over the role of the research officer and the role of the adviser in educational policy innovation. The nature of this conflict fits Mintzberg's (1985) 'rival camps' classification, which he states '... can be the most divisive game of all' (p. 138). The 13 month delay before a policy was formulated in LEA 4 can largely be attributed to this conflict.

Centralisation occurred in all the authorities during the

implementation stage. In LEA 1 the major reason for the rapid creation of policy was the change from negative to positive attitudes by higher tier officers. In particular the director's response to national initiatives on technological change in education. His dominant role in forming a policy had the effect of co-ordinating action and produced rapid results. In LEA 4 the far greater duration before policy was formed can be attributed to the cause of centralisation being the resolution of conflict. Hence, although centralisation was positive in its aims, it was less effective because conflict had already occurred.

These two cases fit Mintzberg's view that centralisation to prevent conflict is usually more effective than centralisation to contain conflict (Mintzberg, 1985). This argument does not hold true, however, for LEA 3. Centralisation to prevent conflict went to the highest tier, the chief executive, and yet there was a long delay before a policy was formally passed.

To explain this delay it is useful to examine the mode of centralisation. In LEA 3 the chief executive tried to encourage policy by presenting the arguments for new technology and by offering to re-allocate resources to allow change. Inducing change in this way worked, but only after some delay. In LEA 4 a similar attempt by the CEO to induce change failed. Subsequently, the CEO resorted to over-riding his subordinates. In LEA 1, the CEO used this mode of centralisation from the outset, generating rapid change.

CONCLUSION

The differential rate of policy innovation displayed in Figure 5.6 indicates some significant variations in educational provision over time and space. With a complex, technological issue, such as the use of computers in schools, there is a particular need for LEA policy to co-ordinate hardware, software, personnel and training. Such co-ordination will be more effective the earlier it is introduced. In this study an attempt has been made to understand why two LEAs (3 and 4) produced a policy relatively early, why LEA 1 created a policy some time later, and why LEA 2 failed to produce a policy for microcomputers.

To understand the differential rate of policy innovation

across the four LEAs a range of concepts from organisation theory have been applied. The comparative studies illustrate that the organisational processes of scrutiny, conflict and centralisation can account for educational policy variations in time and space.

Of the numerous aspects considered some proved more useful to an understanding of policy innovation than others. During initiation an internal origin to scrutiny did not appear to lead as easily to the acceptance of a new idea as suggested by Mintzberg (1985). However, the case with an external origin did suffer resistance, as predicted. Of the various causes of scrutiny, slack resources led to shorter initiation. Waiting for a crisis to cause scrutiny extended initiation. However, individual-level dissatisfaction alone did not account for variation in the initiation stage.

Conflict was important for the duration of the initiation stage. An initial perception of compatibility hastened initiation in comparison to cases where the idea was perceived as incompatible. However, a high level of containment of conflict did not guarantee rapid change just as a low level of containment did not seem to extend initiation. Centralisation also produced mixed results. The level of entry contributed to the rate of change as hypothesised. However, disentangling the effects of the level of entry from the level of impact is difficult.

Variations in the implementation stage were a result of differences in the methods, quantity and quality of scrutiny, as predicted. The effect of committees in slowing change in LEAs 3 and 4 was particularly noticeable. A lack of conflict did not necessarily speed up the rate of implementation, but its presence in LEA 4 did dramatically slow change. In this case, the equality of power of the two individuals in conflict and the cause of the conflict were useful aspects for understanding why the conflict was so intense and so damaging.

Centralisation, in the structural sense of the tier of the hierarchy at which decisions were made, was not important. However, the cause of centralisation was important. Negative attitudes in the top tiers prevented innovation; positive attitudes almost guaranteed it. This was well illustrated in LEA 1 where policy innovation depended on the change from negative to positive attitudes in the senior tiers of the hierarchy. The cause of centralisation cannot explain policy innovation, though. For example, the conflict in LEA 4 prevented implementation despite a high level of

Educational Policy Innovation

centralisation through positive attitudes to change. The mode by which a central decision is exercised was helpful: persuading opponents was less effective than over-riding them.

In short, the timing, duration and outcome of the policy process in the four cases studied reflects the fact that LEAs are organisations. In order to understand variations in educational policies, variations in the organisations creating those policies have to be examined. The ways in which the management of education by different LEAs can lead to variations in educational policy has been explored through a set of concepts derived from organisation theory. The concepts used aid the analysis of processes in organisations. Information is sought and manipulated through scrutiny. Conflicts arise between individuals, groups or departments for reasons more or less closely related to the policy innovation under discussion. Actors within the hierarchy attempt to orchestrate a level of centralisation for the decision that will enable them to control policy innovation to their benefit. Such organisational processes affect the dynamics of policy innovation by LEAs, leading to variations in the nature of educational provision over time and space.

Chapter Six

THE INTERNATIONAL RECRUITING GAME: FOREIGN STUDENT-ATHLETES IN AMERICAN HIGHER EDUCATION

John Bale

INTRODUCTION

In the 1983 American National Collegiate Athletic Association (NCAA) track and field championships at Houston, Texas, the men's 400 metres was won by a student from Jamaica, the 800 metres by a Brazilian, the 1500 metres by an Irishman, the 5000 and 10,000 metres by a Tanzanian, the 400 metres hurdles by a Swede, the pole vault by a Swiss, the triple jump and hammer throw by Englishmen, and the javelin throw by an Icelander. The women's 100 metres and 200 metres went to a Jamaican student-athlete, the high jump to an athlete from Iceland, and the javelin throw to a Norwegian. Foreign students won 15 of the 35 individual events and many others took part and gained placings.

A substantial literature describes the international migration of academic talent and the experiences of students in foreign universities (e.g. Eide, 1970; Spaulding and Flack, 1976; Klineburg and Hull, 1979; Barber, Altbach and Myers, 1984). Such talent migration is frequently described as 'brain drain' and has attracted much interest, analysis and debate in recent decades. However, this fails to include any reference to a small but significant flow of student-athlete migrants to American universities; students who are recruited more for their athletic than their academic talent. The international movement of this particular sub-set of student migrants forms part of the growing internationalisation of the 'trade' in sports-talent per se. Moreover, the study of foreign student-athletes in American universities meshes together the spheres of

geography, education and sport.
This chapter focuses on this under-documented form of talent migration. The context of recruiting is initially described; the sports involved are then briefly examined with a more detailed case study of one sport showing the spatial patterns of national donors and state and college hosts. The chapter concludes with a discussion of the nature of the controversies surrounding international recruiting and the problems associated with their solution.

It is not the purpose of this chapter to 'explain' the phenomenon of international recruiting. Instead, such recruiting can be regarded as an 'explanation' or proof the interactions between the ideological structures that pervade the spheres of sport and education in the world of American intercollegiate sports, a realm which must be distinguished clearly from the recreational sports activity, which tends to characterise British universities and institutions of higher education in most countries.

SPORT IN THE AMERICAN UNIVERSITY

American intercollegiate sport is part of what German sports sociologists term leistungssport, literally 'performance sport', which might be better rendered as either 'highly competitive sport' or, as Guttmann (1978) prefers, 'top-level sport'. Leistungssport is global in organisation in that there are internationally agreed rules and regulations, and international bureaucracies to administer these rules. World records and international competitions are ratified and organised by international committees of various kinds (for example, The International Olympic Committee, the International Amateur Athletics Federation). At this level, sport is undeniably highly commercialised and influenced, if not dominated, by market operations. Players can be bought and sold, big sports events are increasingly produced, packaged and sold like any other commodity on the mass consumer market and can be regarded as 'expressing the quintessential ideology in capitalist society: egoistic, aggressive individualism, ruthless competition ...' (Hargreaves, 1982, pp. 41-2).

There is a danger of overstressing these neo-Marxist perspectives (Guttmann, 1978) and it has been pointed out that 'there are good grounds for thinking that sport is not a homogeneous entity and that there are crucial differences

179

between levels and types' (Hargreaves, 1982, p. 43). However, in so far as it is a global phenomenon whose organisations transcend political boundaries and permit both international co-operation and competition and the international movement and migration of personnel, there are grounds for suggesting that a degree of homogeneity exists in sport. A major feature of sport, like capitalism, is that it is a world system (Galtung, 1984), and movement and interaction are necessary for its survival in its present form. Johnston's (1984, p. 457) description of capitalism applies almost equally to top-level sport:

> goods, capital and labour must be shifted around to realise potentials as they are perceived. The movement of labour (i.e. athletes) brings cultures into contact and provides a potential basis for tension and conflict.

Although sport is a global system, the experiences of sport in different parts of the world are obviously quite different. Soccer played in Warsaw, Indiana is to all intents and purposes the same sport as soccer played in Warsaw, Poland. The same rules and regulations apply to the 400 metres relay if it is taking place in Moscow, Russia or Moscow, Idaho. Sport focuses on winning, competition, record breaking and quantification (Guttmann, 1978) irrespective of global location. Indeed, record-breaking can only exist as a meaningful aim in sport if the nature of the activity is identical among nations at the global level of scale. Very little resistance seems to have existed in the internationalisation of sport. Indigenous sport-like activities in countries of say, Africa, have tended to suffer relative or absolute decline in the face of more westernised activities (Eichberg, 1984), which permit, via their internationally recognised rules, international trade in sports personnel.

The <u>experience</u> of sport at the level of the stadium, swimming pool, gymnasium or rink, may vary from place to place. A basketball game between different university teams in Britain is played according to the same rules as a top-flight intercollegiate game in the USA, but the experiences are totally different, the former being low-key with a handful of spectators and the latter being typified by razzmatazz and boosterism. American sports ideology reflects a number of aspects of American 'national character', among them being what Watson (1970, quoted in Taylor, 1985) called 'freedom to move', 'the mixing of peoples', 'individualism', and a sense of destiny. As Taylor (1985, p. 128) points out, 'individual competition to achieve personal success - log cabin to White House (or Little League to Super Bowl) - is the basis of American liberal ideology'. It has been suggested that one of the main reasons for the great emphasis placed on sports in the American education system is for instilling a success ideology in students at an early age (Sage, 1980, p. 115). Add freedom of movement and the mixing of peoples and one has an ideology fully congruent with the international recruiting of athletic talent. Hence, heterogeneity emerges at the national scale as a result of a national ideological filter that separates day to day experiences of sport at the local level from the reality (i.e. the global scale).

There are, therefore, three geographical scales, namely the scale of reality (top-class sport as practised throughout the world according to an agreed set of rules, which allow international competition), the scale of ideology (the American sports ethos), and the scale of experience (the intercollegiate sports scene). These are not three different things happening at three different scales but a single manifestation of achievement sport 'within which the arrangement of the three scales is functionally important' (Taylor, 1982, p. 24). This idea is illustrated in Figure 6.1. and will be recognised as an adaptation of Taylor's (1982, 1985) view of interdependence in world political geography.

The idea can be illustrated with an example. The implications of sport at the college or local level can be felt when a foreign student-athlete is awarded an athletic scholarship at the expense of a local high school student. Locally, this might appear frustrating or unjust but according to national ideology it is acceptable because winning for the college is paramount. But recruitment of a foreigner could not exist without the global organisation of sport. If sport, and the aims of sports participants, were not essentially the same in Tanzania as in Texas the local experience would be quite different. In other words day to day experiences result from global rather than simply local pressures. The explanation of international recruiting is therefore sought in general structures that characterise and underpin sport everywhere.

The American sport-oriented university is different from institutions of higher education elsewhere. The average attendance at intercollegiate football games at Ohio State University for the period 1952 to 1983 was

Figure 6.1: A Three-tier Format for the Study of Top-class Sport. (Based on an idea by Taylor, 1982, p. 25.)

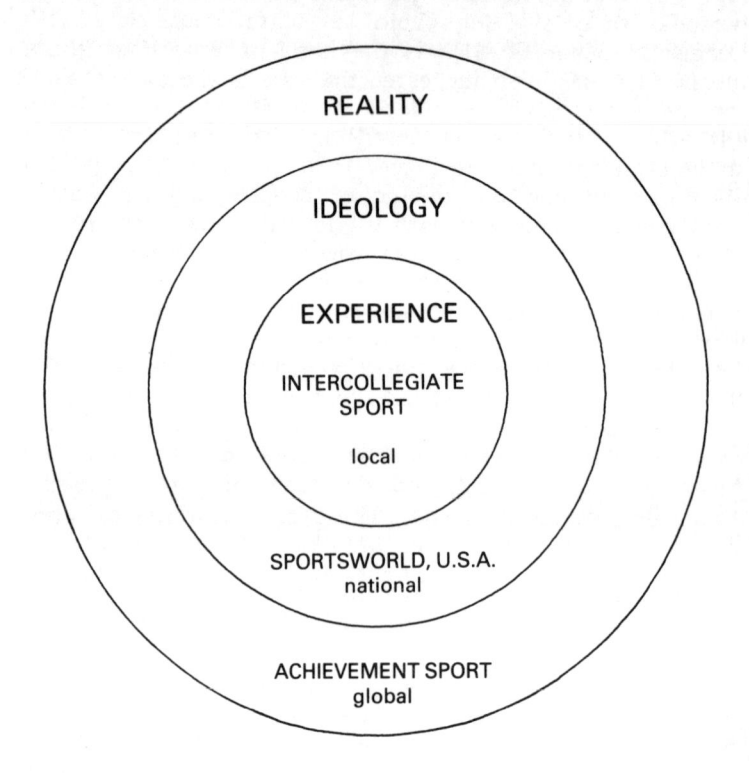

REALITY

IDEOLOGY

EXPERIENCE

INTERCOLLEGIATE SPORT
local

SPORTSWORLD, U.S.A.
national

ACHIEVEMENT SPORT
global

84,681; at the University of Michigan the respective figure was 82,257; eight other universities had average attendances of over 57,000 (Goudge, 1984, p. 87). When the 1986 NCAA basketball championships were held in Dallas, more than $7 million was injected into the local economy (Brady, 1986). In 1983 Oklahoma University spent $2.5 million on its football programme while in 1981 medical costs alone averaged $1,437 per player at Pennsylvania State University (Goudge, 1984, p. 11). In 1985 the 18,000 members of the Clemson University 'booster club' contributed over $5 million to support the university's sports infrastructure (Arbena, 1985).

Statistics such as these illustrate the emphasis placed on sport in America's most sports-oriented institutions of higher education, which has, according to Osterhoudt (1976), contributed to the erosion of the academic fabric of the American university. However, this emphasis may derive from the functions that sport serves in the United States in general. Inter-university rivalry can be viewed as an outgrowth of American ideals of boosterism and place-pride. The inter-place rivalries manifested through sports are widely supported (or internalised) by the American public, 68 per cent of whom agree that school and college rivalries are good because they encourage school pride and loyalty (Miller Lite, 1983). In the USA, colleges in sparsely populated regions often act as substitutes for professional sports teams. In some parts of the country high school rivalries perform the same function, high school football in Texas (Winningham, 1979) and basketball in Indiana (Jenkinson, 1974) being exemplary. The place-boosting nature of sports is therefore well established in the American psyche at a relatively early age and is given greater emphasis than in comparable institutions in other parts of the world.

As Young (1986, p. 8) stresses, 'the solidarity function is central to a sociological understanding of sports'. Likewise, Dunning (1981) observed that sport provides one of the few peacetime occasions when impersonal and mainly functionally bonded units such as universities, cities and nations can unite as wholes. Attachment to place via a sports team provides status through ascription, unusual in achievement-oriented societies. A number of observers (for example, Whannell, 1983, Young, 1986) argue that support for sports teams blurs class differences by emphasising place differences. 'The structures of privilege, inequality and oppression are left intact' (Young, 1986, p. 9) since different social-class groups temporarily unite in support of 'their' team.

In addition to the place-boosting and ideological conservatism promoted by intercollegiate sports, the phenomenon serves other purposes. Revenues from sports sustain the operations of often lavish athletic departments; sports success provides a form of advertising for the university which, it is argued, helps attract academically able students and teaching staff (see, however, Roper and Snow, 1976); and, as we have seen, college sports contribute to the local economic multipliers of entire communities.

Given such an emphasis, the facilities for sports in the major NCAA institutions are extremely sophisticated and superior to those found in many European cities. Superb indoor and outdoor sports provision is the norm and the athletic director is likely to be paid a salary greater than the university president.

RECRUITING

Concern with success in college sports had induced regional recruiting in the early years of this century (Cady, 1978). By the 1930s it had assumed national dimensions. What had formerly been under-the-counter payments offered to recruits were 'legalised' in the early 1950s by means of 'athletic scholarships'. Today these are awarded by many institutions of higher education, including junior colleges, irrespective of students' financial needs. By the 1960s athletic recruiting had become a highly organised business and because of the geographical mis-match between the sources of the best high school talent and the locations of the major 'consuming' universities, considerable inter-regional flows of migrant students linked the major 'exporting' and 'importing' (or 'surplus' and 'deficit') regions. (Rooney, 1969, 1980, 1985). Although the revenue-generating sports of football and basketball are largely, though not wholly (McConnell, 1983), provided for by indigenous talent, many other intercollegiate sports have extended their spatial margins of recruitment beyond the USA. Recruiting per se is regarded by many observers (e.g. Rooney, 1985, Eitzen, 1986) as the bane of college sport and is the source of much controversy. Its extension by the mid-1970s to the global scale has fuelled controversies and problems, the nature of which are discussed later in this chapter.

Why recruit overseas?

It has already been implied that international recruiting is a logical extension of national recruiting. If superior athletes can be obtained overseas, it is in the best interests of the coach and the athletic department to recruit them. The athletic coach occupies a somewhat precarious position in the American university because tenure depends largely on success. One commented: 'Why should I restrict myself to the United States? My job is to win for our school, not develop US Olympic athletes' (quoted in McLaughlin, 1983, p. 43). Another noted that 'those who want desperately to win at all costs will go for foreigners'. (1)

Recruiting overseas talent may be cheaper than trying to attract student-athletes from the USA. One coach said:

> I have a barely adequate recruiting budget. I can get a foreign athlete for maybe a $28 phone call. With a top American prospect I have to bring him in for a visit and write and 'phone repeatedly. I can wind up spending $300 or more on a guy and he might not come anyway. (quoted in Hollander, 1980, p. 70)

Institutions with limited recruiting budgets simply cannot compete with big, prestigious institutions in the domestic recruiting market.

Another coach described how he speculatively wrote to two Kenyan athletes, about whom he had been informed by an academic colleague:

> I figured it was worth the price of a stamp. So I wrote a letter and they both came. Can you believe it? A great hurdler and an NCAA champion for 10c. (quoted in Riley, 1974, p. 7)

In addition, out-of-state fees are waived in the case of foreign student-athletes, making their scholarships less costly than those for American students from outside the state in which the university is located.

A further advantage of recruiting foreign student-athletes is that those who have spent a year or two out of secondary education may be less of a sporting risk because they are athletically more established than an 18-year-old American high school graduate. Foreign student-athletes may provide a kind of 'instant-help' and eliminate the need to establish over a period of time a reputable sports programme. This strategy was adopted by the soccer coach at Clemson University in South Carolina who, unable to attract American soccer talent to a southern location with the lack of a soccer tradition, built up a squad, which in 1976 consisted mainly of foreigners (who accounted for 21 of 22 members). This squad went on to achieve national success. It must be emphasised that the foreign recruit is not a passive pawn at the mercy of a seductive scholarship. Those who are attracted to an American university may already possess a strong sports ideology but are only likely to be successfully recruited if they encounter perceived 'barriers' to their development at home. These might include the conflict between holding down a full-time job and finding sufficient time for training for sport, inadequate facilities or coaching, or lack of athletic competition (Bale, 1987).

The numbers and the sports involved

About 12,000 athletic scholarships are awarded annually by American universities (Edwards, 1984) and because athletes are eligible to compete in intercollegiate athletics for four years it follows that at any time about 48,000 students are in receipt of such scholarships. The total number of scholarships held by foreigners is unknown. It is probable that about 5 per cent of all student-athletes in America are foreign, though this figure will vary considerably among sports and between different institutions. It has been estimated, for example, that about 12 per cent of all NCAA Division 1 soccer players are of foreign origin (Smith, 1986), while in 1985 13 per cent of all 'superior' (2) college track and field athletes came from outside the USA. Numbers recruited to less sports-oriented colleges are likely to be fewer, as are the numbers recruited to the traditional American sports of football and basketball. The above percentages should be compared with the figure of 2.4 per cent of the overall student enrolment in the USA which is foreign (American Council on Education, 1983, p. 29).

Recruiting overseas, while not unknown in the 1950s and 1960s 'took off' in the 1970s. It is estimated that 'the

Table 6.1: Numbers of Foreign Recruits to Big 8 Conference Institutions, 1979-83

Year	Number of foreign recruits	Number of sports
1979	1	1
1980	8	3
1981	27	8
1982	18	5
1983	18	5

Source: Gautt, 1983.

number of appearances by foreign track athletes in NCAA championship meets increased by over 200 per cent' between 1971 and 1978 (Hollander, 1980, p. 81). By the mid-1970s it was widely felt that 'the foreign influx (was) new enough to provoke a major controversy' (van Dyne, 1976). Since the early 1980s the numbers have probably stabilised or even declined (Table 6.1, Figures 6.2 and 6.3) though the impact of foreign athletes in the principal championships reached unprecedented heights in 1986 when 38.7 per cent of points scored in the NCAA track and field championships were by foreigners. (3) This suggests that while the number of foreign recruits may have declined, the quality of such recruits is as high, if not higher, than ever. The decline in numbers may have resulted from legislation designed to reduce the number of 'over-age' athletes (see below) and from the increasing tendency for other nations (such as Canada and Australia) to provide superior facilities for their sporting 'investment'.

TRACK AND FIELD ATHLETICS: A CASE STUDY

The spatial character of international recruiting can be illustrated by the example of men's track and field athletics, the premier sport in the international recruiting game. Data are available for 609 superior foreign student-athletes recruited for the period 1973 to 1985. These individuals represent the extremely talented tip of a pyramid of foreign sporting talent, the exact size of which is unknown.

The International Recruiting Game

Figure 6.2: Numbers and Continental Origins of Superior Foreign Track and Field Student-athletes

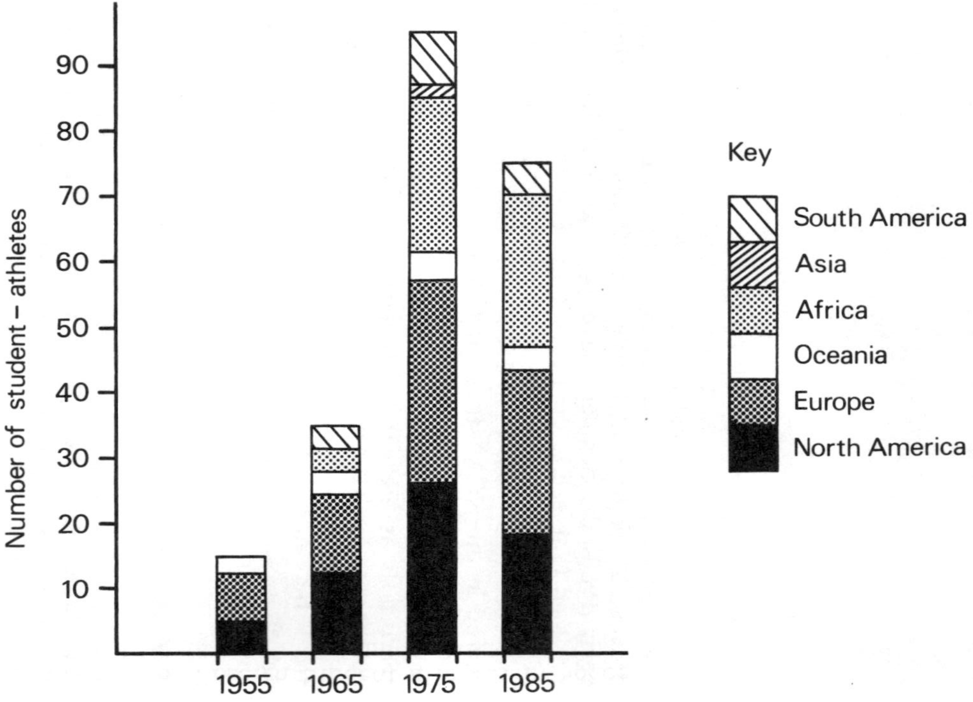

Source: Track and Field News, various issues.

The International Recruiting Game

Figure 6.3: Numbers of Foreign Student-athletes in Soccer and Track and Field Squads, Clemson University, 1970-85

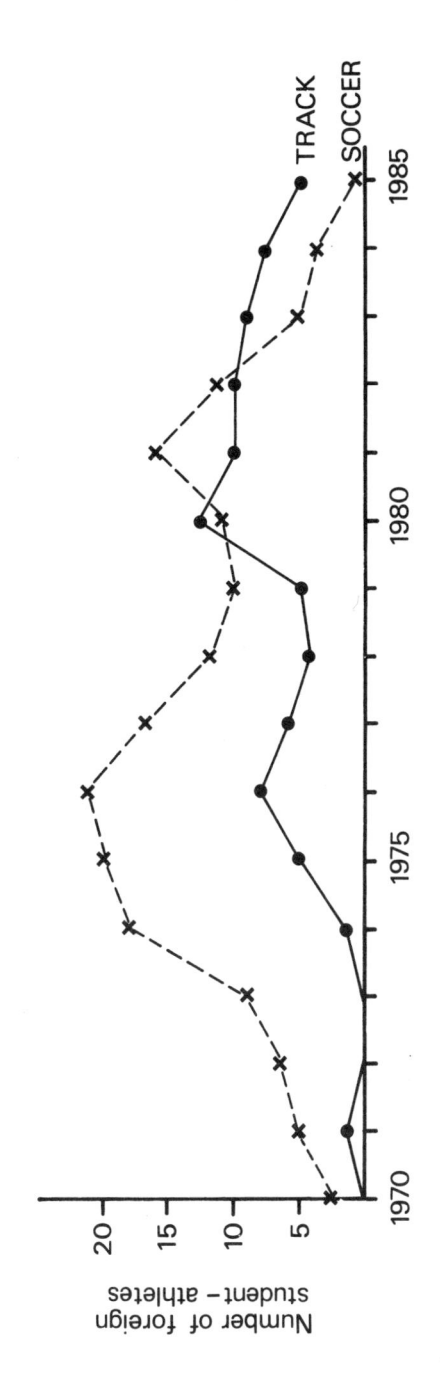

Source: Athletic Department rosters.

Table 6.2: Major National Donors of Superior Foreign Track and Field Student-athletes (male), 1973-85. (n = 609)

Country	number	per cent	S	D	J	T
Kenya	77	12.6	7	66	4	0
Canada	74	12.2	17	24	10	23
United Kingdom	54	8.9	3	41	2	8
Sweden	51	8.3	3	1	7	40
Jamaica	43	7.1	37	3	3	0
Nigeria	34	5.6	20	0	12	2
Eire	32	5.3	0	28	1	3
Norway	25	4.1	0	9	3	13
Bahamas	25	4.1	12	0	12	1
Ghana	18	3.0	9	0	9	0

Event groups (a)

(a) S = Sprints; D = Distances; J = Jumps; T = Throws.

National donors

The number of superior foreign track and field athletes in US universities not only grew rapidly during the 1970s but also came increasingly from countries hitherto untouched by international recruiting (Figure 6.2). In the 1950s and 1960s recruits came almost exclusively from north-west Europe, Canada and the Caribbean. It was not until the emergence of top-rate athletes from Africa, particularly Niger and Kenya (Manners, 1975), that the attention of American college coaches was attracted. The response was dramatic. Whereas in 1965 Africa supplied 8.6 per cent of such recruits, the respective figure for 1980 was 32.6 per cent. Kenya alone has supplied 12.6 per cent of all such students recruited since 1973, the majority being middle and long-distance runners (Table 6.2).

The global pattern of migrants is shown in Figure 6.4. During the thirteen year period under consideration flows of student migrants have come predominantly from Kenya (12.6 per cent), Canada (12.2 per cent), the United Kingdom (8.9 per cent) and Sweden (8.3 per cent). It will be noted that colleges only recruit athletes who will be useful to them, the absence of potential Kenyan throwers or Nigerian long-distance runners, for example, is clearly shown in the event-group specialisms of particular states (Table 6.2). The

Figure 6.4: National Origins of Superior Foreign Student-athletes (male, track and field), 1973-85

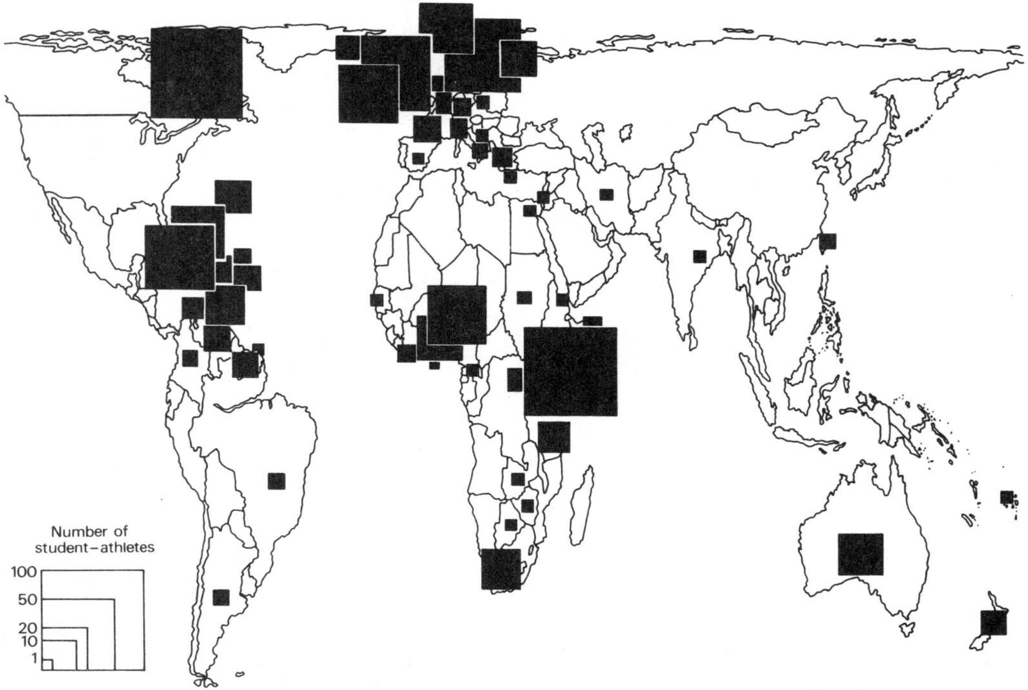

Source: Track and Field News, various issues

Figure 6.5: Campus Destinations of Superior Male Track and Field Student-athletes from (a) Kenya, (b) Nigeria, (c) the United Kingdom and (d) Republic of Ireland

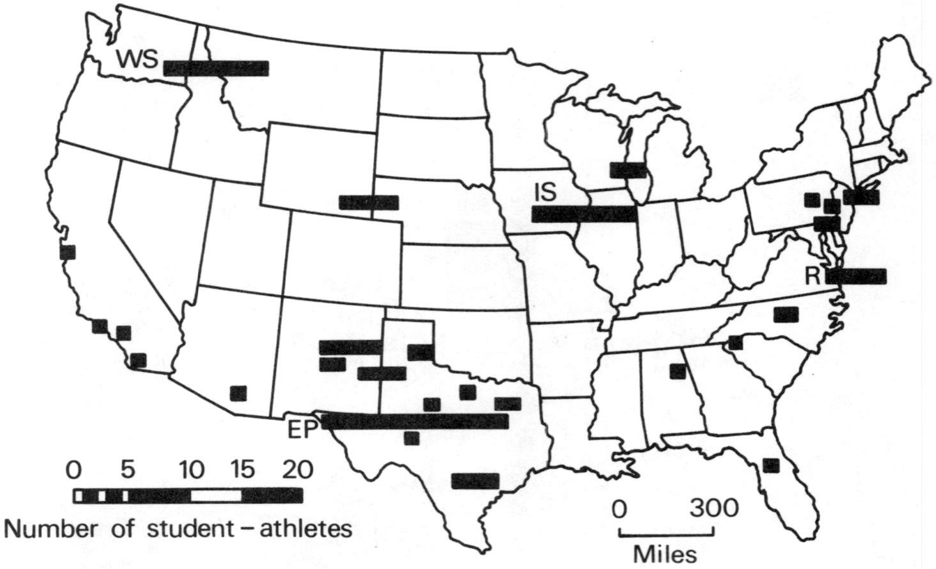

(a) Superior track and field student-athletes from Kenya are found in Universities throughout the USA but 'talent pipelines' have developed between Kenya and the University of Texas, El Paso (EP), Washington State University (WS), Iowa State University (IS) and the University of Richmond (R).

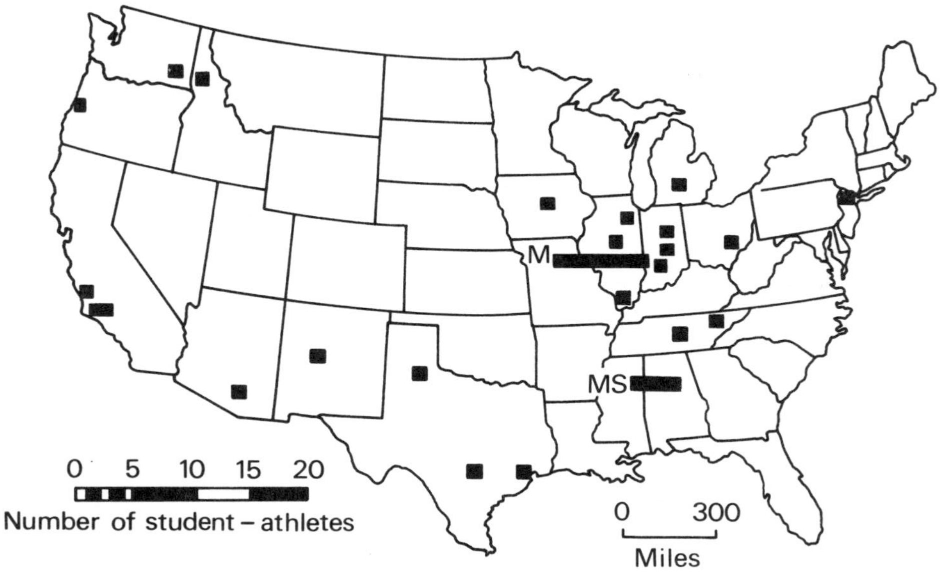

(b) Track and field talent from Nigeria is concentrated at the University of Missouri (M) and at Mississippi State University (MS).

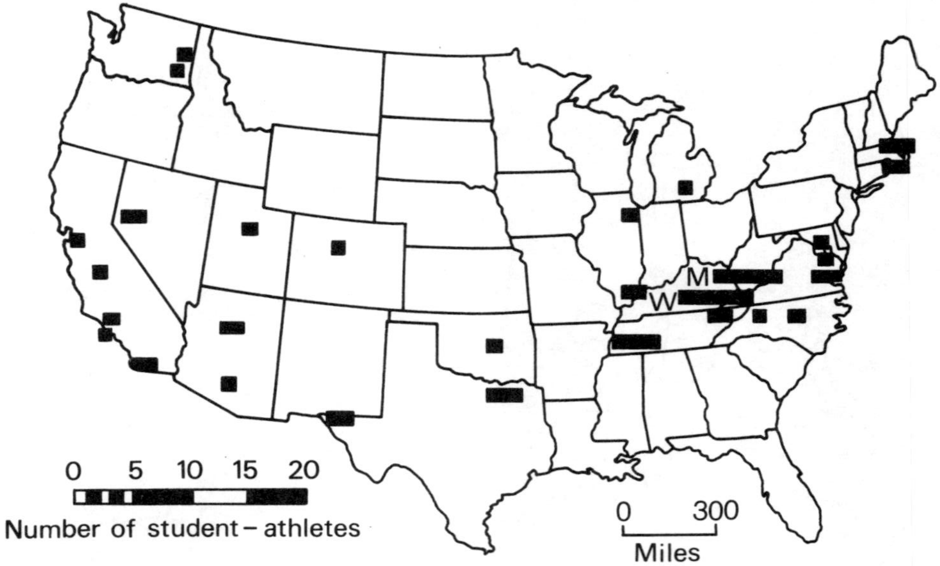

(c) Destinations of superior male track and field student-athletes from the UK are widely distributed over the USA but 'pipelines' have clearly developed at Western Kentucky University (W) and at Murray State University (M).

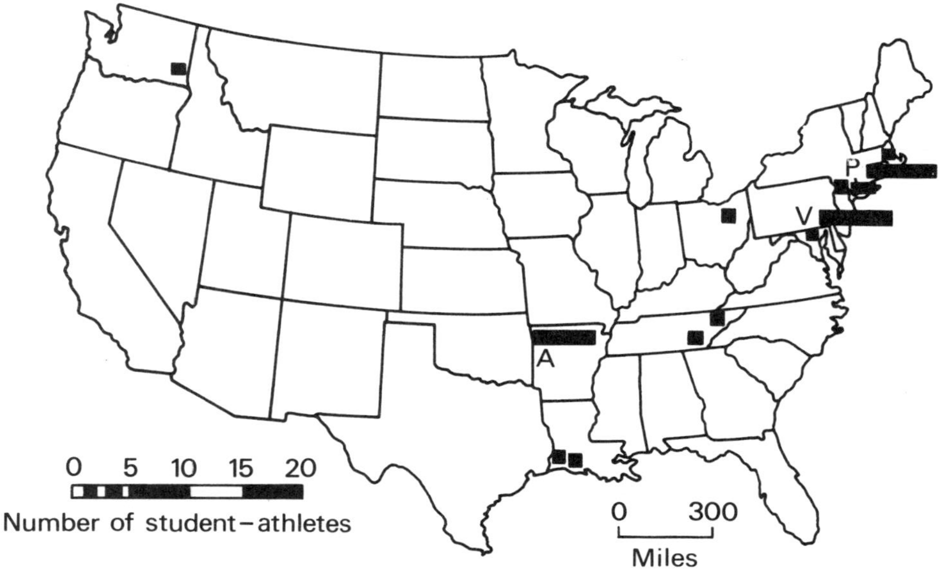

(d) Superior track and field athletes from Republic of Ireland are concentrated at Villanova University (V), Providence University (P) and at the University of Arkansas (A).

emphasis is placed on recruiting proven, not potential talent and the recruiting of athletes yet to prove their worth is regarded as an unnecessary risk. This is analogous to an international division of labour with different countries providing different types of athletes for different 'stages' of the athletic 'production process'. The pattern of origins of foreign student-athletes far from mirrors the overall pattern of migration of foreign (i.e. non-athletic) students to the USA. Most obviously, the preponderance of students from Asia in the overall pattern vanishes when student-athletes alone are considered.

State and college hosts

Universities establishing links with foreign recruits in the 1950s and 1960s did so largely as a result of chance factors. For example, the long-standing connection between Villanova University in Pennsylvania and the Republic of Ireland grew out of a chance meeting at the 1948 Olympic Games between an American and an Irish athlete. Today, however, foreign student-athletes are recruited mainly by direct approaches by the athletic department or on the recommendation of university alumni in their own countries, who act as 'athletic agents'. Frequently a 'friends-of-friends' network grows up. Student-athletes pass on information about their institutions of potential recruits in their own countries (Hollander, 1980, Stidwell and Badecki, 1986) so that a 'talent-pipeline' (Figure 6.5) develops between donor countries and campus hosts. Certain institutions tend to accommodate large percentages of student-athletes from one country. An extreme case is Brigham Young University, which houses 54 per cent of Finland's and 35 per cent of Sweden's American-based track and field athletes. Being a Mormon institution the university is able to establish international contacts through its mission work, a strategy also adopted by Baptist institutions. It is the long-term maintenance of such linkages (another reflection of place-loyalty) that goes a long way towards explaining the geography of foreign student-athletes in the USA.

At the state level the principal concentrations of foreigners are found in a broken arc extending from Texas to Washington (Figure 6.6). Although only seven states recruited no superior student-athletes in track and field, Washington, California, Utah and Texas together account for 41.7 per cent of the total. Few foreign recruits are found in the extreme north-east, the plains states and in much of the south.

Six hundred and fifty-six college destinations were recorded for the 609 athletes identified. The excess of destinations is the result of the transfer of student-athletes between colleges. Transfers most frequently occur among African student-athletes, Kenyans alone accounting for 23 per cent. This is over 10 per cent more than would be expected, given the country's share of athletes being recruited. Such athletes are often initially enrolled at two-year colleges at which they can reach an academic standard acceptable to more senior institutions and also develop greater fluency in English.

The principal campus concentrations of foreign student-athletes are shown in Table 6.3. Four universities account for 20 per cent of foreign student-athletes recruited over the 13 year period. These institutions frequently dominate state recruitment and hence contribute to an explanation of the national pattern.

The development of 'talent-pipelines' is of undoubted importance but it is also noteworthy that the locations of the three principal institutions (El Paso, Provo and Pullman) are each regarded as being relatively undesirable places to live by average Americans (Gould, 1966). Hollander (1980, p. 69) notes that 'many colleges located in remote or sparsely populated regions have little to offer domestic athletes aesthetically'. The track coach at the University of Texas, El Paso put it this way: 'You try and get a kid from any place but a desert area and they're not going to like it (here)'. (4) Implicit in such a comment is that difficulty in recruiting domestic athletes to certain locations has encouraged colleges to recruit overseas.

Women student-athletes. So far attention has been confined to male athletes. Until recently the recruitment of foreign sportswomen to American universities had been almost non-existent, at least partly because of the traditionally inferior status of women's intercollegiate sports. Following the passage of Title IX of the Education Amendment Act of 1972 demanding equality of funding for both sexes, however, funding for women's competitive sports increased (Beezley and Hobbs, 1983) and a steady flow of foreign women athletes has developed. In 1977 the US women's track and

Figure 6.6: Destinations by State of Superior Male Track and Field Student-athletes Recruited from Overseas, 1973-85

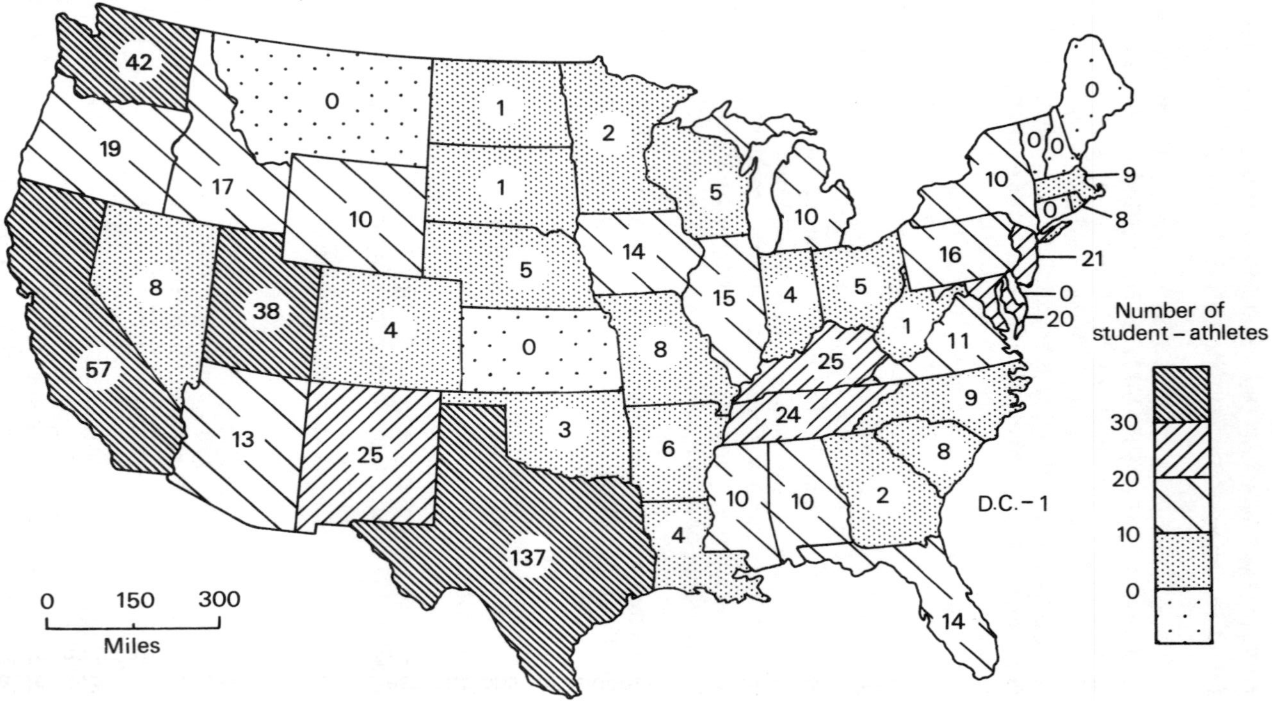

Source: Track and Field News, various issues.

Table 6.3: Principal College Destinations of Superior Foreign Student Track and Field Athletes (male), 1973-85. (n = 656)

Institution	number	per cent	per cent of state total
University of Texas, El Paso	47	7.2	34.6
Brigham Young University (Utah)	35	5.3	94.6
Washington State University	30	4.6	71.4
University of Texas, Austin	21	3.2	15.4
Iowa State University	14	2.1	100.0
University of Southern California	13	2.0	22.8
University of Western Kentucky	13	2.0	52.0
University of Oregon	13	2.0	65.0
Villanova University (Pennsylvania)	12	1.8	70.6

Figure 6.7: Global Origins of Superior Women Track and Field Student-athletes Recruited to US Colleges and Universities, 1977-85

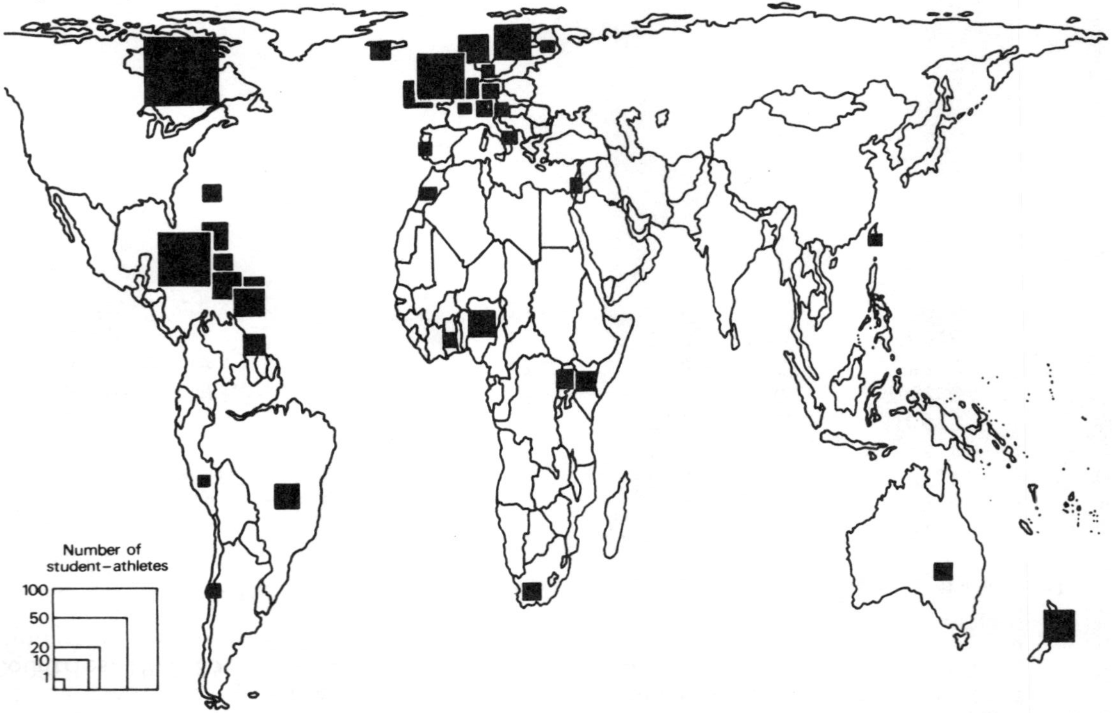

Figure 6.8: Destinations by State of Superior Women Student-athletes Recruited from Foreign Countries, 1977-85

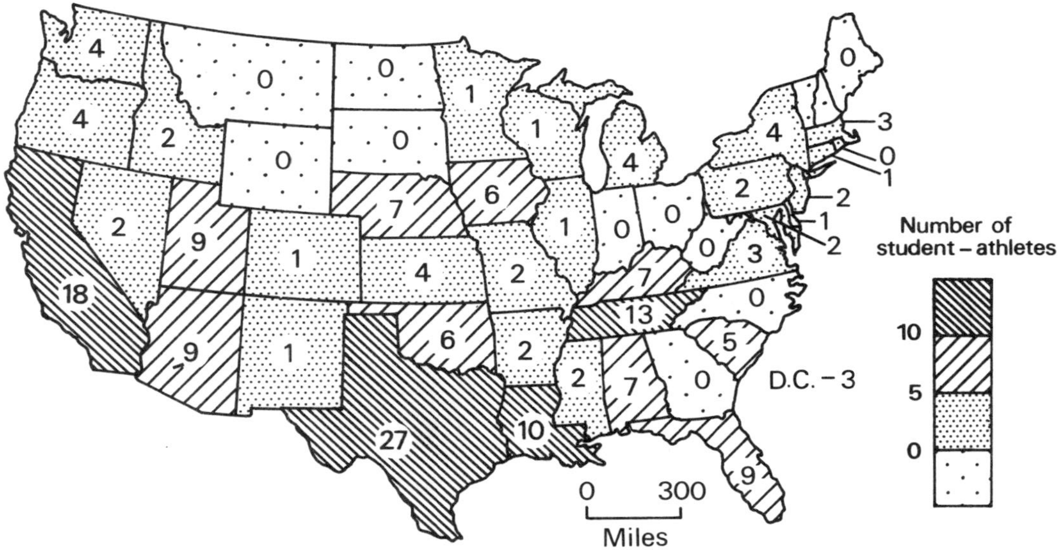

Source: Track and Field News, various issues

field rankings contained only eleven foreigners; by 1979 the respective figure was 32 and by 1986 this had exactly doubled.

The geographic origins of 182 superior foreign women track and field athletes recruited to US colleges between 1977 and 1985 are strongly skewed towards Canada and the Caribbean. Compared with the pattern for men there are few athletic recruits from Africa. Kenya, for example, provided only 1.6 per cent of the total during the nine year period (Figure 6.7).

The three main states of sojourn for foreign women athletes are Texas, California and Tennessee which account for 31.8 per cent of destinations (Figure 6.8). Unlike men's track and field, however, no single university dominates the recruiting race. Tennessee University, a pioneer in track and field for women, and the University of Texas, El Paso each attracted nine (4.9 per cent), Nebraska eight (4.4 per cent) and San Diego State six (3.3. per cent). Whether the geographical pattern will come to mirror that of the men remains to be seen.

Race

According to Edwards (1984) black athletes obtain less than 6 per cent of the 10,000 to 12,000 sports scholarships distributed in the USA. Allowing for the fact that this is an average figure for all sports and that virtually no blacks take part in intercollegiate sports such as swimming, golf or gymnastics, the percentage of all track and field scholarships awarded to black Americans could be between 10 per cent and 20 per cent. Although it is impossible to establish with accuracy the racial mix of athletic immigrants to US colleges, it can be inferred, given the national origins of the superior athletes discussed above, that about 45 per cent of foreign student-athletes in track and field for the period 1973 to 1985 were black, including a number of black athletes among Canadian and British recruits. This is substantially more than would be expected if the proportion of sports scholarships provided for American blacks in track and field was replicated for those from overseas.

CONTROVERSIES SURROUNDING FOREIGN RECRUITING

The patterns described for track and field athletics illustrate two geographical patterns of recruiting: that of the donors and that of the hosts. Other sports will possess different patterns and these require further analysis. However, irrespective of the particular sports, foreign recruiting has produced controversies in the US and in the donor countries, and it is to these controversies that attention now turns.

According to Underwood (1984, p. 182) recruiting 'is an obscene, indecent and disgusting process that demeans coaches and humiliates schools'. Given the pressure exerted on the student at the recruiting stage Zeigler (1979) suggests that it is often impossible for athletes to choose intelligently between alternative offers of scholarships. Most criticism of recruiting has focused on the sports of football and basketball. Eloquent testimonies by observers such as Michener (1976), Rooney (1980) and Locke and Ibach (1982) illustrate graphically the ways in which recruiting is surrounded by dishonest practices and violations of the NCAA rulebook.

Such abuses undoubtedly also apply to the non-revenue sports and to foreign recruiting. Indeed, evidence shows that some foreign recruits themselves accept cheating as a fact of life, forged qualifications and identities being used as a way of obtaining an athletic scholarship (Sojka, 1983, p. 65; Bale, 1987). Some countries have become notorious for sending student-athletes with false records (NCAA, 1984, p. 19). Although such abuses apply to both domestic and foreign recruiting, the primary concern here is with the criticisms and controversies which surround foreign recruiting. Such controversies have been voiced both inside and outside the USA.

Controversy at home

In the USA the recruitment of foreign student-athletes has been the subject of two very different lines of criticism. Some regard the 'importation' of relatively mature foreign students as unfair and argue that colleges who recruit them compete at an unfair advantage over those depending on 18-year-old high school recruits. As one athlete commented, 'The problem is that most foreign athletes turn out to be seasoned veterans and have several years' start on the athlete who's only had high school or JC meets to contend with' (Jordan, 1975, p. 56).

It seems likely that this kind of criticism contributed to the decision of the NCAA to apply to Division 1 universities the rule that every year of athletic competition which students had experienced after their twentieth birthday counted as one year's athletic eligibility. Hence, a student of 25 who had been competing since the age of 20 would be ineligible for intercollegiate competition. This effectively reduced the incentive for colleges to recruit students in their mid-20s (though the ruling did not apply to less sport-oriented NCAA institutions, nor to those smaller colleges administered by the National Association for Intercollegiate Athletics, nor to Junior Colleges). De facto such legislation did discriminate against foreigners since hardly any domestic student-athletes would be affected. The reduction in the number of foreign recruits during the 1980s has already been noted.

The 'unfair advantage' controversy is accompanied by the argument that US high school students are deprived of scholarships if they are given to foreigners. While it is unlikely that the best high school student-athletes would find themselves without scholarships, it seems certain that some good high school students would face a reduction in the number of scholarships which were awarded. For track and field athletics, one coach commented:

> With the number of grants going down and the number of foreigners going up, fewer young Americans will participate in college track under the present system. (5)

A very different form of criticism is that applied by liberal observers of the college sports scene who accuse colleges which recruit black athletes from overseas of blatantly racist attitudes and behaviour. It has been argued that while, say, Swedish hammer throwers would be made welcome in the US, Kenyan distance runners would not, beyond scoring points for their colleges. It is alleged further that African student-athletes 'have been threatened on many occasions with deportation if they don't do as they are told, if they don't race in every meet that comes along' (Ballinger, c. 1981, p. 60). Racial discrimination against foreign black student-athletes is also implicit in the reactions to situations where they fail to conform to certain black sporting stereotypes. American black athletes have traditionally excelled in the 'explosive' events (sprinting and jumping) and it is

> ... not until you have seen black men beating Americans in the long-distances - where black men are not supposed to beat white men - has there been a controversy ... Blacks are supposed to be sprinters. (6)

Controversy abroad

Criticism of the recruitment of foreign student-athletes from the donor countries has been of two types. First, is one that identifies strongly with the achievement ideology of sport and views superior athletes as a form of 'athletic investment'. Viewed this way, the recruiting of athletes is analogous to the 'brain drain'. While athletic performances by foreign students at colleges in the USA generally improve (Bale, 1987), athletes tend to replace allegiance to nation with that to university. They compete at top-level during the university sport season and frequently achieve below-par performances when they return to their own countries in late May or June.

The concern felt in some foreign countries is typified by the comments of the assistant secretary of the Kenyan Athletics Association who has been quoted as saying:

> The American coaches want to take anyone who can run. Agents come over here and try to take schoolboys away from their homes before they are ready. (Rodda, 1984)

Such student-athletes are lost as national or regional role models and as representatives of their own country and instead become parts of the American collegiate, and often subsequently, American professional sports (and cultural) scene.

During the recruiting process it does not appear that bright foreign student-athletes are alerted by American recruiters to the fact that their degrees, should they obtain them, may be of limited value on the European job market (Bale, 1986). For example, in Britain holders of American bachelors' degrees are not regarded as 'graduates' with regards to teachers' salary scales (Taylor, 1986). Foreign student-athletes are subtly pressurised into accepting athletic scholarships without the full implications for future employability being made clear. One British student-athlete commented:

> When I returned to Britain my degree did not help me. That is why I returned to the States where I am currently pursuing an MA in English. (Bale, 1987)

Although graduation rates among many American student-athletes are notoriously low (for top-class footballers it is around 30 per cent), a sample of European student-athletes indicated that 60 per cent had obtained, or expected to obtain, degrees during their four year period of athletic eligibility (Bale, 1987). This is not very different from the 66 per cent of the typical American student population which graduates during a four year period (Mihailich 1982, p. 117).

After graduation or completing a period at university, foreign student-athletes need to decide whether to remain in the USA or return home. Staying in America may be short term, in order to capitalise on remaining athletic prowess, or in extreme cases may be permanent with accompanying naturalisation. However, the probability of remaining in America after a period as a student-athlete seems likely to vary considerably between nationalities and cultures. The greater the 'cultural distance' between students and their nations of origin, the greater the probability that they will return home following their period of domicile in America. For example, of a sample of foreign track and field athletes (about 25 per cent of whom were Africans) in the USA, 59 per cent planned to return home after college (Hollander, 1980), but for a European sample only 31 per cent were certain that they would not remain in America in their post-college years (Bale, 1987).

A second kind of criticism is of a more ideological nature and views athletic recruiting as a form of 'cultural imperialism'. Kidd (1973) argues that foreign recruiting is a form of the cultural colonialism of much of the world, presenting recruits with negative images of their own countries. In extreme cases, traditional cultural and religious values can be over-ruled in the interests of the university athletic department. A runner from Somalia, for example, was successfully persuaded to modify the fasting requirements of his Moslem faith in order to take part in weekend sporting events (Jenkins, 1985, p. 23). Such an infusion of western ideas forms part of what Peet (1986) describes as the destruction of regional cultures and the imposition of value systems associated with the west. Having adopted western sports, countries from the economic periphery become dominated by, and increasingly dependent on, the cultural core. Hence, for example, 'virtually the whole of the Tanzanian national (track and field) team trains at UTEP' (Stidwell and Badecki, 1986, p. 294).

Many donor countries seem more than willing to send athletes to the USA. This is especially true in the former British West Indies where long-term dependence on American college sports scholarships has contributed to the underdevelopment of facilities at home. However, with dependency on US college training, countries like Jamaica and Trinidad have been able to reproduce a continuous line of world-class athletes, though in a narrow range of events. Such dependency is far from inevitable as the case of the more diversified and superior per capita sporting 'output' of Cuba clearly shows (Bale, 1985).

IMPLICATIONS

Various solutions have been proposed in response to these criticisms in international recruiting. Some centre on the establishment of athletic scholarships and 'institutes of sport' in countries that have traditionally had donor status. Canada and Australia are candidates for such approaches. However, this solution is impossible for the majority of the principal donor countries. Athletic recruitment from the Caribbean and much of Africa is therefore likely to continue unless it is either curtailed in the USA or controlled by potential and a tacit rejection of dependency on US colleges for the production of their international and elite athletes. There is currently a suggestion that Kenya is attempting to implement some sort of 'control' on American recruiting, the national athletics coach stating that efforts are being made to prepare 'athletes in Kenya, and not relying on the results achieved at American universities' (Rodda, 1987).

Recruiting per se is generally regarded as the biggest problem in college sports. Any reforms, aimed principally at domestic recruiting, would have implications for recruiting overseas. It has been suggested that recruiting should be spatially restricted to a sphere of influence based on the number of high school athletes available and that coaches should be physically restricted to this geographical area, though communication outside the sphere of influence could be continued by telephone or letter (Underwood, 1984). As shown above, such a proposal might increase rather than decrease the foreign influx since the well established linkages between colleges and countries do not depend upon face to face contact with the recruit.

Suggestions relating specifically to foreign recruiting include the elimination of <u>athletic</u> scholarships for foreign students and the banning of foreign students from NCAA championships. An extreme view is expressed by a coach at Indiana University who said that 'We should try to eliminate the foreign athlete from competition and if we can't do that we should eliminate him (sic) from scholarship assistance'. (7) In addition, it has been suggested that colleges should only be allowed to recruit foreign student-athletes in proportion to their overall number of foreign students.

None of these proposed 'solutions' take into account the ideological scale shown in Figure 6.1. Given the ideological foundations of sport in American education where, if Snyder and Spreitzer (1981) are correct, winning is primary and individual development is secondary, recruiting of talent is likely to continue. Rule changes regarding recruiting are likely to be merely cosmetic, given the pressure on many athletic departments. The pressure to succeed for both university coaches and foreign student-athletes are reflections of American sports ideology which consists of a rabid sense of place pride and competition on the one hand, and of sport's achievement ideology, with its emphasis on improved performance on the other. Given limited opportunities in their own countries, the international migration of sports talent is unlikely to stop. In other words, suggested reforms of the American college sports system tend to be rooted at the scale of experience (Figure 6.1), failing to appreciate the significance of national ideology and global sporting reality.

CONCLUSION

This chapter has attempted to explore a uniquely American educational phenomenon, namely the recruitment of foreign student-athletes on sports scholarships. While the international movement of professional sports personnel has become widespread in recent years, it is only in the American system that the migration of sporting talent is so integrated into the national education system. The geographical patterns of donors and hosts for one sport in which such international recruiting has become widespread in recent decades have been described. However, such a narrowly empirical examination is subject to the limitations of the analyses of geography of sport employed by Rooney (1974) and Bale (1982). This chapter has taken it as axiomatic that 'there is an isomorphism between the competitive sport system and the world system' (Galtung, 1984, p. 13) and has combined traditional empirical analysis with a broader discussion of the context in which international recruiting occurs. It has concluded that the importing of foreign sports talent helps increase institutional visibility and enhance university win-loss records. At the same time such migration contributes (in a small way) to the erosion of national culture and to the reduction in autonomy of many parts of the world. It has been suggested that American college sport is an ideological representation of the global phenomenon of achievement sport and that Taylor's three-tier model is useful in examining the place of sport in the American education system.

NOTES

1. Quoted in Track and Field News, 30 (4), p. 56 (1977).
2. 'Superior' is defined as having a performance capable of ranking in the annual US top 50 in any athletic event. These data have been published annually in Track and Field News for nearly 40 years.
3. Quoted in Track and Field News, 39 (6), p. 58 (1986).
4. Quoted in Track and Field News, 30 (4), p. 56 (1977).
5. Ibid.
6. Ibid.
7. Ibid.

Part Two

SOCIAL ISSUES IN EDUCATION

Chapter Seven

BLACK AND WHITE YOUNG PEOPLE AND EMPLOYMENT IN BRITAIN

John Eggleston

INTRODUCTION

Prior to large-scale industrialisation the experience of work was indivisible from the experience of family, community and society. It is only during the past century and a half that paid employment, for most citizens, has been taken apart from the day-to-day life of family and community and transferred to separate institutions - factories, shops, offices, workshops and warehouses. This is not to say, of course, that other forms of real work do not exist - notably in the home (see for example Pahl, 1984). Such institutions are increasingly 'closed': for reasons of complex technology, security, privacy, hygiene or hazard they are only accessible to those who work therein and within their prescribed working hours.

Yet the twentieth century has seen a further development in the nature of the experience of paid employment. Not only is it a separable part of human experience, but it is also one that is not being made available to all human beings. When twentieth century societies first experienced mass unemployment it was believed that this was but a temporary phenomenon caused by short-term 'malfunctionings' of the economic mechanism such as depression or recession. Now it is realised that unless effective alternative strategies are identified and adopted, such 'malfunctioning' may become a permanent feature: unemployment has become a structural feature of modern society. Many young people now have very limited prospects of paid employment - this is particularly true of special categories such as those living in inner-city areas or members of minority ethnic groups. (For a detailed discussion of the employment opportunities of minority ethnic groups see Eggleston, 1986.)

YOUNG PEOPLE AND PAID EMPLOYMENT

In this new situation major problems arise for young people. By far the majority are beyond the reach of any school 'remedy' and it is misleading and dangerous to imply otherwise. But some remedies have considerable relevance for the work of schools. One is that in many countries unemployment, especially for the young, co-exists with unfilled vacancies in many areas of work, which require skills, understandings and attributes not generally possessed by school leavers. Thus there are shortages of young people for vacancies in the 'servicing trades' responsible for the maintenance of motor cars, television sets and other domestic appliances, building maintenance and even gardening and window cleaning. There are also recurring shortages of candidates for higher level work in computing, electronics and a range of scientific and creative occupations. Of course, not all of these shortages are 'real', some are 'tactical' in that they are used to rationalise an unwillingness to employ young people with low initial productivity, but there is little doubt that many do exist.

A second problem is that young people who leave school and do not experience work often seem to find it increasingly difficult to obtain it. Potential employers believe that some kind of atrophy develops: just as the muscles in a broken leg lose their power, so a total lack of work experience is believed to diminish the capacity to satisfy the very requirements of work such as industry, responsibility and punctuality.

A third, and perhaps the most fundamental, problem is closely associated with the second; it is that work experience provides the basic contexts for 'normal' life. These include the use of time, the achievement of social 'standing' with its rights and duties and many of the attitudes and values that underpin participation in all the other human contexts offered by society. We may express the situation in two ways. One is that vocational identity is the key to social identity. The other is that work is the central instrument of social control in modern societies. Without the experience of work, how can the individual

Employment and Race

develop an adequate social identity and how can the society exercise the social control over its members necessary to achieve stability and continuity? The loss of a driving licence is a severe, even incapacitating, penalty for many people in paid employment; it may be of little consequence to an unemployed person who does not even have frequent access to the use of a motor car.

THE EXPERIENCE OF PAID EMPLOYMENT

We have now come to the crucial nature of employment. Like most human experiences, it has been taken for granted while its existence seemed assured. We have come to see its importance more clearly when its availability is at risk.

Most young people see work as the key to the achievement of full masculinity or femininity. Willis's study of working-class boys in an English comprehensive school in an inner-city area depicts the social pressures on the boys to take their place on the shop floor and so earn the acceptance of the community to which they belong (Willis, 1978). These boys need to prove themselves amongst their work-mates as capable of facing and surviving the realities of the factory floor with its 'hard and brutalising' conditions. Willis writes:

> The lads are not choosing careers or particular jobs, they are committing themselves to a future of generalised labour. Most work - or the 'grafting' they accept they will face - is equilibrated by the overwhelming need for instant money, the assumption that all work is unpleasant and that what really matters is the potential particular work situations hold for self and particularly masculine expression, diversions and 'laffs' as learnt creatively in the counter-school culture. These things are quite separate from the intrinsic nature of any task. This view does not contradict, for the moment, the overwhelming feeling that work is something to look forward to ... the lure of the prospect of money and cultural membership amongst 'real men' beckons very seductively as refracted through their own culture. (pp. 99-100)

Although Willis's study is concerned specifically with male roles a number of other studies of girls and work identities

215

indicate similar connections (for example, Davies, 1984).

As such studies clearly show, of even greater importance than specific occupational roles is the set of understandings and the self-image that individuals bring to roles. This _identity_ with which individuals imbue roles is crucial to the way they are played, modified and developed, and to the personal future within them. A label, such as machine operator, is but an incomplete guide to human behaviour in work: the identity with which the incumbents fill the role is the key component. How do individuals perceive themselves as machine operators? Have they chosen the work or is it a forced decision? If the former, what are his alternatives? Are they realistic or only based on fantasy? How do they adjust to the role in the absence of alternatives? What are the implications for other social behaviours? Fundamentally, is the vocational identity, with all its consequences, compatible with ego and self-image? Does it affect the exercise of power? If it does not, how may greater compatibility develop within the role?

The development of vocational identities is complex in modern society. In early, labour-intensive industrialisation, when large numbers of workers were required to perform routine and repetitive tasks, individual identity seldom came to exercise a dominant influence on production. Their self-image was of relatively little consequence to most employers. Young people were fitted into their roles in conditions Durkheim describes as 'mechanical solidarity'; the role transcendent, the individual subordinate.

The concept of identity alerts us to an alternative process. It is one in which young people may 'contract in' to both the specific job and the labour market generally, rather than to accept them passively. This new approach is highly relevant to some aspects of contemporary social conditions. It is compatible with the expressed views of young people who wish to 'count for something' in society rather than to be 'on the receiving end' of 'the system'. But it is also appropriate for the needs of some sectors of modern industry, which call for human beings not to act as 'machines', but to use their capacity to adapt, adjust and initiate. For such occupational roles an active vocational identity rather than a passive vocational role is highly preferable.

Unless an acceptable vocational identity can be achieved, then life for the individual is likely to be at best incomplete or compartmentalised; at worst, frustrating, enervating and incompatible.

THE ACHIEVEMENT OF WORK IDENTITY

It has already been noted that, until recently, most vocational identities were acquired by predominantly informal means. The learning of occupational roles literally began in the cradle as the child saw parents at work in homes, farms and workshops. The phrase 'like father like son' epitomised not only the informality of learning, but also the predictability of the vocational role that awaited most young people. The circumstances of the parents determined the future role of the young and the learning appropriate to it. Such identities were strongly reinforced by the norms of the community which defined, often with great precision, such things as woman's work and man's work; noble work and base work. Definitions of this kind were sometimes strongly reinforced by initiation ceremonies as a prelude to entry to adult vocational roles and still feature in some apprenticeship schemes.

Informal mechanisms for achieving vocational identities are, however, not always appropriate in modern dynamic societies, where occupational structures are changing rapidly and in which it may be possible for young people to have sufficient knowledge of the available roles in sufficient time to learn them and identify with them in anticipation. A characteristic problem of all advanced industrial societies is the rapid growth of new occupational groups, such as electronics engineers, television crews, and salesmen, advertising and sales personnel, which has meant that many young people enter work to undertake roles for which they have been able to achieve little or no preliminary identification. New generations of vocational identity regularly commence with each new initiative in technology and commerce.

SCHOOL AND VOCATIONAL IDENTITY

Schools have usually played only a small part in helping young people to achieve vocational identity. Though in the past half-century, they have come to exercise a major role in helping to identify talent through the examination and accreditation systems, there has been little attempt to assist the young in achieving the identities to accompany the examination qualifications. There has been even less attempt to help those without examination qualifications to achieve such identities. This has led to many problems. Not only have many young people lacked an adequate identity for work, but also for the other aspects of life that are linked to work. There has, for example, been remarkably little preparation for such activities as leadership in the workers' unions - roles that undeniably play a central part in modern societies. As a result, there are major problems in identifying leaders for these bodies at both local and regional level with important consequences for the day-to-day running of our occupational and economic systems. Political and community identities also have seldom received the attention they deserve; potential leaders here too are often in short supply.

A determining element in vocational identity has commonly been the social background of the young. Many writers have drawn attention to the small part played by schools in orienting young people for work. Becker (1963) has suggested that school makes little impact other than to offer legitimation of the differences brought about by home and community. As Willis (1978 p. 1) says: 'The difficult thing to explain about how middle class kids get middle class jobs is why others let them. The difficult thing to explain about how working class kids get working class jobs is why they let themselves.'

Bourdieu (1972) sees this to be a consequence of dominance of social and cultural reproduction processes that schools reinforce but do not change. Many writers, such as Lazerson (1971) and Bowles and Gintis (1976) have come to see the growing potential importance of schools as a transition institution into the labour force; an institution that 'accredits' young people with the various needs of the labour market (including unemployment) and achieves the necessary correspondence between supply and demand. Grubb and Lazerson (1981) demonstrate ways in which even new strategies of career education have, in practice, been used to stratify the school system, and to separate lower-class and ethnic minority youth from their white and middle-class peers.

ETHNIC MINORITY YOUNG PEOPLE AND WORK: A CASE STUDY

So far we have explored the mainstream analyses, which almost inevitably lead to the view that, notwithstanding the prevailing structural conditions, young people lacking work constitute a 'problem'. The opportunity to explore such matters more fully arose in a study entitled The Educational and Vocational Experiences of 15-18 Year Old Members of Minority Ethnic Groups, and now published as Education for Some (Eggleston, Dunn and Anjali, 1986). Young blacks, commonly find themselves in some of the least favourable positions in the labour market and the object of the study was to search for reasons, including why the school attainment and paid employment opportunities of black adolescents were, overall, markedly inferior to those of their white peers. Through detailed work with teachers, students and members of the minority group communities, a picture has been assembled of the pathways of the young members of the minority ethnic groups through school and beyond and their consequences. With a budget of £180,000, the project team worked with a cohort of 593 black and white young people, including 157 pupils of South Asian and 110 of Afro-Caribbean ethnic origins attending 23 comprehensive secondary schools in Bedford, Birmingham, Bradford and London. Most were born in Britain, almost all had lived here for more than five years. (A full statistical profile of the population is to be found in the published report.)

Many of the findings confirm and add extra emphasis to what teachers, social workers, pupils and parents increasingly suspect: that low achievement of black pupils is very frequently a consequence of the social system of which schools are an important element, rather than something that is inescapable and inevitable. The team found striking differences in the experiences of black and white pupils, for example the willingness of schools to enter black and white young people for examinations. Afro-Caribbean boys were only half as likely to be entered for any CSE or 'O' level examinations as those of all other groups of pupils together. Teachers' views of their black pupils, even though clearly based upon ethnic prejudices were nonetheless accepted and implemented by the 'official' mechanisms of schools and colleges. A linked study by Cecile Wright (1986) of two additional schools in another local education authority added further dramatic evidence on the attitudes of teachers.

A first step was the collection of teacher explanations for the low achievement of black pupils. These explanations were attributed in a blanket way to all black pupils, although it was generally qualified by remarks which suggested that they were more directly relevant to Afro-Caribbeans, particularly the boys and that the Asians compensated for the 'problem' by 'sheer hard work' and 'parental pressure'. The 'explanations' ranged through the full gamut of low academic and work aspirations, low attendance, poor understanding of the labour market, low motivation and minimal effort and application. Many teachers were prepared to accept these explanations as being the end of the matter and an indication that their professional responsibilities despite good intentions could take them no further. However, as these were analysed it became increasingly clear that most were not causal factors but consequential ones.

The next area of exploration was with young people themselves. Most display a very clear knowledge of the educational and occupational system and in particular the likely pay-offs of different kinds of examination results. In their fifth year at school more black than white young people were expecting to undertake a one-year sixth form course, usually to enhance their 'O' level or CSE stocks. A greater proportion of Afro-Caribbean pupils than all others wanted to go to colleges of further education. A high proportion of students from Asian backgrounds were expecting to take 'A' levels and were envisaging spending three further years doing so. A high proportion of all black pupils expected to resit their fifth year public examinations in the following year in school or college.

Of even greater interest was the fact that most black young people interviewed had a very clear knowledge of what the schools system had offered to friends in their own community and of the kind of jobs that might be available for them. In general they had a remarkably logical perception of participation in the school system; their apparent lack of effort or even of attendance was usually matched to a realistic appraisal of the consequences of so doing. More perceptibly than white children, they were not prepared to waste time on activities that offered little hope of a useful pay-off. Maybe in this way their lack of long term 'cultural' commitment to the school system was enabling them to take a more objective assessment of their expenditure of time and energy. However, their objectivity was to some extent clouded by an understandable fear of unemployment. For many black children the stigma of unemployment was of far greater concern than for white children and hence continued education was for many, particularly Asian boys, a means of avoiding the 'reality' test of the employment market. However, in almost all cases these children shared an objective awareness of the choices available and for the most part pursued educational and occupational goals that were realistic in terms of their ability. This can be seen in one of the many interviews reported where David Dunn, (Researcher) is talking with Mostaq Khaliq:

DD: What O levels have you signed up for at the colleges?
MK: Biology, physics, maths and chemistry.
DD: So a full spread ...
MK: and English as well ...
DD: and basically you're not expecting to get O levels this coming term?
MK: Might get one or two - CSE Grade 1's
DD: So what sort of grades are you expecting to get and in what subjects?
MK: In maths about 3 or 4 or better - in English I might get 2 or 3 but in physics and biology I should get 1.
DD: And you're doing CSE in physics and biology but you're expecting Grade 1's?
MK: And Communication Skills that's E2L English as a Second Language you can only get Grade 4, only a Grade 3 in that ...
DD: Maximum of Grade 3. Are you doing English?
MK: Yeah I'm doing English I might just get Grade 2 or 3 in that and there's another - Community Studies - I should get Grade 3 or 4 I don't know.
DD: So you've got a spectrum, you could certainly work up to several O levels this time next year. You obviously can't tell me what you want to do but you tell me what the advantages are of going to ... taking O levels and the advantages the other way round.
MK: The first job I really want to do is get an apprenticeship as an electrical engineer but I don't think I'll be able to get one now.
DD: Have you applied for any?
MK: No, not really - 'cos all teachers say you won't get in - I haven't really found out for meself, I should do that.

221

And if I go to ... the only snag is that I don't really like getting me hands dirty and working with oil and all that - I don't know if I'll get used to it or not. If I have to do that all me life I don't know if I'll like it or not. And O levels at ... I've got to do a course first, that's a foundation course, a City and Guilds then I could do O levels or do O levels straight off. The thing is if I do O levels straight off I wouldn't have reached O level standard so I might not be able to do the foundation course but there'd be an advantage in that - I'd have more attention than I'd have in the college so I might be able to pass them - I don't.

DD: Let's go back to first principles. Is there any job that you'd really like to do?
MK: Yea electrical engineer ...
DD: ... rather than automotive ...
MK: That's what I'd rather do.
DD: When did you decide you wanted to do that?
MK: About 2 or 3 months ago.
DD: What makes you want to do that, what is it about it?
MK: I just like messing about with electrical things, you know I've done quite a few things at home, and go to electrical classes some times and all that.
DD: So by an electrical engineer, what sort of job?
MK: I mean by mending television, videos and tape recorders really, washing machines and all appliances, hoovers and all that.
DD: Servicing ...
MK: Repairs and all that.
DD: You into hi-fis and all that?
MK: Yea.

(Eggleston, Dunn, Anjali, 1986, pp. 359-60)

It became clear that the 'explanations' based upon the low motivation and understanding attributed to black young people were largely incorrect.

This stage was followed by investigation of what seemed to be some of the more fundamental reasons for low attainment. These sprang very much from the low expectations with which black children were surrounded. In part this was due to racist attitudes expressed on the part of the teachers, some even less disguised to us than we had expected. Even where these expectations were not explicit, they were sometimes deeply embodied in the 'hidden curriculum' of schools and could be seen in the surprised manner with which teachers and heads spoke of the achievements of some of their black pupils, implying that this was so unusual as to be worthy of special mention. Also the attribution of special prowess, for example, to black adolescents' prowess in sport, often contained the implicit assumption that it was only in such areas that they could be expected to display talent. The 'barrier' use of language was also a factor in a number of schools; here language difficulties experienced by non-mother-tongue English speakers tended to be subtly exploited rather than overcome and used as a further vehicle for differentiation. Both at and below sixth-level there was evidence that ethnic minority pupils may be placed on courses and entered for examinations at levels significantly below those appropriate for their abilities and ambitions. In careers literature it was noticeable that the most prestigious careers available were usually illustrated by pictures of white persons performing them; only in the lower status jobs did black people appear in the illustrations in any number. And the other resources of the schools such as books, pictures, films, music and much else frequently reinforced the superiority of white achievement. Careers officers often acted to reinforce impediments. This has been clearly demonstrated by Brown (1985) who quotes the comments of a careers officer in a school with a relatively high proportion of pupils of Asian descent:

> Asians are a real problem because they always want to be doctors, lawyers and brain surgeons ... what's spoilt it this year is that one of them has made it (referring to a pupil of Asian descent who had been accepted by a university) (...) At this school they are always two jumps ahead ... those that should be applying for apprenticeships want to go to university. (p. 679)

Not surprisingly, black adolescents not uncommonly demonstrated the validity of the self-fulfilling prophecy by reacting in manners, speech and behaviour that appeared to justify the differential expectations and attitudes that surrounded them. In so doing, they fell neatly into the trap of appearing to justify the superficial explanations we encountered and which reinforced their feelings of powerlessness within the school system.

Young people, and often their parents, reacted in two

predictable ways. One was simply to drop out and abandon the system either at the minimum leaving age or in practice, before. But a very large number stayed on in the belief that, notwithstanding all the impediments, full-time schooling and the qualifications associated with it provided the best opportunity of success. Indeed, if there is a single theme running through the experiences of young people from the ethnic minority groups it is the determination of very large numbers to persevere with their education in the hope of improving their prospects and obtaining their desired occupations. This persistence showed not only in staying on but also in their willingness to undertake extra schoolwork, to attend Saturday schools, to participate in continuing further education and to aspire to higher education.

Even here the path was still paved with difficulty. Afro-Caribbean young people in particular found it difficult to get into college, those who actually succeeded did so after more applications and more rejections than whites and generally only by obtaining details of college opportunities by informal and incomplete methods rather than directly. The young people in the cohort displayed little awareness of special 'access' programmes to enter college or higher education institutions. Much the same impediments arose even in participation in YTS schemes and the 'loss' of black young people in the transition from school to work or YTS was notable. Within YTS schemes, there was a differential pattern in actual participation in that fewer black young people found places on the more attractive schemes based on employers' premises (Work Experience on Employer's Premises - WEEP).

Yet notwithstanding the impediments a surprisingly high proportion of black young people achieved formal qualifications in the end. This was pointed out with considerable satisfaction by many teachers who rather triumphantly asserted that, 'You see, we eventually get them there in the end!' Implicit in such statements was frequently a subtle reinforcement of prejudice in that it was seen to demonstrate that black young people take longer to 'make it' than whites. But the emptiness of this boast has been shown in a recent article by Krutika Tunna (1985) where it was pointed out that if the results achieved at 16 are taken alone, then there is a considerable difference in the opportunities of black and white young people.

The study concludes with many recommendations to schools, the career services, education authorities, the

Employment and Race

Manpower Services Commission and the DES which are too numerous to summarise in this chapter. Overall it recognises that professionals and their institutions cannot fundamentally change the labour market nor eradicate structural unemployment, it argues that they certainly can enhance the employability of many black and white young people and even develop their entrepreneurial and occupational skills far more fully as well as removing the impediments to achievement in more conventional areas. The key to this is to escape from the view that any category of young people can, or should be, defined as 'a problem'. In doing so, professionals can help to create a considerably more just and equitable distribution of opportunity than now exists, and play a considerably more positive role than many teachers have so far been prepared to concede possible. But the positive role can only be achieved by an all round reappraisal of what is offered to young people in schooling - and particularly by more appropriate diagnosis of their capabilities, motivations and situations. Simply to introduce a new subject 'work' into the school curriculum is, by itself, likely to achieve only very modest benefits.

Chapter Eight

EDUCATIONAL ATTAINMENT IN GLASGOW: THE ROLE OF NEIGHBOURHOOD DEPRIVATION

Catherine L. Garner

INTRODUCTION

Using data on some 3,000 young people who left school in Glasgow in 1979/80 this chapter assesses the effect of neighbourhood deprivation on individual attainment by modelling the contribution that it makes over and above the effects of the individual's home background and the particular school attended.

The interrelationships between home, school and neighbourhood have long been acknowledged in the literature but there has been little progress until recently in disentangling them. Over twenty years ago Douglas raised the issue in The Home and the School:

> Perhaps it is the type of area rather than the standard of housing that is important. Middle-class children, even if their home circumstances are bad, are likely to mix with other middle-class children who come from families where education is valued. In contrast manual working-class children in similarly substandard homes will often live in poor neighbourhoods where there is little interest in learning, so that both they and their parents may be discouraged by the apathy and disinterest around them. Unfortunately since our information concerns households and not neighbourhoods we cannot look further into this question. (Douglas, 1964, p. 67)

At about the same time Wiseman concluded that 'educational attainment ... is apparently affected by neighbourhood factors, school factors and home factors' (Wiseman, 1964, p. 173). He also commented that to understand these complex interrelationships better, would require multivariate and multi-level data, appropriate methods of analysis and a multi-disciplinary approach.

The existence of spatial variations in educational attainment was further highlighted by Taylor and Ayres (1969) and later formalised in a model of attainment by Byrne, Williamson and Fletcher (1975). They argued that earlier models of attainment failed 'to distinguish between those variables relating to educational attainment which describes individuals and those which relate to the properties of the system in which people find themselves' (p. 29). Their 'socio-spatial model' combined the influence of social, economic and political processes in the local area, as mediated through schooling and resource provision. This innovatively drew together social and spatial structure as recursive elements in a model of educational attainment. However, since their analyses used aggregate data, they were unable to disentangle the separate effects of the model's components and have been criticised for their ecological interpretations (Hutchison, 1975).

Nevertheless, their multi-level conceptualisation of the problem was important and they lacked only multi-level data and methods of analysis to make further advances. Since then, progress in empirical research has been impeded by technical constraints in computing and data linkage and by a general reluctance among many social scientists to employ area-level data for fear of committing the ecological fallacy. A recent study of educational attainment and occupational aspirations of children in Manchester (Moulden and Bradford, 1984) overcame these problems. But it was on a small scale. They used questionnaire data on 674 pupils from two schools, linked to area data from the 1971 Census of Population. This study showed that residential environment contributed a significant amount to the explanation of educational outcomes over and above the influence of home background and individual characteristics. With only two schools in the study, however, the effects of schools, as distinct from neighbourhoods, could not be systematically modelled.

The present study, which is larger and uses more recent area-level data, extends this investigation of the importance of neighbourhood. The linkage of data sources was made simple and systematic for the first time because the areal framework for the 1981 Census of Population in Scotland, was based on postcodes (De Mellow, 1979; Rhind, 1983). The model used here acknowledges the multi-level nature of the processes which influence attainment and draws on data appropriate to this multi-level structure. Four levels of influence could be modelled; the individual, the home, the school and the neighbourhood. However, true individual-level measurements are limited in the available data. The various measures of socio-economic status (SES) elide individual and home background measurements and therefore restrict the modelling to three levels.

The lack of data measured unambiguously at the individual level, as distinct from the level of the family or home, poses a threat to the specification of the model and increases the chance that other variables might assume spurious significance. Hauser (1970) argues that many contextual (group) effects assume their significance because they pick up unmeasured individual effects in poorly specified models. This is a particular problem where levels higher than the individual are constructed from aggregates of individual-level data. The neighbourhood data used here have the virtue of being derived from a separate source and measured directly. (1) It is the lack of a control for individual ability which is the most important single omission. A recent study examining school contextual effects has shown that the effects of home and school-level variables tend to be over-estimated when there is no control for individual ability on entry to school (Willms, 1987). In Willms' study coefficients were reduced by the inclusion of a verbal reasoning test (VRQ) score, although the contribution of family background variables remained significant. This is a problem that cannot be resolved in this study but the reader should bear it in mind throughout.

A further problem lies in the conceptualisation of the multi-level model and of its constituent parts, for any individual (or group) is assumed to be independent of the values for other members of the same level and independent also of other levels (McPherson and Willms, 1986). This 'atomistic' assumption may arbitrarily mis-specify 'relational' aspects of individuals or groups within and across levels. SES measures, for example, can reasonably be regarded as measuring attributes of an individual (the atomistic assumption), and attributes of the relationships that such measures entail. Although an atomistic approach allows progress in analysis which a purely relational approach inhibits, it does pose the danger that such a model will wrongly attribute characteristics to the members of any one level. As McPherson and Willms write,

> the constant danger is that we will wrongly 'freeze' aspects of the relations ... and attribute them to the atomistically conceived (individual). Equally dangerous is the possibility that we will fail to notice other aspects of (individuals) and their relationships or that we will notice them but assign them to the wrong level ... or that we will assign them to the right level but measure them inadequately. (ibid., pp. 285-6)

In the context of the home, the school and the neighbourhood, boundaries between the levels can be artificially drawn to allow a multi-level specification. But because, in reality, such levels exist in relation to each other and are not atomistic, it is impossible to assert that variables will capture only the variation associated with that level to which they are assigned. This is apparent time and again when the model here is specified. Bearing these problems in mind we can now proceed to describe the constituents of the model.

The home and the individual

Home background factors measured at the level of the individual are in a sense wrongly attributed to that level since they are more correctly properties of the group of individuals which make up the family or household unit and could, as such, constitute another level in the model. However, this distinction becomes blurred when examining the influence of the characteristics of a group (family) on an outcome at the individual level (attainment) when the individual is part of that group (i.e. the SES measures may be proxies for both relational and atomistic aspects of the individual and their situation).

Home-based factors can be broadly subdivided into material and cultural influences. Of those discussed by Mortimore and Blackstone (1982), only a few can be substituted by the data available here, and the material/cultural distinction that they indicate cannot be made. Father's social class is widely recognised to be of prime importance and its relationship with inequality in educational attainment has been an important focus for research over the past three decades (Douglas, Ross and Simpson, 1968; Boudon, 1973; Tyler, 1977; Halsey, Heath and Ridge, 1980; Gray, McPherson and Raffe, 1983; Raffe, 1983; Willms, 1986). Although social class cannot be directly measured, it has become common practice to use father's occupation (variously coded) as the most reasonable proxy. This occupational measure incorporates both socio-economic divisions within the social structure (Halsey 1975) and associated differences of attitude between social groups.

Father's social class may capture part of any neighbourhood effect since social class (father's occupation) measured at the level of the individual family is not independent of the social class (types of fathers' occupations) in the area. The social-class segregation of residential neighbourhoods is well known. However, social structure and its spatial manifestation accounts for more than just social class (father's occupation), and it is therefore unlikely that all area differences can be accounted for by social class measured at the home level.

Father's occupation may also be a proxy for other characteristics within the home, for example, father's occupation (or lack of it) will partly determine the level of material provision of the home. Inadequate material provision can have severe consequences for children's attainment (Wedge and Prosser, 1973; Barnes and Lucas, 1975). Paternal occupation may also be related to general health and health care within the family (Black 1980; Jarman, 1983; Riddell, 1985). Poor health and recurrent illness predicates irregular school attendance with a concomitant lowering of performance.

Numerous studies over the past two decades have detailed other home-based factors which influence attainment (Bernstein, 1962; Douglas, 1964; Central Advisory Council for Education (England) (CACE), 1967; Robson, 1969; Rutter, Tizard and Whitmore, 1970; Kelsall and Kelsall, 1971). Rutter and Madge (1976) give a comprehensive review. Of the factors they highlight, parental education and family size can be modelled from the data available here.

The school

At the school level, research into school effectiveness has

combined data for pupils with data on schools and has increasingly made use of a multi-level specification. Current research in this area is attempting to take account simultaneously of influences both within and external to schools at a variety of levels (Raudenbush and Bryk, 1986). Analyses have distinguished school-process effects from contextual effects. The latter are the effects of the collective properties of the pupils within a school on an individual's performance. These effects are determined by the pupil body within the catchment of the school and are therefore closely related to the characteristics of home area. As Gray et al. write, 'it may be inappropriate to seek too precise a distinction between, on the one hand, the effects of the schools themselves and, on the other, the effects of the characteristics of their catchments' (Gray et al., 1983, p. 262). However, by separating the school and the area conceptually, the analysis can be performed in such a way as to estimate minimum and maximum contributions of school and area to the explanation of educational attainment (see below). The definition of school contextual effects (Willms, 1985, 1986) means that school variables will capture part of the effect of neighbourhood. Once again the multi-level conceptualisation of the problem allows us artificially to partition the effects of one level from that of another. However, although we may statistically separate school and neighbourhood and conceptually distinguish them, the underlying causal mechanisms remain confounded. One particularly pertinent finding of school-effectiveness research has been to show that there are differences in the relationship between family background variables (such as social class) and educational attainment in areas with different local school systems (McPherson and Willms, 1986). This means that schools are not independent of the communities which they serve since 'pupils are not randomly allocated to schools, nor schools to neighbourhoods' (ibid., p. 286). It is also important to realise that neither are people allocated randomly to neighbourhoods but are subject to socio-economic and spatial constraints, controlled by 'urban gatekeepers' (Pahl, 1970) and by the workings of the urban housing market both public and private.

The only school variable which can be represented here is school membership, which is modelled as a dummy variable for each school. By definition the school dummies capture all the variation associated with schools whether through school processes, contextual effects or differential resource provision. However, the method of analysis (see below) does not allow for any variation between schools in the relationship of background factors to attainment within schools. Thus the analysis is not 'multi-level' in the sense that this currently obtains in research on schooling (see Aitkin and Longford, 1986; Goldstein, 1986; Raudenbush and Bryk, 1986).

The neighbourhood

The term 'neighbourhood' may be applied to a range of area scales and no fixed definition could or should be applied. What is crucial is to take account of processes at the appropriate area scale at which they operate. Further, when data at different scales are combined in the examination of individual outcomes, it is important not to be constrained in consideration of the scale at which potentially significant social processes operate. In this study it is the immediate local area surrounding the home which is likely to be of crucial importance, since it is within this milieu that young people grow up. Both the physical character of the home area, such as housing conditions, and the social milieu, are likely to be influential. The home area and the school are the prime focus within which young people define their reference group, which in turn is involved in determining the role expectations of the individual including their attitudes to education. As the Plowden report stated, the importance of the local social environment in the formation of attitudes to education should not be overlooked:

> In a neighbourhood where the jobs people do and the status they hold owe little to their education it is natural for children as they grow older to regard school as a brief prelude to work rather than as an avenue to future opportunities. (CACE, 1967, vol. 1, p. 50)

In a study of attitudes to education Robson (1969) found that for 'working-class areas' the conflict between the 'educational ethos' and the 'ethos of the community' tended to produce negative attitudes to education. These examples suggest that the influence of neighbourhood is less to do with the physical environment (although undoubtedly this plays some role) and more to do with the social environment where the influence of groups or individuals on others is promoted through spatial proximity and day-to-day contact (Robson, 1969). In assessing the importance of neighbourhood influences on attainment the choice of variables used to describe an area is critical. As a data source, the Census of Population contains a large number of possible indicators and therefore it is essential to select those that best represent the underlying processes thought to operate at this level. Moulden and Bradford (1984) drew on the list of variables used by Wiseman in his Manchester study (Wiseman, 1964). When subjected to principal components analysis their study produced a first component strongly related to socio-economic structure. Although this captures a large amount of the variation between residential areas, the aim here is to represent a broader concept and therefore an indicator that combines a range of environmental characteristics was chosen. Given the study's focus on Glasgow (see below) it seemed appropriate to use an index of deprivation.

The definition of multiple deprivation used here is that drawn up by the Housing and Urban Renewal Research Unit of the Scottish Development Department to identify areas of special need in Scotland in 1981. (2) It combines characteristics of the physical environment with social and economic aspects of the population living in an area and should therefore provide a reasonable proxy for the type of neighbourhood effects under examination. This measure has several advantages, for not only is it based on a substantial programme of research to identify areas of need in Scotland (Duguid and Grant, 1983) but it is widely used by policy makers at national, regional and local levels.

The use of deprivation indices to define large areas within cities for area-based programmes has been criticised because large 'deprived' areas have often been wrongly classed as worse off than a 'severely deprived' single enumeration district (Duguid and Grant, 1983). In this study each enumeration district score is treated separately. This has been shown elsewhere to provide a more sensitive and sensible use of this type of data (Tunley, Travers and Pratt, 1979).

SPECIFICATION OF THE MODEL

Design

Data sources
The data used in this study come from two sources. The individual-level data on young people's educational attainment and their personal and family backgrounds come from the 1981 Scottish School Leavers Survey (SSLS). This survey is one of a series of of biennial surveys conducted by the Centre for Educational Sociology at the University of Edinburgh in conjunction with the Scottish Education Department. The particular data used here come from questionnaires sent out in April 1981 to young people who had left school in Scotland in the academic session 1979/80. The survey covered leavers from all secondary schools in Scotland and was sent to 37 per cent of all 1979/80 leavers. Of these leavers 88 per cent agreed to take part in the study but a further four per cent of the questionnaires were returned as 'undelivered'. The response rate for pupils who received the questionnaire was 89.6 per cent (for further details of the survey, sampling and response rates see Burnhill, 1984; Weston, Lamb, Burnhill and Garner, 1984). All analyses employ a design weight to take account of biases arising from non-coverage.

The second source of data is the 1981 Census of Population, which provides area-level data at various scales of aggregation for the whole of the country. (3) The two data sources were linked through the postcode of the address at which survey respondents were contacted (Garner, 1984). This link therefore permits the description of the respondent's immediate neighbourhood or surrounding environment in terms of the characteristics of the population in the home enumeration district. This method cannot allow for past mobility of respondents' families and therefore length of residence in the current home area. However, since most urban moves are short distance ones, particularly within the local authority housing sector (4) (Garner, 1979; Forbes, Lamont and Robertson, 1979), this is unlikely to be a serious problem.

The study is focused on those school leavers in the 1981 SSLS who left from the 69 schools within the Glasgow division of Strathclyde Region. Each leaver is therefore attributed membership of the last school attended. In terms of home area, some of the leavers came from outside the physical boundaries of the division but were considered eligible for inclusion through their attendance at divisional schools.

Glasgow

The decision to focus on school leavers from Glasgow was made partly for logistical purposes and partly because Glasgow, as a city, is intrinsically interesting, offering a wide variation in neighbourhoods, schools and types of individuals. By restricting the study to an administrative division of one education authority (EA), between-EA differences in resource provision or in educational policy and philosophy are excluded for EA schools. (5)

In terms of attainment Glasgow is below the average for Scotland. Even after adjusting for social-class composition, Glasgow's mean attainment score is still below the national average (Willms, 1985). The Scottish Tertiary Education Advisory Council (STEAC) report on the Future Strategy for Higher Education in Scotland noted concern over the low levels of school-leaver qualification for higher education in Strathclyde and Glasgow in particular. In 1982-3, 20 per cent of school leavers in Strathclyde gained the minimum entry qualifications for higher education (three or more SCE Highers). This was one per cent below the national average. But in Glasgow, only 17 per cent gained this level of qualification (Scottish Education Department, 1985).

In schooling terms, Glasgow division has the largest number of schools of any administrative area in Scotland and research has shown that it also has the highest level of school effects in Scotland. The estimate for contextual effects in Glasgow is 0.56 compared with values from 0.25 to 0.45 in the rest of Scotland (Willms, 1986). A description of school catchments in Glasgow from 1981 Census data showed wide variations in terms of the level of adult unemployment, the percentage of single-parent families and the proportion living in local-authority housing (ibid.). In the same study Glasgow was shown to be 25 per cent of a standard deviation below the mean for Scotland in terms of a composite SES measure and to have the greatest between-school segregation on that same measure.

The variation in the composition of school catchments reflects the range of residential environments within the city. At the bottom end of the scale Glasgow is well known for its long history of deprived neighbourhoods. As early as the 1960s Glasgow had a policy of slum clearance in which vast areas of the central city were cleared of buildings and people. In the mid-1970s a study by the Department of the Environment (Holtermann, 1975) once more highlighted Glasgow's premier position in the league table of deprivation. Since that time, area-based policies of positive discrimination for areas of multiple deprivation have been implemented in forms as diverse as housing action areas, educational priority areas and neighbourhood schemes. Although these policy initiatives have undoubtedly helped in the fight against deprivation in Glasgow, recent studies using the 1981 Census of Population have shown that the problem of deprivation in the city remains severe, although its nature and spatial distribution have both changed (Department of the Environment Inner Cities Directorate, 1983; Glasgow District Council, 1983; Sim, 1984).

In studying Glasgow it is thus essential to remember that we have a unique setting where two decades of government policies have been at work attempting to ameliorate the worst effects of deprivation within schools and neighbourhoods.

Measures and definitions

Two dependent educational outcome variables were defined in terms of formal qualifications. Although there is debate about how outcomes from the school system should be measured, this basis was employed because young people leaving school and entering the labour market or further education are still judged on their formal qualifications (Main and Raffe, 1983; Raffe, 1984). The first measure is a general attainment score (TOTSCEP) which covers 14 categories describing the number of O-grade and Higher awards at the A to C level. Awards on the range A to C are officially recognised as passes on the Highers examination. For pupils obtaining no A to C awards at O grade, account was taken of any SCE O-grade awards at the D or E grade. This variable captures both attainment and length of schooling since Highers cannot be taken until the fifth or sixth year, that is in the first or second year of non-compulsory schooling. This variable was scaled using a logit distribution for re-expressing grades (following Mosteller and Tukey, 1977) carried out by Willms (1986). He rescaled

Educational Attainment in Glasgow

this variable for all leavers in the 1981 SSLS by dividing the logit scores by the standard deviation for the total school population thereby obtaining scores for the entire 1981 sample with a mean of zero and a standard deviation of one. (6)

The second educational outcome measure was based on the 14 category scale recoded to create a dichotomous variable (THREEHI), which scores one for those with three or more passes at SCE Higher grade and zero for others. This was chosen since it represents the nominal formal qualification level for entry to higher education and as such was of particular interest in the light of the STEAC debate.

The independent variables in the model were selected to represent the three levels discussed above.

Home

Social class. Social class is represented by father's occupation (RGSC) scaled on the Registrar General's Occupational Classification (Office for Population Censuses and Surveys, 1980). It was defined here by a set of five dummy variables. DCLASS1, DCLASS3N, DCLASS3 and DCLASS4 take the value of one respectively for school leavers with fathers in professional and intermediate (RGSC I and II), skilled non-manual (RGSC IIIn), skilled manual (RGSC IIIm) and semi- or unskilled jobs (RGCS IV and V). DCLASS6 identifies those with no fathers, those for whom no father's occupation was reported and those (including the armed forces) whose father's occupation was not classifiable. In the analysis DCLASS4 is taken as the reference category and coefficients on DCLASS1, DCLASS3N and DCLASS3 are predicted to be positive and to be powerful in their influence on attainment.

Mother's and father's education. These are represented by two dummy variables MUMED and DADED. They are constructed from length of parental schooling and therefore are substitutes for the level of parental education. These variables are scaled one for parents who stayed on at school beyond 15 and zero for others. Coefficients on these variables are predicted to be positive.

Table 8.1: Deprivation Score: Constituent Variables

Socio-demographic indicators:

1. Single-parent families - households containing at least one single-parent family with dependent child(ren) as a percentage of all households.
2. Large households - households with four or more children as a percentage of all households.
3. *Elderly households - households containing persons of pensionable age only as a percentage of all households.

Economic indicators

4. Unemployment - economically active residents aged 16 or more seeking work as a percentage of economically active residents of the same age.
5. Youth unemployment - economically active residents aged 16-20 seeking work as a percentage of economically active residents aged 16 or more.
6. The permanently sick - residents aged 16+ who are permanently sick as a percentage of all residents aged 16+.
7. Low earning socio-economic groups - residents economically active or retired who are classified by the Registrar General into socio-economic groups 7, 10, 11, 15 or 17 as a percentage of all residents who are economically active or retired.

Housing indicators

8. *Amenity deficiency - households without exclusive use of either a bath or an inside WC or both as a percentage of all households.
9. Overcrowding - households below the occupancy norm as a percentge of all households.
10. *Vacant dwellings - household spaces classified in the Census as 'other' vacants as a percentage of total household spaces.
11. *Level and access (1): The very elderly - elderly households containing at least one person age 75+ on the first floor or above with no lift for access as a percentage of all households.
12. Level and access (2): The under-fives - households containing at least one person aged 0-4 on the first

Table 8.1: continued

floor or above as a percentage of all households.

* these four variables have very small weightings and therefore have comparatively little impact on the deprivation score.

Source: Based on Duguid and Grant (1983).

Family size. This is represented in the model by a dummy variable, LFAM, which takes the value one for those school leavers who have four or more siblings and zero for others. This variable is predicted to have a negative effect on educational outcomes.

Sex of respondent. This is the only unambiguously individual-level measurement in the data available here and is included since there are well-known gender differences in attainment and attitudes to schooling (Willms and Kerr, 1987). Moulden and Bradford (1984) found that residential environment was a more important influence on education for girls than for boys. Early analyses were done separately for males and females and, although differences were found between the sexes in the relationship of background variables to education, the differences were small and with regard to residential environment were, if anything, contrary to the findings of Moulden and Bradford. GENDER is scored zero for males and one for females.

Schools
To control for the differential effects of schools across the city a set of dummy variables, S1 to S69, representing school membership was constructed. There are 69 schools in Glasgow division of which twelve were grant-aided or independent in 1981. The school (S45) with the mean on deprivation closest to the mean for Glasgow as a whole was chosen as the reference school.

The individual coefficients for the 69 school variables will not be reported here since the purpose is not to distinguish the effect of individual schools on attainment but only to assess their importance as a group, relative to the other variables in the model.

Table 8.2: Pearson Product Moment Correlations for Background Variables with SCE Attainment and Neighbourhood Deprivation for School Leavers in Glasgow.

	SCE attainment	Deprivation index
SCE attainment (TOTSCEP) (a)	-	-.471
Social Class		
RGSC I + II (DCLASS1)	.403	-.346
RGSC IIIn (DCLASS3N)	.126	-.154
RGSC IIIm (DCLASS3)	-.089	.049
RGSC IV + V (DCLASS4)	.121	.133
RGSC nec (DCLASS6)	-.209	.214
Mother's education (MUMED)	.243	-.202
Father's education (DADED)	.275	-.215
Family size (LFAM)	-.215	.277
Sex of respondent (GENDER)	-.015	.024
Deprivation index (DSCORE)	-.471	-

N = 3080

Notes:
(a) Names in brackets refer to the shorthand names given to variables for analysis.

Source: 1981 SSLS and 1981 Census of Population.

Neighbourhood
The deprivation index. Twelve variables from the 1981 Census of Population were drawn from three broad groupings: socio-demographic indicators, economic indicators and housing indicators (Table 8.1). The individual indicators were combined into a single deprivation score by taking the first factor from the all-Scotland analysis. For each enumeration district within the study area the values of the twelve indicators were obtained from the Small Area Statistics of the 1981 Census of Population. These variables were then standardised to have a mean of zero and a

standard deviation of one; weighted by the factor score coefficients from the all-Scotland study are then summed to give a deprivation score for each enumeration district in Glasgow. The enumeration district deprivation scores were linked to the respondents from the survey through home postcodes, thus attributing to each individual a measure of multiple deprivation in their home area. Since the all-Scotland study was designed to give a national score with a mean of zero and a standard deviation of one it is possible to compare the present area of study to the national profile. For the Glasgow area defined here, this score has a mean of 0.224 and a standard deviation of 1.095, showing that the average level of deprivation for Glasgow is 22 per cent of a standard deviation higher than the average for Scotland.

The variables described above are the basis of the model of attainment examined here. The relationship of the independent family background variables with SCE attainment and the deprivation score is shown in Table 8.2.

Strategy for analysis

Separate analyses will be performed for the two outcome attainment measures. For the first, (TOTSCEP), an ordinary least squares (OLS) regression model will be fitted using an hierarchical specification. Such a specification permits two types of testing. Firstly, by entering variables into the model in pre-specified groups, separate significance tests can be made for the different levels of the conceptual model. Secondly, when explanatory variables are associated, the proportion of variation explained by each variable depends on the order in which they are entered into the model. This means that when associated variables or groups of variables are reordered, some assessment can be made of their minimum and maximum unique contributions. In this situation of interrelated variables, the most stringent test of the contribution of neighbourhood can be made by entering the deprivation index into the model after all other groups.

The use of OLS regression admits certain assumptions which may not be valid here, in particular, the model is additive and thereby constrains the relationships between outcome measures and background variables to be the same within and between levels. The validity of this assumption has already been questioned for schools in different areas, but is one which cannot be overcome in the present study. A

Table 8.3: Regression of SCE Attainment on Home, School and Neighbourhood in Glasgow: Contributions of Variable Groups

	R^2	Percentage increase in R^2
Home: (DCLASS1, DCLASS3N, DCLASS3, DCLASS6, MUMED, DADED, LFAM, GENDER)	.245	24.5
School: (S1 to S44, S46 to S69)	.360	11.5 (6.7) (a)
Neighbourhood: (DSCORE)	.386	2.6 (7.5)

Notes:
(a) Figures in () represent the percentage change in R^2 for schools and neighbourhood when entered in an hierarchical model in reverse order.

Source: 1981 SSLS and 1981 Census of Population.

multi-level regression model would be required to allow for such variation in the relationship of outcome and background variables. A recent study of school effects which makes a direct comparison of OLS and multi-level regression models found a high correlation between the two sets of estimates although those from the multi-level regression were more precise (Willms, 1987). This finding provides some reassurance that the proposed form of analysis is not inappropriate.

Since the second outcome attainment measure (THREEHI) is a dichotomous variable it is more appropriate to use a form of analysis that makes explicit use of the fact that the dependent variable has a binary (0/1) nature. The technique used here will be probit analysis (Maddala, 1983). This has been used previously to analyse similar data for school-leaver unemployment (Garner, Main and Raffe, forthcoming). (7)

Table 8.4: Regression of SCE Attainment on Home, School and Neighbourhood in Glasgow: Tests of Significance

Variable group tested	Unrestricted residual sum of squares	Restricted residual sum of squares	n-k	q	$F_{q, n-k}$
	1792.77		3002		
Home		1939.61		8	30.75*
School		1986.97		68	4.75*
Neighbourhood		1869.69		1	128.84*

Notes:
* significant at $p < 0.01$

Source: 1981 SSLS and 1981 Census of Population.

ANALYSIS AND RESULTS

The general attainment score (TOTSCEP) was regressed on the specified input variables using OLS regression. (8) The model is powerful in explaining educational outcomes, the coefficient of determination (R^2) being .39. A higher coefficient would not be expected for a model that does not include any measure of individual intelligence/ability.

Table 8.3 shows the increase in R^2 as groups of specified variables enter the model. Individual/home variables account for 24.5 per cent of the variation in educational attainment. School effects are extremely important adding 11.5 per cent to the model and the deprivation score being added last contributes an additional 2.6 per cent (entered before all other variables the deprivation score accounts for 22 per cent). All groups of variables add significantly to the explanation of educational outcomes as shown by the tests of significance given in Table 8.4.

If the order in which school variables and neighbourhood variables are entered is reversed, neighbourhood accounts for 7.5 per cent of the variation and schools add a further 6.7 per cent. The minimum unique contribution of schools and neighbourhood can be said to be 6.7 and 2.6 per cent respectively.

Educational Attainment in Glasgow

Table 8.5: Regression of SCE Attainment on Home, School and Neighbourhood Variables in Glasgow

Home:	Coefficient	SE	tstat
RGSC I + II (DCLASS1)	0.536	(.056)	9.60*
RGSC IIIn (DCLASS3N)	0.317	(.064)	4.97*
RGSC IIIm (DCLASS3)	0.058	(.039)	1.50
RGSC nec (DCLASS6)	-0.130	(.045)	2.89*
Mother's Education (MUMED)	0.080	(.047)	1.69
Father's Education (DADED)	0.150	(.052)	2.92*
Family Size (LFAM)	-0.185	(.033)	5.62*
Sex of respondent (GENDER)	-0.028	(.029)	0.96
School: (a) (S1 to S44, S46 to S69)	-	-	-
Neighbourhood: Deprivation index (DSCORE)	-0.204	(.018)	11.35*
Constant	-0.221	(.133)	
R^2	.386		
Adjusted R^2	.370		
F	24.50		
N	3080		

Notes:
(a) Coefficients are not reported for individual schools.
* significant at p <.01

Source: 1981 SSLS and 1981 Census of Population.

The coefficients for individual variables are shown in Table 8.5. This shows that six variables out of the ten (school membership variables are not reported here) are significant. When compared with having a father in a semi-skilled or unskilled occupation, those with fathers in professional, intermediate and skilled non-manual jobs have a marked positive advantage for their educational outcomes. Having a father in RGSC I or II (all other things being equal) results in an increase of over half a standard deviation in attainment. This is equivalent to getting four O grades rather than one since a difference of 0.10 on the TOTSCEP score is approximately equivalent to one O-grade pass at bands A to C. (9) Those with fathers in the non-classifiable category have a relatively greater disadvantage. Father's education also has the predicted positive association and a substantial effect on outcomes. Having a father who has stayed on at school beyond the minimum leaving age can add 15 per cent of a standard deviation to the outcome score. Family size similarly has the predicted effect with those coming from families with five or more children being disadvantaged by about 19 per cent of a standard deviation (almost two O grades).

The area deprivation score is also powerful, with a difference of one standard deviation on the score, resulting in a 20 per cent difference in attainment scores (i.e. two O grades). Table 8.6 shows the attainment differentials between selected areas within Glasgow in terms of standard deviation units on the dependent variable. Since Glasgow has an average level of deprivation some 22 per cent of a standard deviation higher than Scotland as a whole, this results in a lowering of educational attainment by four per cent of a standard deviation on TOTSCEP. The Glasgow deprivation effect is equivalent to about half an O grade.

However, as Table 8.6 shows, this average for Glasgow conceals a wide variation across the city. For some areas of the city the 'deprivation effect' is substantially more serious. Young people from Easterhouse (postcode-sector G34.0) suffer a lowering of their educational outcomes by almost 40 per cent of a standard deviation on TOTSCEP. This means that the effect of deprivation in the neighbourhood in Easterhouse is associated with a reduction in attainment of young people who live there ceteris paribus by up to three O grades. It is a very similar story for those in Drumchapel and Blackhill. There are, however, parts of Glasgow where neighbourhood gives a substantial positive advantage. For example, in Kelvinside, Bearsden and Giffnock the neighbourhood effect is associated with a positive advantage of around two O grade passes. These

Table 8.6: Contribution of Neighbourhood Deprivation to Differential Attainment in Glasgow

Selected Areas (a)	Mean Deprivation Score in Standard Deviation Units	Predicted Attainment Differential (b)
Glasgow	+0.21	−0.04
Easterhouse	+1.88	−0.38
Drumchapel	+1.68	−0.34
Blackhill	+1.35	−0.28
Castlemilk	+1.10	−0.22
Priesthill	+1.08	−0.22
Pollokshaws	−1.00	+0.20
Dowanhill	−1.10	+0.22
Kelvinside	−1.20	+0.24
Bearsden	−1.30	+0.26
Giffnock	−1.34	+0.27

Notes:

(a) The named areas correspond to the following postcode sectors:

Easterhouse (G34.0); Drumchapel (G15.8); Blackhill (G33.1); Castlemilk (G45.0); Priesthill (G53.6); Pollokshaws (G43.2); Dowanhill (G12.9); Kelvinside (G12.0); Bearsden (G61.1); Giffnock (G46.6).

(b) The attainment differential is measured in standard deviation units of TOTSCEP. The predicted differential is calculated by multiplying the mean score on the deprivation index for each area by the OLS coefficient (−.204) on neighbourhood deprivation.

Source: 1981 SSLS and 1981 Census of Population.

Table 8.7: Probit Analysis of Attaining/Not Attaining Three or More SCE Highers Passes in Glasgow (summary)

Unrestricted log-likelihood	Restricted log-likelihood	q	Chi-square (a) (q)	Test on
-988.93	-1030.1	8	82.34 (b)	Home
	-1091.9	68	205.94	School
	-1017.6	1	57.34*	Neighbourhood

Notes:
(a) critical values at = 0.01 for χ^2 with the following degrees of freedom are:
(1) 6.63 (4) 13.28 (70) 100.4
(chi-squared = -2* the change in log-likelihood)
(b) all groups are significant at $p < .01$.

Source: 1981 SSLS and 1981 Census of Population.

effects are based purely on the contribution of neighbourhood (deprivation index) to educational outcomes and say nothing about the home background factors or schooling of the young people from such areas. Home and school influences are removed (held constant) in the calculation of the OLS coefficient on deprivation. This is not therefore a comment on the quality of schooling in any area but rather a statement about the context in which schools operate.

The wide range of deprivation within Glasgow means that it is not altogether sensible to speak of a 'Glasgow effect' since for two people, one living in Easterhouse and one living in Giffnock (the extremes within Glasgow with a difference on the deprivation score of 3.22 standard deviations), the difference in educational outcomes associated with deprivation alone (ceteris paribus) would be 65 per cent of a standard deviation. That is the difference between getting one O grade (in Easterhouse) and five O grades (in Giffnock). Given the importance of qualifications in obtaining employment this difference is not inconsiderable. Indeed it has been shown elsewhere (using the SSLS data) that pupils who left school in 1981 with only one or two O grade awards had less than 70 per cent employment rate whereas about 85 per cent of the pupils with five or more O grades in the A to C range found employment (Raffe, 1984). Variations across Glasgow are mirrored by variations within many of the larger areas given in Table 8.6. In Easterhouse for example, the individual enumeration district scores within the larger postcode-sector range from some with a score of over three standard deviation units to some with scores less than one. The difference in attainment associated with this is almost as large as the differences across Glasgow. This change in the level of deprivation and quality of environment over relatively short distances is one that has been noted previously in relation to local authority housing estates (Garner, 1979; Tunley et al., 1979) and one that supports the view that positive discrimination initiatives should be targeted at a more local scale than is currently the practice in area-based policies.

The results for the probit analysis on THREEHI are shown in Table 8.7. This testing parallels that done for groups of variables in the OLS model given in Table 8.3. The chi-squared statistic is used to measure the significance of the difference between the log-likelihood for the

Educational Attainment in Glasgow

Table 8.8: Probit Analysis of Attaining/Not Attaining Three or More SCE Highers Passes in Glasgow

	Co-efficient	SE	tstat	OLS Equivalent
Home:				
Social Class				
RGSC I + II (DCLASS1)	0.565	(.11)	4.98*	0.085
RGSC IIIn (DCLASS3N)	0.271	(.13)	2.02	0.041
RGSC IIIm (DCLASS3)	0.019	(.09)	0.20	0.003
RGSC nec (DCLASS6)	-0.021	(.12)	0.18	-0.003
Mother's Education (MUMED)	0.114	(.09)	1.23	0.017
Father's Education (DADED)	0.294	(.09)	2.96*	0.044
Family Size (LFAM)	-0.140	(.08)	1.71	-0.021
Sex of Respondent (GENDER)	-0.184	(.07)	2.71*	-0.028
School: (a) (S1 to S44, S46 to S69)	-	-	-	-
Neighbourhood: (DSCORE)	-0.363	(.05)	7.23*	-0.054
Constant	-0.919			
χ^2	841.16			
Convert to OLS	0.150			
N	3080			

Notes:
(a) Coefficients are not reported for individual schools.
* significant at $p < .01$.

Source: 1981 SSLS and 1981 Census of Population.

Table 8.9: Definition of Advantaged and Disadvantaged School Leavers and their Probability of Qualifying for Entry to Higher Education

Advantaged	Disadvantaged
Father in RGSC I or II	Father in RGSC IV or V
Mother's education - beyond 15	Mother's education - not beyond 15
Father's education - beyond 15	Father's education - not beyond 15
Family with fewer than 4 siblings	Family with more than 4 siblings
Male	Female
Living in an area with mean deprivation score equivalent to Bearsden	Living in an area with mean deprivation score equivalent to Easterhouse

Probability of getting 3 or more SCE Highers

disadvantaged (home) disadvantged (area)	0.03
disadvantaged (home) advantaged (area)	0.22
advantaged (home) disadvantaged (area)	0.26
advantaged (home) advantaged (area)	0.70

Source: 1981 SSLS and 1981 Census of Population

unrestricted model where all variables are entered and the log-likelihood for the restricted model where the contribution of the omitted category can be assessed. All groups of variables are seen to be significant.

The probit coefficients are more difficult to interpret than OLS coefficients since the influence of a variable on the probability of a person obtaining three or more Highers passes depends not only on the size of the estimated parameter but also on the characteristics of that person. One way to aid interpretation is to convert the parameters to approximate OLS coefficients by multiplying each by the 'convert to OLS' factor. The final column in Table 8.8 gives these converted parameters and allows similar comparisons to those made for the general SCE score to be made for obtaining three-plus Highers or not. Those young people with fathers in non-manual occupations retain an advantage, having a better chance of obtaining three or more Highers although the probability is only 8 per cent greater for those in RGSC I and II and 4 per cent greater for those with fathers in RGSC IIIn compared to those with fathers in unskilled or semi-skilled jobs. Father's education still remains a strong positive influence on attainment, with those whose fathers remained at school beyond the minimum leaving age of 15 years having a 4 per cent higher probability of obtaining three or more Highers. The 'deprivation effect' for Glasgow as a whole reduces the probability of getting three or more Highers passes by 1 per cent as compared to Scotland as a whole. The 'deprivation effect' for Easterhouse is a reduction in the probability of qualifying for higher education of some 10 per cent. (This is considerably lower than that noted for the general attainment score but the outcome variable, being dichotomous has less variability.) Young people from Drumchapel and Blackhill have reduced probabilities of some 9 per cent and 7 per cent respectively, while those from Kelvinside, Bearsden and Giffnock (ceteris paribus) have an increased probability of obtaining three or more Highers passes of some 7 per cent. This means that the probability of becoming qualified for higher education increases by some 17 per cent between Easterhouse and Giffnock.

A more elegant method to allow interpretation of the estimated parameters from the probit analysis is to define advantaged and disadvantaged stereotypes and to calculate the probability of these stereotypical individuals obtaining three or more Highers. (10) Table 8.9 shows the definitions used for advantaged and disadvantaged individuals and their associated probabilities of obtaining the nominal entry qualifications for higher education. This combines home and neighbourhood effects but omits schools. A school leaver with an advantaged home background living in an advantaged area has a 70 per cent probability of qualifying, whereas a school leaver with a disadvantaged home background living in a disadvantaged area has only a 3 per cent probability. This is a dramatic difference but is primarily related to the difference in personal characteristics between individuals defined here as advantaged or disadvantaged.

CONCLUSIONS

The analysis conducted here has shown that deprivation in a young person's home neighbourhood has a negative influence on his or her educational attainment. This is an influence which operates over and above the influence of home and school. The effect is considerable. For those young people from the most deprived neighbourhoods in Glasgow, deprivation is associated with a reduction in general attainment of up to three O grades and a reduction in the probability of qualifying for higher education of some ten per cent.

Since the principal aim of the analysis here was to establish the importance (or lack of importance) of neighbourhood as an influence on educational attainment, the 'deprivation effect' has been examined primarily in isolation from the effects of home and school. Thus in assessing the neighbourhood's influence on attainment the contribution has been stated in terms of 'all other things being equal'. This means that the effect of all the other variables in the model such as social class, parental education and family size have been removed before neighbourhood is assessed. However, because there is an unhappy coincidence of home and neighbourhood characteristics which negatively influences educational attainment in deprived neighbourhoods, the young people living there are doubly deprived. First by their home circumstances and second by where they live. The magnitude of this combined disadvantage is shown in the calculations of the probability of entering higher education

(Table 8.9).

The present study has not attempted to comment on the effectiveness of individual schools but they too play an important role in any individual's attainment and it indeed may be that the schools attended by young people from deprived areas help to alleviate their disadvantage from home and neighbourhood. This, however, cannot be taken further in the present study.

In assessing these conclusions, however, it must be remembered that the influence of neighbourhood cannot be causally separated from home and school, irrespective of the ability conceptually or statistically to distinguish it. The influences on educational attainment obtaining at the different levels are, in reality, relational and although the application of models which assign atomistic properties to each level facilitate statistical analysis they are artificially partitioning the real world. The deprivation index after all is not measuring some abstract 'environmental determinism' but is a summary of the condition of the population living within a neighbourhood and includes, as part of that measure, the family whom we are measuring at the level of the individual. Therefore, although the neighbourhood data provide information which is not merely an aggregate of the individual data measured here, it subsumes the individual family within its measurement. Given this, the interpretation of the results here must be treated with caution. Although neighbourhood has been shown to be an important influence in the model specified here, it must be remembered that first we can never be absolutely certain that we are not mis-attributing influence between levels and secondly that the model specified here is one which does not include any individual measure of prior attainment. To overcome these doubts, future analysis requires to be carried out on data where some measure of ability or prior attainment is available, using a multi-level regression model, since such methodology begins to incorporate relational aspects of the world which it models. This anlaysis is currently being planned.

The limitations of the present study, however, need to be put in the perspective of what has gone before. The present analysis has extended past research and has verified that educational attainment is influenced by some factor or factors which can be captured by neighbourhood variability. To policy makers the fact that neighbourhood matters at all should be sufficient to encourage further investigation and policies for neighbourhood improvement. Present policies to tackle neighbourhood deprivation have had limited success, for area-based policies can only alleviate the symptoms of neighbourhood deprivation. They are unable to solve the underlying structural causes. Unemployment, youth unemployment and single-parent families contribute the greatest weight to the deprivation index and all reflect aspects of the wider social and economic structure. Neighbourhood deprivation is the end result of procesess whereby groups and individuals with similar (in)abilities to compete in the urban markets of housing, employment and education are constrained to live in spatial contiguity. That the characteristics of these spatial groupings (neighbourhoods) matter for educational attainment confirms neighbourhood as an important element in the equation of educational outcomes.

NOTES

The research on which this chapter is based was supported by the Economic and Social Research Council (Grant Nos D00232070 and C0028004) and the Scottish Education Department (Grant No. JHH/219/1). The analysis, conclusions and opinions are solely those of the author. I would like to thank Andrew McPherson and other colleagues in the Centre for Educational Sociology at the University of Edinburgh for their comments on earlier drafts of this paper, and Caroline Clark, Moira Burke, Joan Hughes and Linda MacDonald for their preparation of the manuscript.

1. A test of the robustness of the regression coefficients using two randomly selected subsets showed that the coefficient for the area-based data was stable. Both random groups produced a coefficient within the range of $\pm$ one standard error of the coefficients reported here. This gives some reassurance that the relationship is not spurious.
2. George Duguid of the Housing and Urban Renewal Research Unit at the Scottish Office, supplied details of the construction and weightings for the deprivation index. I am most grateful for all his help in this.
3. The Small Area Statistics for the 1981 Census of Population are made available to researchers through the Edinburgh University Data Library. Copyright of these data

Educational Attainment in Glasgow

is vested in H.M. Stationery Office on behalf of the Crown, and may not be reproduced without permission. The data were accessed through the computer package SASPAC.

4. In 1981, 63 per cent of all housing in Glasgow city was local authority housing (1981 Census of Population: Key Statistics for Urban Areas, Scotland: HMSO, 1984).

5. The present study includes independent and grant-aided schools but an early analysis on only the EA schools gave very similar results to those reported here. All coefficients were within ± one standard error of those reported here.

6. My thanks are due to Doug Willms who allowed me to use his rescaled TOTSCEP score.

7. The probit analysis was done using the computer package LIMDEP.

8. The model can be represented by the equation

$$Y_i = \beta_o + \beta_h H_i + \beta_s S_i + \beta_1 N_i + \varepsilon_i$$

where
Y_i = the scaled educational outcome score, for the ith respondent (i = 1 ... 3080)
H_i = the vector of individual/home variables,
S_i = the 68 dummy variables representing school membership,
N_i = the deprivation score representing the neighbourhood
ε_i = residual,
β_h is a vector of coefficients that indicate the relative advantage or disadvantage of having particular family characteristics as compared with the stated reference categories and β_s is a vector of 68 coefficients that indicate the relative advantage or disadvantage of attending a particular school rather than the reference school. β_1 is a coefficient showing the effect of deprivation in the home environment on the general educational outcome score.

9. Scaled TOTSCEP values with their equivalent qualification levels:

-2.03   'No awards'
-0.63   'O grade D or E'
-0.24   '1 O grade A to C'
0.08   '2 O grades A to C'
0.31   '3 O grades A to C'
0.51   '4 O grades A to C'
0.67   '5 O grades A to C'
0.85   '6 O grades A to C'

Educational Attainment in Glasgow

   1.08   '1 Highers pass'
   1.35   '2 Highers passes'
   1.64   '3 Highers passes'
   2.04   '4 Highers passes'
   2.76   '5 Highers passes'
   4.41   '6 Highers passes'

10. My thanks are due to Brian Main who allowed me to use his program to calculate these probabilities.

Chapter Nine

CATCHMENTS, SCHOOLS AND THE CHARACTERISTICS OF TEACHERS

M.H. Matthews, Anthony Airey and Lesley Tacon

INTRODUCTION

A number of studies of education have focused upon children in their social and environmental setting (see review by Herbert, 1976; Williamson and Byrne, 1979). Geographers have been particularly concerned with the influence of environmental factors on a child's school performance (Robson, 1969; Moulden and Bradford, 1984; Garner, in this volume). In this way geographers have stressed the importance of the family and the home, the neighbourhood and the peer group. Similarly, sociologists have viewed disadvantage and adversity largely in terms of these environmental factors, which are seen to affect a child's life chances in dramatic ways (Tyler, 1977; Mortimore and Blackstone, 1982). A stereotype of the educationally under-privileged urban child has emerged: one who has parents of low socio-economic status, lives in poor housing, and lacks access to values and attitudes conducive to educational achievement (Byrne, Williamson and Fletcher, 1975; Robinson, 1976). The principal outcome has been the recommendation and justification of area-based policies designed to compensate children for their environmental and social disadvantages (Central Advisory Council for Education, 1967; Halsey, 1972; Field, 1977).

In all of this research less attention has been given to the school and its teachers. However, some studies have focused either on the school and the range of facilities and curricula it offers (King, 1971, 1974; Williamson and Byrne, 1977) or have examined the school's staff and their attitudes and expectations of pupil attainment (Rist, 1970; Eggleston,

1977). A paucity of data exists on the backgrounds, experiences and qualifications of the teaching profession at the school level. Even those studies that have singled out teachers as a vocational group in order to consider their promotional, motivational and career structures have neglected the issue of intra-urban spatial variation (Hilsum and Start, 1974; Lyons, 1981). This lack of attention is surprising especially in the context of educational policy initiatives aimed at redressing areal imbalances through positive discrimination. Following the recommendations of the Plowden Committee Report of 1967 the DES made provision for LEAs to identify 'schools considered ... to serve areas of educational disadvantage'. A consequence of Social Priority designation was that teachers would receive supplementary allowances in order to compensate them for their difficult working environments, in the hope of attracting staff who would be keen to confront the challenges associated with multiple social disadvantage. In this way the school's catchment may not only influence the types of pupil attending a school, but it may influence the kinds of teachers who choose to work in these areas and the managerial decisions of staff selection. Through such mechanisms it can be anticipated that schools of different kinds in different locations would comprise different sets of teachers. The areal basis required to investigate these issues is indicative of the potential contribution of geographers to educational research and policy.

A number of American case studies have considered the relationship between teacher characteristics and the school catchment. In Chicago, Kerner (1968) ranked public high schools by the socio-economic status of the population of the surrounding neighbourhoods and found that in the ten lowest ranking schools 37 per cent of the teachers were not fully qualified and the median length of teaching experience was approximately four years. In contrast, in the ten highest ranking schools less than one per cent of the teachers were not fully qualified and the median length of teaching experience was over twelve years. These socio-economic contrasts correspond to findings based on ethnic indicators. Both Baron (1971) and Mladenka (1980), also working in Chicago, note that schools in white, more middle-class areas of a school district generally had more experienced and better qualified teachers, good teacher-pupil ratios and higher spending on staffing. Quite the reverse had been found in black and lower class areas of the city (Sexton,

1961).

Similar disparities were noted by Levy, Meltsner and Wildavsky (1974) in their influential study of elementary school resources in Oakland, California. Comparing white, middle-class neighbourhoods with nearby black areas they observed that white children in 'rich' schools had teachers with longer experience: in schools with the greatest proportion of white students, one out of every two teachers had 13 or more years' experience, whereas in schools with the greatest proportion of minority students the ratio was only one in five and a quarter of staff had taught for less than three years. There was a corresponding variation in degree attainment: more than 40 per cent of all teachers in upper-income white schools had a masters degree compared with only a fifth of those in low-income, black districts. The reasons for such contrasts related to teachers' preference and Oakland's transfer policies. The District generally permitted teachers with seniority to transfer freely in the system and most of the teachers who wanted to move came from predominantly minority and poor schools: 'they wanted to move to what they perceived as easier or more rewarding jobs in upper income schools' (Levy et al., 1974, p. 78).

Owen (1972) comments that there seems little doubt that, based on a variety of criteria, pupils at schools with more middle-class, white enrolments tend to get higher quality teachers than schools with more lower class or black entries. Guthrie (1971) points out that quality in this context refers not only to teachers' experience but also to their intellectual capacity. In a study of Detroit schools, he correlated teachers' verbal skills (a surrogate measure of IQ) with student social class. The conclusion was that students of higher social class were being exposed to teachers of higher verbal skill and therefore, 'presumably teachers of greater intellectual capacity' (Guthrie, 1970, p. 3458).

In the British context evidence of this kind has been less forthcoming. An exception is the work of Little (1977, pp. 66-7) who articulates three concerns: 'the difficulty of recruiting teachers in inner city schools; the difficulty of retaining teachers in inner city schools; the difficulty of recruiting and retraining experienced teachers in inner city schools'. A survey of the Inner London Education Authority (ILEA) revealed a turnover rate among teachers more than twice as high as the UK average: of permanent teachers who resigned, 77 per cent of the men and 87 per cent of the women had been teaching in their last school for less than five years. By contrast Little estimated that the national average for teacher turnover (the percentage of teachers in a school for less than three years) was 25 per cent. Consequently, difficult urban schools faced the joint problem of high staff turnover and few teachers with more than a limited amount of teaching experience. Little found that in the most disadvantaged school in ILEA 75 per cent of the staff had been at the school for less than one year; in the school ranked 50th the proportion was 67 per cent and in the school ranked 100th it was nearly 50 per cent.

This chapter reports on a project which was set up to consider the influence of school catchments on the characteristics of teachers in schools in Coventry. The first stage examines whether there are differences between teachers working at inner-city and outer-city schools or between Social Priority and other schools, with respect to such characteristics as qualifications, experiences and attitudes towards education. Such aggregation may mask within-group variation. Accordingly, the next stage examines data on teachers at the level of the individual school. Ecological explanations of variation between schools are considered by correlating catchment area data with staff profiles in each school. In the concluding section the results of these stages are used to provide an assessment of the effects of catchments and existing area-based and school-based policies on the teaching profession. Lastly, an interactive model is postulated, which identifies those processes which are instrumental in shaping the staff profiles of a school. In particular, two broad sets of processes are highlighted: the influences of educational management and individual decision-making on the part of the teacher, both of which take place against a backcloth of policy aimed at compensating disadvantaged catchments.

METHOD

Study area

The study area constituted Coventry LEA, which administers 16 comprehensive schools. These were set up during the early 1970s. As there has been more than a decade of adjustment, this ensures that the present structure of teachers within schools is not simply a legacy of the previous system. Within the city there are a wide

Catchments, Schools and Teacher Characteristics

variety of neighbourhoods ranging from multi-cultural, inner districts to low density, middle-class suburbs. The secondary schools are all neighbourhood based and so their catchments reflect such spatial contrasts. In 1986, less than three per cent of parents preferred that their children were allocated other than to their neighbourhood school. In recognition of this, Coventry LEA has implemented a range of positive discrimination policies, favouring those schools drawing from the more deprived catchments. These include the designation of Social Priority schools and the establishment of a strong community framework. In the mid-1980s, falling school rolls have prompted plans for school closure, but at the time of the survey only a small percentage of staff had been redeployed between schools within the city.

School sample

The sample consisted of eight comprehensive schools differentiated by their location and Social Priority designation (Figure 9.1). In some cases there was no choice: for example, there is only one inner-city, non-Social Priority school. This approach was considered to be methodologically sound since it avoided the problems of drawing a representative sample from each school. Table 9.1 provides information on selected social and economic indicators, taken from the 1981 Census, which illustrates variations between the catchments of the schools used in this survey.

Questionnaire survey

The survey was carried out between October 1985 and March 1986 and was coincident with a period of industrial action by teachers in schools. In order to ensure that the questionnaire was well received by staff, support was gained both from the local authority and local teacher union leaders.

Within each school, every member of the full-time teaching staff was invited to participate in the survey. The overall response rate was 98 per cent, reaching at least 96 per cent in each school. A total of 526 interviews were completed. The questionnaire sought to establish each teacher's qualifications and training, career history and school experience. Reasons for choosing, staying and moving

Table 9.1: Selected Social and Economic Characteristics of School Catchments in Coventry (per cent)

School	Location	Social Priority status	Children aged 0–15 in lone parent families	Ethnicity: residents born outside UK	Housing amenities: households lacking bath or inside wc or with neither
A	Inner	No	3.0	4.0	4.6
B	Inner	Yes	5.0	27.6	6.2
C	Inner	Yes	2.0	17.7	7.1
D	Outer	Yes	5.9	4.4	0.9
E	Outer	Yes	6.2	3.8	0.8
F	Outer	No	2.2	6.5	2.2
G	Outer	No	2.5	2.1	0.6
H	Outer	No	1.3	4.3	1.2
Whole city			2.6	7.6	2.7

Table 9.1: continued

Overcrowding: > 1.5 people	Unemployment	Non owner-occupiers	Households with no car
1.5	11.5	47.1	59.1
3.3	14.0	56.8	67.6
1.9	9.4	26.5	46.9
1.0	12.2	57.6	48.1
1.7	13.1	58.6	51.7
0.6	7.2	27.6	38.7
0.3	7.7	28.7	32.2
0.2	4.9	12.0	24.5
0.9	8.9	33.6	42.7

Source: 1981 Census data adjusted to school catchments

Catchments, Schools and Teacher Characteristics

Figure 9.1: Classification of Schools by Location and Social Priority Status (number of staff interviewed)

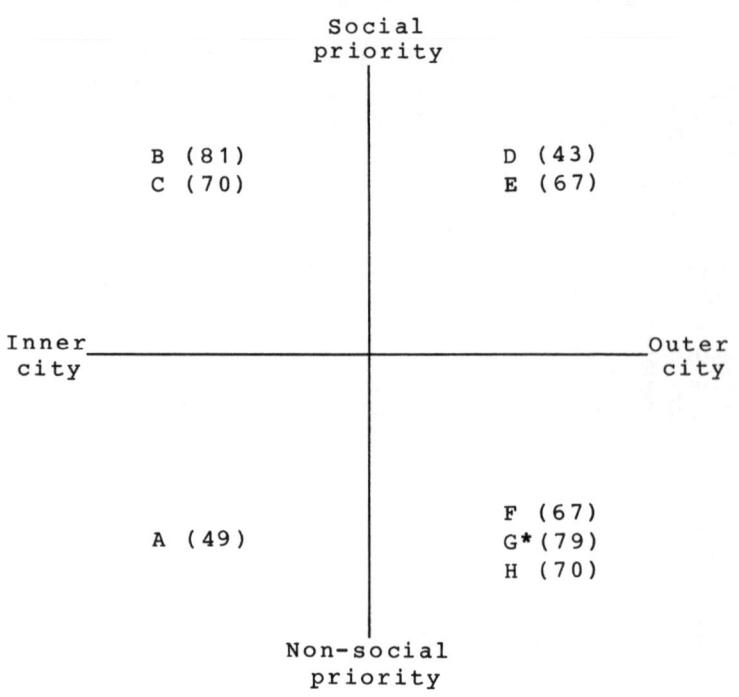

```
                          Social
                         priority
                            |
          B (81)            |         D (43)
          C (70)            |         E (67)
                            |
                            |
Inner_____|_____Outer
city                        |                       city
                            |
                            |
                            |         F (67)
            A (49)          |         G*(79)
                            |         H (70)
                            |
                        Non-social
                         priority
```
* Single-sex

schools were explored, as well as attitudes towards such issues as the needs of the school and future professional expectations. Altogether 112 variables were derived for analysis.

Analysis

The analysis is organised in three parts. First, the characteristics of teachers in inner-city and outer-city schools and Social Priority and other schools are compared. Secondly, inter-school differences in staff profiles are highlighted. The third section, attempts to relate these differences to the characteristics of catchment areas. In these ways, the effects of catchments and of area-based and school-based policies on the characteristics of the urban teaching profession are evaluated.

RESULTS

School catchment patterns in Coventry

This section focuses on the similarities and the principal contrasts between teachers located in different areas in Coventry and compares the characteristics of staff in Social Priority and other schools. The analysis focuses upon aggregate data within the framework shown in Figure 9.1. Whenever appropriate, the data have been tested by chi-squared analysis. Clearly there are limitations to this approach. With such a small number of schools statistically significant differences between any of the four sampling cells may be due to the disproportionate effect of one school in one of the areas. Accordingly the tabulated date (Tables 9.2 to 9.4) are disaggregated to the school level to highlight within-group variation.

Similarities in the characteristics of teachers in inner-city and outer-city schools

The results reveal strong homogeneity within the urban teaching profession, contrasting sharply with the American experience. The survey revealed no significant difference between inner-city and outer-city schools with respect to the age, sex, qualifications or experience of teachers (Table 9.2). A large proportion of teachers are aged in their thirties and the workforce is dominated by males: Coventry mirrors the national age-sex structure of the profession. Most teachers were found to possess either B.Eds or PGCEs. Furthermore, locational disparity was not evident in the number of schools at which teachers had worked or the length of teaching service. Typically, staff had taught at only one or two schools, with a mean of eleven years in their present job. In addition, promotional prospects, both in terms of gaining scaled posts within a school and upward moves involving a school change, did not vary spatially. In both inner- and outer-city schools the number of teachers achieving internal promotion is less than 50 per cent and a similar proportion enhance their position by moving schools. Accordingly, there is no support for the notion that many staff choose inner-city schools to obtain scaled positions before moving elsewhere.

Attitudinal variables also show little spatial variability. Few staff, less than seven per cent, acknowledge that they

Table 9.2: Similarities in Selected Characteristics of Teachers Working in Inner- and Outer-city Schools. Table shows percentages for sample, (aggregate frequencies) and (individual school percentages).

Variables	Schools Inner-city (A,B,C)	Outer-city (D,E,F,G,H)
Age: proportion aged 30-39	48% (96) (51%, 40%, 55%)	43% (157) (41%, 36%, 43%, 51%, 42%)
Female teachers	44% (88) (39%, 48%, 41%)	40% (130) (40%, 40%, 51%, 24%, 49%)
Qualifications: B.Ed or PGCE	62% (134) (71%, 59%, 59%)	64% (200) (56%, 78%, 65%, 59%, 59%)
School experience: < 2 schools	61% (122) (59%, 63%, 60%)	58% (189) (40%, 58%, 61%, 70%, 60%)
Length of teaching service (in years)	11.4	11.7
Promotion in present school	43% (86) (47%, 39%, 45%)	46% (150) (48%, 47%, 42%, 49%, 44%)

Table 9.2: continued

Promotion with a school move	39% (78) (37%, 41%, 37%)	42% (137) (45%, 43%, 37%, 48%, 39%)
Reasons for becoming a teacher: career motives	72% (144) (73%, 74%, 70%)	73% (238) (71%, 70%, 75%, 71%, 77%)
Involvement in extra-curricular activity	85% (170) (90%, 85%, 83%)	87% (284) (86%, 88%, 79%, 92%, 89%)
Participation on INSET: <5 years	59% (118) (67%, 52%, 56%)	62% (202) (70%, 61%, 63%, 63%, 56%)

Table 9.3: Differences in Selected Characteristics of Teachers Working in Inner- and Outer-city schools. Table shows percentages for sample, (aggregate frequencies), (individual school percentages) and chi-squared (χ^2) values

Variables	Schools Inner-city (A,B,C)	Outer-city (D,E,F,G,H)	χ^2 (df1, p<0.05)
First career	67% (134) (67%, 63%, 74%)	75% (164) (74%, 76%, 82%, 70%, 73%)	4.3
Age began training: <23	54% (108) (57%, 53%, 52%)	40% (130) (40%, 29%, 43%, 31%, 46%)	10.0
Reasons for choosing school: lcoation and type	39% (78) (39%, 40%, 38%)	29% (95) (33%, 25%, 34%, 28%, 30%)	7.2
Thought of leaving teaching	49% (98) (47%, 43%, 57%)	66% (215) (69%, 64%, 61%, 62%, 67%)	8.9
At present school too long	34% (68) (22%, 36%, 37%)	46% (150) (49%, 49%, 46%, 47%, 36%)	7.3
Teachers expressing disbenefits of school catchments	20% (40) (18%, 17%, 24%)	35% (114) (30%, 36%, 33%, 37%, 37%)	13.8

Table 9.4: Differences in Selected Characteristics of Teachers Working in Social Priority and Other Schools. Table shows percentages for sample, (aggregate frequencies), (individual school percentages) and chi-squared (χ^2) values

Variables	Social Priority (B,C,D,E)	Schools Other (A,F,G,H)	χ^2 (df1, p <0.05)
School experience: >1 type of school	66% (172) (66%, 68%, 69%, 61%)	47% (125) (52%, 53%, 42%, 44%)	8.2
Prefer not to teach in SPS/(again)	6% (16) (6%, 4%, 7%, 7%)	40% (100) (25%, 36%, 58%, 31%)	85.8
Scaled posts: scale <2	78% (204) (80%, 77%, 82%, 75%)	68% (180) (72%, 66%, 67%, 68%)	4.9
Involvement in extra-curricular activity in the community	57% (149) (49%, 60%, 73%, 44%)	48% (127) (65%, 48%, 41%, 46%)	3.9

drifted into teaching: most, more than 70 per cent, emphasise the importance of career motives such as, the sense of fulfilment of working with children or enjoyment of their chosen subject. Commitment to their present school and pupils was strongly evident in all areas. This professional outlook extends to active participation in out of school activities and to attendance on in service training (INSET) courses both curricular and extra-curricular in nature. Teachers, in general, shared a positive perception of the value of such activities to their career development.

Differences in the characteristics of teachers in inner-city and outer-city schools

This pattern of broad uniformity amongst teachers is, however, disturbed in a number of ways (Table 9.3). For example, an interesting contrast is found between the inner- and outer-city in terms of the route members followed into teaching. Whilst most teachers, in both locations, followed a traditional entry, undertaking professional training either straight from school or after graduation, a significant proportion of inner-city teachers entered the profession after initially following another career. As a result, 54 per cent of those working in the inner-city commenced teacher training after the age of 23, compared with 40 per cent in outer-city schools. Thus, teachers with wider experience seem to be positively attracted to the challenges that inner-city schools present. At the same time, the headteachers of such schools might also be alert to the benefits such teachers can bring and therefore favour their appointment.

Staff in inner-city schools are drawn more by the locational and educational needs of the catchment. The multicultural setting of these catchments is seen as an asset, heightening the professional challenges and rewards of the work. Conversely, outer-city staff favour coeducational schools with less cultural diversity and measure professional satisfaction in terms of academic performance and success.

At the same time, inner-city teachers seem more content with their job, fewer staff expressing a wish to leave teaching. Almost two-thirds of those working in suburban neighbourhoods had thought about giving up teaching in the last five years, compared with less than 50 per cent in the inner-city. Nearly half of those interviewed in the outer-city felt that they had stayed in their present school longer than expected and many frequently bemoaned the lack of labour mobility in the profession. In comparison, 66 per cent of inner-city staff expressed satisfaction with their current school and most teachers in these areas felt less trapped by their working environment.

Such evidence further suggests that locational factors are considered by teachers in their school selection. This is substantiated when teachers were asked to nominate the 'three worst and best catchments' in Coventry. Suburban staff were more highly opinionated and keenly sensitive to the disbenefits of school catchments. Many had clear ideas about which areas of the city displayed these negative characteristics. By contrast, inner-city staff were seemingly immune to these adverse perceptions and highlighted the positive benefits of working in these environments. In consequence, staff in both areas asserted that in general their catchments were the most desirable and those elsewhere were less attractive.

Comparison of the characteristics of teachers in Social Priority and other schools

Disparities between Social Priority and other school teachers are also evident (Table 9.4). First, Social Priority staff have wider school experience than their counterparts, with 66 per cent of their members having taught in more than one type of school. By contrast nearly half of those interviewed in non-designated schools had experience of only one kind of school, mostly large co-educational comprehensives. The second variation reinforces the notion that such staff are highly selective in their choice of school systems. When asked whether they would teach in a Social Priority school a significant 40 per cent replied negatively, whereas only 6 per cent of current Social Policy teachers would not work in such a setting again.

Two further contrasts relate to the different nature of Social Priority school provision. As expected the availability of scaled posts is higher within designated schools: four-fifths of teachers are on Scale Two or above, compared with other schools, where a third of the staff are on the minimum level. This is one of the ways in which area-based policy achieves spatial compensation. Associated with this system of scaling is the requirement that teachers involve themselves in activities in the surrounding community.

Accordingly, Social Priority school teachers are more engaged in catchment events outside the school, 57 per cent taking part in some regular extra-curricular programme, compared with less than 50 per cent of their counterparts in other schools.

Summary

From these results it is clear that the strong relationship between areas and the characteristics of teachers hypothesised is not supported by the Coventry case. Unlike many American studies there is little evidence of marked spatial variations in the age of composition, sex composition and level of qualifications of the teaching force. Few differences were found between teachers in inner-city and outer-city schools and those in Social Priority and other schools. Out of the 112 variables considered for analysis only eleven yielded statistically significant differences and of these seven were attitudinal in character. The implications of these findings are discussed in the last part of this chapter.

School patterns in Coventry

Cross-sectional analysis of the characteristics of teachers based on data aggregated within the spatial framework shown in Figure 9.1 provides only a partial insight into school-based variations. Important differences may be obscured by the level of aggregation: some contrasts may only become evident at the level of individual schools. In order to examine school differences the composition of the teaching force and the experiences and attitudes of teachers are considered in turn.

Composition of the teaching force

Considerable variation emerges in particular charcteristics, concealed by the spatial framework. Disaggregation of the data at the school level reveals marked inter-school differences in sex, age and qualification (Table 9.5). For example, sex composition ranges from schools with male/female parity to those with less than 25 per cent female staff. This can be explained in part by the retention of one single-sex school (for boys), at which the percentage of male

Table 9.5: Composition of the Teaching Force at Each School

	Sex: female %	Age ≤30 %	Age ≤40 %	Qualifications: non-degree and vocational %	degree %	higher degree %
School						
A	39	33	16	20	71	8
B*	48	27	33	30	59	11
C*	41	19	26	35	59	6
D*	40	19	40	33	56	12
E*	40	43	21	16	78	6
F	51	24	33	32	65	3
G	24	20	29	32	59	9
H	49	29	29	26	59	16
Overall	41	27	20	28	63	9

*Social Priority school

Catchments, Schools and Teacher Characteristics

Table 9.6: Experience of Teachers at Each School

School	First career %	Age began training ≤23 %	Years in teaching ≤5 %	≤10 %	School experience: No ≤3 %	Type ≤3 %
A	67	57	33	14	41	22
B*	63	53	25	23	37	33
C*	74	52	16	24	40	26
D*	74	40	9	30	60	44
E*	76	29	33	19	42	19
F	82	43	24	27	39	24
G	70	31	14	20	30	22
H	73	46	16	14	40	26
Overall	72	44	21	21	41	27

* Social Priority school

teachers is particularly high. By contrast, the school with the second lowest proportion of women teachers was formerly a girls' grammar school prior to its comprehensive status, suggesting legacies can be diluted quickly.

Age profiles show even greater diversity. Some schools have high proportions of young staff whereas others are characterised by a more mature age structure. For example, the percentage of teachers under 30 varies from 19 per cent to 43 per cent. Similarly, the percentage of teachers over 40 varies from 16 per cent to 40 per cent. However, the relationship between the two distributions is not always inverse (see Table 9.5).

Turning to teacher qualifications, the bulk of staff in all schools were qualified to degree level, most with additional teacher training certificates, although proportions of teachers with these qualifications varied from 56 per cent to 78 per cent. When higher degrees are added to this category some of these differences become less exaggerated. However, in one school 84 per cent of staff were qualified in this way, compared to 65 per cent in another. Sharper contrasts are found in the employment of staff with non-degree or vocational certificates: schools varied from those with more than one-third to those with less than one-fifth of their staff with such qualifications.

Experiences of teachers
Disparities between schools are also evident with respect to teachers' professional experience (Table 9.6). The two characteristics, 'whether teaching was a first career' and 'the age at which teacher training commenced' are closely related. For most staff, teaching was their first career. However, levels vary between schools from 82 per cent to 63 per cent suggesting that a significant proportion of teachers in some schools did not follow the direct route into the profession. This is confirmed by the high proportion of teachers in some schools who began their training after the age of 23, an age by which the majority of traditional entrants would have qualified as teachers.

Diversity is also evident in the number of years in the profession and the range of school types at which staff had worked. In one school more than 90 per cent of teachers had more than five years' experience, with at least three-fifths having worked in three or more different sorts of school environments: in another, a third of the staff had worked five or less years in the profession and 42 per cent had only limited experience of different types of school.

Attitudes of teachers
Eight attitudinal variables are examined, five relating to the school at which the teacher was employed and three relating to teaching in general (Tables 9.7 and 9.8).

For most teachers, factors such as the nature of the school's catchment and Social Priority status were only secondary considerations when seeking teaching opportunities. However, as already shown, 40 per cent of those working in the inner-city specify a conscious decision to do so. Elsewhere, both in Social Priority schools and the outer-city, school location is given by no more than a third of staff as a decisive factor.

Teachers' intention to stay at their present school was high, with little inter-school variation. This is probably a realistic recognition by many secondary school teachers of current constraints upon career mobility. Yet a substantial minority of teachers, exceeding 45 per cent in four schools, felt that they had been at their present school too long, compared with another where little more than a fifth expressed the same doubts. There is some suggestion that schools with the youngest teachers are those with the highest rates of satisfaction.

Table 9.7: Attitudes of Teachers Towards their Schools

School	Reasons for choosing school: location and type %	Intention to stay at present school %	At present school too long %	Involvement in extra curricular activity %	Involvement in community activity %
A	39	90	22	90	65
B*	40	95	36	85	49
C*	38	87	37	83	60
D*	33	91	49	86	73
E*	25	96	49	88	44
F	34	93	46	79	48
G	28	92	47	92	41
H	30	91	36	89	46
Overall	33	92	40	87	53

* Social Priority school

Table 9.8: Attitudes of Teachers Towards the Profession

School	First career choice %	Thought of leaving teaching %	Participation on INSET: 5 years %
A	55	47	67
B*	57	43	52
C*	61	57	56
D*	72	69	70
E*	61	64	61
F	67	61	63
G	59	62	63
H	71	67	56
Overall	63	59	61

* Social Priority school

The great majority of teachers appear committed to their school and its pupils. Over 80 per cent of all teachers were actively involved in extra-curricular events, with only slight inter-school variation. However, rates of involvement in community-based programmes varied from 41 per cent to 73 per cent. The general trend for teachers in Social Priority schools to be more involved in community activities, obscures the lower involvement rates at two of these schools (A and E). In these two cases community initiatives are the responsibility of particular staff.

Attitudes towards the profession show equally complex patterns of variation, often unrelated to school type and location. Whilst the majority of teachers assert that teaching was their first career choice proportions vary between schools from 57 per cent to 72 per cent.

In an attempt to examine professional commitment, staff were asked if they had ever thought of leaving teaching. In six out of the eight schools most staff expressed strong disillusionment with teaching. The two remaining schools were both found in the demanding environments of the inner-city, although only one had Social Priority status.

Voluntary staff participation on INSET was categorised as an attitudinal rather than an experiential variable because it suggests differences in outlook. Many teachers had attended courses in the last five years, but in some

Table 9.9: Correlation Matrix: Catchment Area Data and the Characteristics of Teachers (significant correlations, critical value: r = ± 0.63 p= <0.05)

Variables	A	B	C	D	E	F	G
1.		+0.69					
2.							
3.							
4.							
5.			+0.86				
6.							
7.							
8.		+0.71					
9.		+0.74	+0.88				
10.							
11.			−0.68				
12.		−0.83					
13.							
14.			−0.71				
15.							

Characteristics of teachers
1. Sex: female
2. Age: <30
3. Qualifications: non-degree and vocational
4. First career
5. Training >23
6. <5 years teaching
7. >3 school experience
8. >3 school type
9. School choice: location and type
10. Intention to stay at present school
11. At present school too long
12. Involvement in extra-curricular activity
13. First choice career
14. Thought of leaving teaching
15. Involvement on INSET

Catchment area data
A   Children aged 0-15 in lone parent families
B   Residents born outside UK
C   Housing amenities: households lacking bath or inside WC or with neither
D   Overcrowding: >1.5 people per room

Table 9.9: continued

E   Unemployment
F   Non owner-occupiers
F   Households with no car

schools rates were little more than 50 per cent, whereas in others the rate reached 70 per cent.

Characteristics of school catchments: an examination of ecological correlates

What emerges at an aggregate level of analysis is the variability between staff in different schools. Schools develop their own teacher profiles for reasons other than those of Social Priority designation and inner/outer-city location. In consequence, schools of similar status and location may show marked contrasts with respect to the characteristics of their teachers. This can be further examined by considering the catchment area data for each school to see whether these provide a more sensitive explanation of the variation between schools. A more local approach may reveal relationships between the characteristics of staff and the catchment area obscured by the more aggregative approach.

Correlation analysis of selected catchment area data derived from the 1981 Census (Table 9.1) with the characteristics of teachers (Tables 9.5 to 9.8) at the school level reveals few linkages (Table 9.9). Only two of the seven catchment components show significant relationships.

First, schools located in catchments with the highest percentage of persons born outside the UK (ethnicity of residents) generally have the largest proportion of women teachers, staff who have taught in more than three types of school and personnel who have consciously chosen their working environment according to the school's location and designation. Conversely, staff in these schools are least involved in extra-curricular activity within the community. It would seem that the multicultural setting of these schools has had some influence upon the characteristics of the teaching force.

Secondly, schools drawing upon catchments with low housing amenity (households lacking bath or inside wc or with neither) have significant proportions of staff who were

279

late entrants into teaching and chose their school because of its location and designation. In addition teachers within these catchments show high levels of commitment both to the school and the profession, in the sense that they feel that they have not been at their school too long and have not thought of leaving the profession.

The remaining characteristics of the catchment area provide no significant correlations. The lack of relationship at this local level suggests that ecological explanations for variations between schools can be dismissed. Other processes clearly shape staff profiles within schools. Of these the role of school managers in the selection process and the aspirations and ambitions of individual teachers seem important. These wider considerations provide a managerial and behavioural perspective to the original spatial framework used in this survey.

DISCUSSION

The initial part of this study investigated whether there were differences between teachers working at inner-city and outer-city schools or between Social Priority and other schools. Few significant contrasts were found in the characteristics of teachers working in these different environments. At this level of aggregation a broad pattern of uniformity was revealed.

From these findings it is possible to provide an evaluation of aspects of existing area-based and school-based policy. Clearly, the strong inter-neighbourhood contrasts repeatedly shown by American studies are not evident in the Coventry case. The absence of such spatial disparity in the UK can be explained by crucial differences in the financing and administration of the respective education services. In the USA education administration is highly fragmented. Local school districts are major decision brokers often conferring considerable advantages on suburban residents through the provision of lavish facilities and the control of school entrants. British LEAs, such as Coventry, have a wider, more unitary focus and as a result administer a full range of city schools. Furthermore, the Rate Support Grant (RSG) still provides a means of compensatory financial assistance, averting the worst features of the American variable revenue experience (Cox, 1979). This is not to suggest that intra-LEA school contrasts cannot arise. The RSG is far from perfect and not itself designed to ensure intra-LEA homogeneity. Little (1977) has shown that important differences can be found between inner-city and suburban schools. What is important in the British context is how LEAs respond to and implement policies aimed at compensating schools located in disadvantaged catchments.

In this study the uniform nature of the characteristics of teachers between the sampling cells suggests that Coventry LEA has been successful in compensating disadvantaged catchments. Coventry LEA has been in the forefront of community-based education (Society of Education Officers, 1975). It has been quick to seize upon central government inner-city initiatives and designate its schools for preferential allowances. To this extent Coventry LEA's positive approach to area-based and school-based policy has minimised disparities between the characteristics of teachers across its city schools.

There is, however, a contrary view (Field, 1977). If compensatory policy is to have a positive effect it is not enough to achieve parity in the characteristics of teachers working in schools in different locations and of different priority status. Instead schools in disadvantaged catchments should contain significant proportions of staff with backgrounds, experiences and outlooks particularly suited to tackle their special problems. For example, this may include teachers with certain vocational qualifications or wider teaching experience. One strand of Social Priority designation is the provision of higher pay in order to attract better qualified staff to these schools. In these terms, the evidence from this study, using only compositional, experiential and attitudinal criteria, suggests that Coventry has not fully met these compensatory requirements. Accordingly, policy implementation in Coventry is better described as a qualified success. This may also reflect a failure on the part of the DES to adjust Social Priority allowances in line with current rates of pay. At present this allowance for teachers is little more than £200 p.a., increasing to only £276 after two years. Minimal adjustments have been made since the early 1970s. In this study many Social Priority teachers claimed that they were unaware of these financial benefits and it is not surprising that none specified income incentives as a reason for school selection.

The second part of the analysis disaggregated the data

Catchments, Schools and Teacher Characteristics

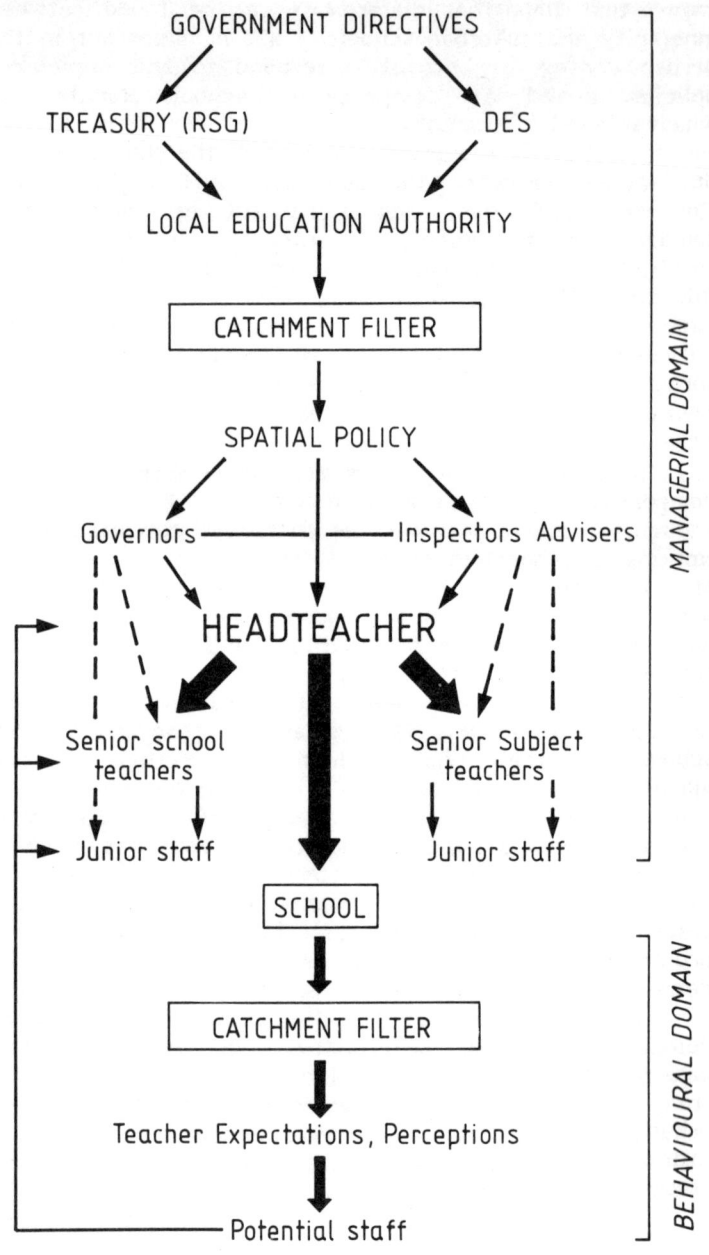

Figure 9.2: Teacher Characteristics and the School: an Interactive Model

to the level of the individual school. At this finer scale differences were found between schools in the composition, experiences and attitudes of teachers. Simple correlations between staff profiles and the characteristics of catchment areas provided few ecological relationships. This school-based focus suggests that there are other processes at work which shape staff profiles. It is likely that factors such as the policies of educational management and individual decision-making on the part of the teacher are important in this respect. Figure 9.2 summarises the processes at work at the school level.

In terms of the managerial domain a set of composite influences can be recognised with the school's catchment acting as an intervening filter. At the highest level, central government issues finance and directives to LEAs, directly through the DES and indirectly via the Rate Support Grant. The LEA interprets and transmits these initiatives in the light of its own priorities. This may operate to the advantage of some catchments, as shown in this study by the designation of Social Priority schools.

Secondly, at the school level, several agents are important in translating and modifying these policies in the appointment of teachers. Amongst these, the headteacher has a pivotal role, with assistance from advisers and governors. Together, their perceptions of the needs of the school and its catchment and the relevant teacher qualities required to address these needs are crucial in the selection of senior staff. In their turn, the senior management of the school translate their collective priorities in the appointment of junior staff. This appointment system relies heavily on the qualifications, experiences and attitudes of the candidates.

Teachers, as individual actors, also influence outcomes in what might be termed the behavioural domain. Their perceptions of good and bad catchments, school status and professionally-satisfying environments will influence their decision-making and application for school posts.

The culmination of the interaction between these domains is to dilute the effect of area-based and school-based policy. In consequence, the initial spatial and policy framework of this study has only partially explained intra-urban teacher profiles in Coventry. Future work intends to examine these school-based processes as well as widen the study to focus on inter-LEA differences.

NOTES

The authors wish to thank Coventry LEA for permission to undertake the survey, in particular, A. Simpson, Research Officer, Forward Planning Department; the headteachers and staff of the eight anonymous comprehensive schools for their patience and co-operation and the Nuffield Foundation for their generous grant.

Chapter Ten

TECHNICAL AND VOCATIONAL EDUCATION INITIATIVE CRITICISM, INNOVATION AND RESPONSE

Les Bell

INTRODUCTION

By September 1986 most local education authorities (LEAs) were taking part in the Manpower Services Commission's Technical and Vocational Education Initiative (TVEI). The initiative was announced in the House of Commons by the Prime Minister in November 1982. Four months later a National Steering Group, consisting of representatives from industry, trade unions, educational organisations, local authorities and institutions of further and higher education, had chosen the first 14 projects which were to commence in September 1983. A year later the number of Authorities involved in the scheme had grown to 62. By September 1986, 80 per cent of all LEAs were involved in the scheme. The pace of change has been nothing short of remarkable. A noisy political and educational debate has surrounded this policy innovation. While nearly all educational authorities are now involved in TVEI schemes, it might also be argued still that only a small number of schools and pupils are affected by vocational initiatives funded by the Manpower Services Commission (MSC), since only a very limited number of secondary schools in each LEA (between five and ten in most cases) are involved in each project. Within each school a group of about 25 students in the fourth and fifth years, and a similar number in the sixth form (where one exists), will follow TVEI courses.

The implementation of TVEI has required schools to adopt a new approach to managing the curriculum and a new role has emerged: school TVEI co-ordinator. The rapid spread of TVEI and the responses within participating schools has been such that significant changes have taken place in those areas of the curriculum on which TVEI has focused. In this chapter it will be argued that schools' responses to TVEI have to be understood as a reaction to the criticism implicit in the initiative. These responses are mediated through the internal organisational and managerial structures which are commonly found in schools and that have been created to manage this innovation, particularly the establishment of the post of school co-ordinator. These factors produce a range of responses in schools, which might be determined by the extent that staff in schools involved in the TVEI project have come to terms with the inherent conflicts and ambiguities within TVEI. These conflicts and ambiguities stem from the criticisms of secondary education embodied in the projects and from the attempts being made by schools within the project to come to terms with the problems being caused by the contraction of the education service, caused by declining pupil numbers.

TVEI may be more significant for secondary education in England and Wales than is at first apparent. The actual number of schools and the pupil groups within those schools are small, but the aims of the project are far-reaching. TVEI is based on a radical critique of the current curriculum and pedagogy embodied in the educational provision for pupils in the 14- to 18-year-old age group. The main thrust of TVEI is to bring about change in:

(a) the content of what is taught;
(b) related pedagogy and forms of assessment;
(c) experiences of, and preparation for, the world of work for young people; and
(d) the structuring of educational provision for pupils approaching the school-leaving-age and beyond.

The impetus for these changes were part of a revaluation of the position and purpose of education in society. This revaluation had two main thrusts. The first was concerned with the nature and purpose of education in a post-industrial society. The second focused more sharply on the relationship between education and employment.

EDUCATION IN A POST-INDUSTRIAL SOCIETY

Jamieson (1986) has argued that in the late 1950s and early

1960s, there was a view that in a modern economy the quality and efficiency of the working population very largely depended on the education system. The restructuring of schools along comprehensive lines was begun, at least partly because it was believed that such a system would make better use of the 'pool of ability', and thus ultimately benefit the economy. By the mid-1970s, however, the faith in education as a contributor to economic well-being had ebbed away. The oil crisis of the early 1970s helped to usher in a new economic analysis that saw education, alongside other state services, as part of a policy of social engineering that was syphoning off wealth from the economic heart of the society. It was at this time that the macroeconomic analysis of economists and politicians of the political right were brought together with the microanalysis of employers. Employers focused on their problems with young employees. Although several social institutions were implicated in the problem, for example, family life and the mass media, it was the schools that were directly blamed. After all, the schools were directly responsible for the fact that 'children these days couldn't add up and spell' and employers felt justified in expecting the schools to educate for employment, since they were paying for them through taxation and rates. These cries of anguish contributed significantly to the growing mood of disillusionment with education. At the same time, some economists were arguing that the attitudes being engendered by education to careers in industry, together with the enormous cost of the education system, were producing a situation in which education was a significant causal factor in the shift of resources away from the wealth creating private manufacturing sector to the non-productive service sector (Bacon and Ellis, 1976).

This ambivalent relationship between education and industry, or, more accurately, between education and the world of work, is nothing new in historical terms although, as Eggleston has argued,

> (i)n the recent past the experience of work was indivisible from the experience of family, community and society. It is only during the past century that work, for most citizens, has been ... transferred into separate institutions (which) are only accessible to those who work therein and within their prescribed working hours. (Eggleston, 1982, p. 3)

Thus work became separated from preparation for work and, in the longer term, work became separated from the rest of daily life. As a result the education system has tended to concentrate on the selection of pupils for entry into the occupational structure, either directly into employment or indirectly after further or higher education. It has, at the same time, played a socialising role to the extent that it has influenced the attitudes of young people towards the world of work and, therefore, has influenced their occupational choices. The selection process has long been criticised for being ineffective and wasteful and, by extension, inappropriate, since the status of school subjects tends to increase as they move away from utilitarian or pedagogic roots and become more academic. Similarly a critique has developed of the attitudes that schools transmit about the world of work. This finds its expression in Industry Year and in a variety of attempts to change or influence the school curriculum, one of the most significant of which was TVEI (Crompton, 1987).

EDUCATION AND EMPLOYMENT

At the same time as schools were facing this radical revaluation of their nature and purposes, they were also being faced with, and blamed for, widespread unemployment, particularly among young people. For several years now Britain has had more than 3 million people registered as unemployed. This overall figure masks significant regional variations. It also conceals the high proportion of young people within that total. Although the problem of youth unemployment is common to all EEC countries, Britain has one of the highest totals in Europe (Wallace, 1986). A set of positive policies were required to deal with this situation.

In 1976 the Work Experience Programme was introduced to provide unemployed 16- to 18-year-olds with first-hand experience of working life. In 1978 this was superseded by the Youth Opportunity Programme (YOP) and the Special Temporary Employment Programme (STEP). YOP was originally conceived as a short-term response to the crisis of youth unemployment and offered low-level training rather than unskilled temporary work. Although not strictly a continuation of education, it was training that was offered and not a job. Its successor, the Youth Training

Scheme (YTS), has a similar ethos. STEP, on the other hand, was designed to provide temporary jobs on schemes of benefit to the community and replaced the earlier (1975) Job Creation Programme (JCP). By the end of the 1970s, therefore, unemployment among school leavers was not only recognised as being a problem but schemes were being developed to alleviate it. Within schools, however, less was happening. Even as late as 1980 the DES, in A Framework for the School Curriculum made no mention of unemployment and little of new technology.

Nevertheless changes were about to take place, although it was not until the launch of TVEI that the extent of the potential changes became apparent. Thus attempts to meet the prevailing situation were, at best, piecemeal. They were essentially marginal to the education service as a whole and had little impact on pupils before they approached the statutory school leaving age. With the introduction of TVEI came a project which was neither piecemeal nor marginal. It concentrated on the curriculum provision and pedagogy for those pupils in the most crucial years of secondary education.

THE TECHNICAL AND VOCATIONAL EDUCATION INITIATIVE

When the funding for the first 14 projects was announced it came from an unexpected source. The new initiative was not located within the Department of Education and Science which had overall responsibility for the nation's education system. The initiative was to be controlled by the MSC. Thus it was placed outside the usual DES-LEA-schools network of educational influence. This was particularly surprising since the project was intended to penetrate the secret garden of the curriculum, from which teachers, through their professional associations, had managed successfully to exclude the DES since 1944.

A total of £46 million was available for the first round of projects (MSC, 1984) to defray the additional expenditure LEAs required to educate young people under the scheme. In the event, 14 local education authorities submitted successful bids. A further 46 local education authorities were successful in the second round. All the LEAs were committed to having at least four cohorts of students entering the scheme. MSC funds for each project were

Technical and Vocational Initiative

allocated to meet the costs of additional staffing, premises, equipment and consumables, and of features such as residential and work experiences which were to be integral parts of all projects. Projects varied in their allocation of funds, but on average over 60 per cent of MSC resources for project expenditure was to be used for staffing, the major element of which was additional teaching staff. In the first year, however, the need for equipment meant that under 50 per cent of expenditure was related to staffing. Each authority developed proposals to help its teachers to equip and adapt themselves to meet the changing needs of the students within the project. The additional staffing resources allowed teachers to be released from time to time for various staff development courses. The allocation of funds for premises and equipment varied between projects, and between schools in any one project, according to the needs of the individual scheme and its participating schools. In most cases, expenditure on premises was related to adaptation and refurbishment of existing buildings rather than new buildings. By 1984 it was known that a further £100 million was available for those LEAs who had submitted proposals. Thus the education service was seen by some to have found its gift horse.

TVEI was providing a new source of funding for education in the secondary sector at a time when morale was low and, therefore, when change was difficult. Contraction was becoming endemic in the system. The popular view among teachers, espoused by their professional associations, was that the share of national resources being devoted to education was too low and was diminishing to an unacceptable level. The inducements offered by TVEI were such as to encourage LEAs, headteachers and many teachers to look more favourably on an initiative that would require teachers not only to change what they were doing in their classrooms, but also to allow their activities to be subject to the scrutiny of local and national teams of evaluators. It seems that, at all levels within schools, teachers were willing to accept externally imposed criteria and, at least tacitly, to concur with the criticisms levelled at existing educational practice.

TVEI, CRITERIA AND CRITICISM

In order to be accepted, TVEI proposals had to be innovative within the strict terms of the MSC's conceptualisation of appropriate curriculum development for the 14 to 18 age group. They had to be cohesive in the sense that learning is a developmental process. They had to be cost-effective, and contain opportunities for a variety of cross-institutional collaboration. They had to be manageable, both within the school and within the LEA and, lastly, they had to be capable of replication within the input of resources which the MSC provides through its TVEI Unit for the initial courses. These criteria show that the MSC is attempting to develop, through TVEI courses, a particular view of good educational practice (MSC, 1984). In particular, TVEI programmes have to demonstrate that they are relevant to the needs of the appropriate age group, to the world of work, and to the future changing demands of the labour market. The courses have to be integrated in the sense that they should transcend traditional subject boundaries, encourage initiative, problem-solving abilities, and other aspects of personal development. A deeper understanding of the economies of late twentieth century industrial society is to be encouraged by courses that promote a positive view of industry and commerce. Pupils should be given experience of the 'World of Work', and courses should have a strong, but not exclusively, vocational element fostered through (a) the course content, (b) the provision of work experience, and (c) the involvement of representatives of local industry in the planning of programmes. It has been claimed by its proponents that TVEI has introduced another way of thinking to the world of education. When the notions of good practice that are embodied in the criteria for programmes are examined, this statement can be seen to have some force. On the other hand it has been argued by headteachers within at least one LEA that the main significance of TVEI is that, for the first time, an opportunity has been provided for change to be managed effectively and funded adequately.

The essential feature of TVEI as a curriculum innovation is that it is concerned not merely with the content of the curriculum but with its delivery and the ways in which that delivery is organised and managed. The development of economic and industrial awareness, therefore, becomes crucial to the processes of education and with those very sets of attitudes upon which the establishment of successful links between industry and education must rest. In order to meet the relevant criteria, TVEI courses should focus on learning as a process rather than on bodies of knowledge as ends in themselves. A comprehensive understanding of any one curriculum area has to give way to 'learning how to learn'. The teacher is no longer the source of knowledge. He or she becomes a partner, with the student, in structuring, negotiating and guiding learning processes. TVEI thus emphasises the need, which Tomlinson (1986) has identified, for the teaching profession to develop new skills and to change the emphasis that it places on existing ones. Learning has to become more active and experiential. New forms of assessment based on profiles and criteria, rather than examination papers and norm-based tests, are being developed as part of TVEI. Above all, new forms of school organisation will emerge to enable more flexible forms of learning to take place. The tyranny of the timetable will need to be broken and school management will have to become more responsive to the needs of pupils and the wider community, especially where schools have to co-operate with each other and with other organisations.

Current criticisms of, and dissatisfaction with, existing educational provision and practice form a significant part of this pressure for change. In TVEI such criticisms focus on three areas: curriculum content, pedagogy and the status of technical and vocational subjects in schools.

(i) In the area of curriculum content the objectives of TVEI are to widen and enrich the curriculum in a way that will prepare young people for work, and to develop skills and interests that might help pupils to learn. Such activities are expected to be developed on a cross-curricular basis and to spread to areas such as English, Languages and Mathematics. Implicit here is a move from a knowledge or subject-based approach to a skills and techniques-based approach to education.

(ii) Related to this is the explicit intention of TVEI projects to develop student centred approaches to learning across the whole of a student's school experience, thereby bridging subject areas and transcending the boundaries of TVEI. This change in pedagogy is regarded by many as the main unifying influence within the initiative and one which will effect a change in emphasis towards more active learning across the curriculum.

(iii) These developments are also designed to improve the teaching of technical and vocational subjects within the

Technical and Vocational Initiative

curriculum and, more specifically, to raise the status of those subject areas among parents, pupils and teachers. This can only be achieved by encouraging more pupils to follow such courses and by creating more space for such courses within the curriculum. However, pupil numbers are in decline, resources are limited and in a full curriculum that is tightly timetabled across the school day, the only way to put in something new is to leave something out.

Thus, it can be argued that some of these changes can only take place at the expense of other teachers and of other subjects. Further changes planned as part of the TVEI extension programme from 1988 onwards may involve all or most teachers in rethinking strongly held beliefs about their traditional subjects and the methods used to teach them. How then have schools coped with the introduction of TVEI? This question is addressed in all TVEI projects by the local evaluators, since all schemes are subject to detailed monitoring and evaluation.

THE CONTEXT OF LOCAL EVALUATION

The data that form the basis of this chapter have been collected as part of the local evaluation exercise on the TVEI programme in one West Midlands LEA. The data have, therefore, to be interpreted in the light of a methodological context within which a local evaluator has to operate. This context is determined by two main factors. First, the totality of TVEI evaluation, and secondly, the nature and extent of the local evaluation.

The national evaluation

The national evaluation of the TVEI programme consists of three main strands.

(i) A programme of monitoring and evaluation is directly mounted and funded by the MSC over the life of the initiative. This involves two main sub-programmes:
 (a) curricular development, based on case studies, involving a comparative and longitudinal analysis of students, teachers and schools; and

(b) the organisational aspects of the scheme, and the achievements and experiences of those involved, based on cohort studies of TVEI students, and surveys of teachers and LEA staff.
(ii) Studies, which are aimed at influencing progressive developments and promoting good practice.
(iii) The establishment of four TVEI databases (financial, operational, curricular and statistical).

It is within the context of this national evaluation that a local evaluation team has to operate. There are considerable problems of overlap and duplication between the survey studies planned by the National Foundation For Educational Research (NFER) for the initiative-wide evaluation, and those planned for some LEA evaluations. The evaluation division of the TVEI Unit has provided detailed guidelines for local evaluation exercises to avoid unnecessary duplication, but the nature of the national evaluation appears to be so extensive and detailed that some overlap is almost inevitable. This need to try and avoid overlap is a significant constraint on some local evaluation projects.

Local evaluation of TVEI

The National Steering Group suggested that the overall aims of the independent studies of each LEA project should be:

(a) to enable each LEA to have regular independent feedback concerning its own projects;
(b) to enable an independent assessment, which can be widely disseminated of each project as an entity;
(c) to give further insight into the particular features and implications of individual LEA projects; and
(d) to support the national evaluation.

Local evaluators were exhorted to concentrate on curriculum content and organisation, the pupils themselves, the teachers, the schools and the LEAs, the impact on industry, trade unions, parents and the wider community.

At the same time, it was suggested that LEAs will want to ensure that this work did not duplicate other studies, and that it could be carried out on 1 per cent of the LEA's total TVEI budget. The effect of all this was to raise expectations

Technical and Vocational Initiative

within the LEAs as well as within the schools. These were not normally met by local evaluators, since they could not possibly cover the five subject areas in any detail, let alone concentrate on particular aspects of individual schemes. Furthermore, it was suggested that evaluation studies should be based on rigorous methods of investigation, incorporating, for example, cohort and longitudinal studies, in-depth interviews, group discussion, observational methods and action research. Such methods could be supplemented by surveys of students, teachers, employers and parents, statistical data, applicable documentation and relevant factual evidence such as educational records and students' profiles.

The importance and relevance of local evaluation proposals may not always have been clear to those people responsible for writing the proposals at the time of writing. At least one group of evaluators has developed an awareness of what can be done within the standard local evaluation budget. Experience of producing five evaluation proposals over the last year has shown that the negotiations about specific details of the evaluation activity have come to play a more and more significant part in drawing up the contract. The approach to the evaluation adopted here recognises that the main purpose of the exercise is the provision of information, analysis and insight which may contribute to the LEA's decision-making about TVEI, and its development. Two principles follow from this.

(a) The emphasis of the evaluation programme is qualitative rather than quantitative.
(b) The evaluation programme has to be formative in the sense that the evaluators expect to contribute regular feedback on TVEI as it is being implemented, rather than at the end of the period.

In order to achieve this, the local evaluation on which the following case study is based has taken the form of an examination of agreed elements of TVEI in one LEA. These elements were the organisation and management of the project at the scale of both the LEA and individual school (curriculum content and teaching and learning styles). The evaluators produced an annual report for the LEA at the end of each of the first two years of the project (Merson and Bell, 1985, 1986). This will continue throughout the remaining three years of the project.

TVEI, SCHOOLS AND RESPONSES: A CASE STUDY

The process of evaluation can provide a valuable insight into how schools respond to a new curriculum initiative. The case study concentrates on the organisation and management of the project through which the responses of the schools were mediated. It examines the perspectives of headteachers, some problems of implementation, the school co-ordinator as manager and the responses of three schools to the project. The project on which this case study is based is organised around seven schools, offering TVE option areas to 256 pupils within the scheme. The TVE options are Manufacturing Technology, Commerce and Business Studies, Food Technology, Caring Studies and Media Technology. The schools, four in the north of the LEA and three in the south, were chosen for their experience in the TVE curriculum or related areas. Each TVE option is the equivalent of two or three conventional fourth year options (in the first year) and requires seven hours of timetable time each week. To enable pupils to transfer between schools all TVE options are offered at the same time, occupying two mornings each week. Starting and finishing times, which could vary by as much as 45 minutes, are co-ordinated and allowance made for significant travelling time.

A total of seven additional staff were appointed to the participating schools in the first year of the project, funded from MSC resources. A project director with full-time responsibility for TVEI was appointed from within the LEA. She had previously been a deputy-head and had the distinctive experience of a one year's industrial secondment. The director is based at the Education and Industry Centre in the north of the LEA. Each participating school has a TVE co-ordinator on Scale 3 or 4, responsible for administration, curriculum development, assessment, counselling and liaison with the consortium. This required new skills. The role also required co-ordination between different elements of the curriculum and demanded considerable external liaison and co-operation. In every school, however, it was the headteacher who gave the initial impetus to the initiative.

The headteacher's perspectives of TVEI

Each of the headteachers in the seven schools had played a part in drawing up the LEA's proposal, and each was instrumental in writing the option proposal for his or her own school. They all saw the project as a significant opportunity to enhance the curriculum in their schools and to involve their staff in a well-funded curriculum innovation project, which could be used for developing further initiatives within their schools. They recognised that this particular development was taking place at a time of scarcity of resources, retrenchment and low morale and, thus, it provided opportunities for growth and development that might not have been otherwise available. They justified the participation of their school in the project in a number of different ways, four of which are important.

(i) The provision of increased vocational opportunities for many pupils. This might be linked with work experience, in order to give pupils a better understanding of the world of work, and therefore enable them to operate more effectively within that world in the future.

(ii) The provision of opportunities for pupils to work in different environments, in different settings, with different teachers. This applied both to pupils who selected an option provided by their own school, and to pupils who chose to travel to another school. One headteacher in particular welcomed the opportunity that the project provided for teachers and pupils to work together unhampered by conventional timetabling, by the length of the school period or by other general factors of school organisation. The TVEI project therefore, was seen as an opportunity to explore alternative ways of structuring teaching and learning within the overall organisation of a comprehensive school.

(iii) The provision of opportunities for teachers working on the project to develop different teaching styles and to explore a variety of ways of organising their work as well as the work of the pupils. This has stimulated and motivated colleagues as well as providing them with an opportunity to reflect on their preferred teaching styles. It has not only meant a shift to pupil-directed learning but it has meant, in some cases, that curriculum content has been organised on a modular basis and that more informal forms of teaching and learning have been adopted. This has contributed to the career development of the teachers involved in the project.

Technical and Vocational Initiative

(iv) The provision of the opportunity for teachers to extend their existing curriculum, develop new aspects of the curriculum and to incorporate new materials into the curriculum. Most frequently mentioned by the heads was the need to relate the curriculum to future technology, and to the world of work. This was to be facilitated by the development of new ideas and materials, the purchasing of equipment, the provision of new buildings or the adaptation of existing buildings, and in some cases, the availability of extra staff and other resources. Headteachers also saw that the project provided an opportunity for the cross-disciplinary work that they were already trying to encourage within their school, but which was quite difficult without some of the extra resources and the organisational and administrative changes TVEI had brought into the schools.

Clearly, the various rationales developed by the seven headteachers to explain the involvement of their schools in TVEI tended to be similar to the stated aims of the TVEI programmes.

Some problems of implementation

It is likely that the heads tended to play down the wider implications of the changes involved. They all claimed that they saw the project as an opportunity to do many of the new things that they wished to do, as well as a vehicle for obtaining the resources and creating the necessary organisational and administrative structures to do more effectively that which they were already trying to do. No innovation can be successful unless it can be based, at least in part, on what those involved believe ought to be done. Equally no innovation can be implemented without encountering a number of problems and difficulties, and it is to these problems which we now turn.

Briefly listed are some of the main problems that were encountered by the schools.

(i) In a minority of schools the reaction of some non-TVEI staff created problems. Some teachers believed that the introduction of TVEI had an adverse effect on their own departments, particularly through its effect on

option choices. Where pupil numbers are falling these effects are exacerbated. There has also been some philosophical and ideological opposition to MSC involvement in education and to the control it exerts over TVEI resources, as well as to the accountability and evaluation requirements incorporated into the TVEI project.
(ii) There was a general failure to predict exactly how much time would be required for various aspects of the project. The amount of time school co-ordinators, headteachers and others would need to devote to TVEI was seriously underestimated. Some schools underestimated how much staff time was needed to teach a particular course. Some schools misjudged the extent to which the school co-ordinator would have to devote time to TVEI, whilst others found difficulty coping with the considerable demands made by TVEI in the form of paperwork.
(iii) The consortium arrangement created some timetabling problems and will continue to do so as the project develops and as new groups of pupils are incorporated. The need to have all TVEI courses taught at the same time in all the schools has had an effect on the whole organisation of teaching in some schools, and has affected option choices arrangements in all schools.

These problems were dealt with through the structures set up to manage the project. Each school tended to respond to them in its own way. However, embodied in the organisational and management procedures in each school are the various reactions to the criticisms of secondary education that are implied in TVEI projects. At the same time the way in which each school copes with the integration of TVEI into its existing structure exemplifies a set of attitudes towards, and expectations about, the initiative.

The school co-ordinator as manager

TVEI is integrated into the school organisation through the activities of the school co-ordinator and of the people planning and teaching the courses. However, there was no common pattern to the ways in which school co-ordinators actually worked, nor was there any agreement about the extent to which they should devote their time to TVEI work. Furthermore, it was clear that different mechanisms are used in different schools for monitoring the TVEI courses during the year. For example, in one school, the co-ordinator is a member of, and therefore reports to, the school's senior management team. In a second school the co-ordinator liaises through a deputy-head, producing written reports at the request of the headteacher. This school also has regular meetings between the head and the co-ordinator on a fortnightly basis, supplemented, as in any other school, by the steering group meetings. In a third school the TVEI co-ordinator is regarded as a head of department and a head of year. The co-ordinator has responsibility for academic and pastoral development of the pupils following the TVEI course. He reports directly to the headteacher in the same way that other heads of departments do. It is clear, however, that in this school, as in most others, more is required of the co-ordinator than is required of heads of non-TVEI departments. This is partly because of the demands of the project itself, partly because more information has to be provided for outside agencies and partly because there is a great deal more money to spend. In a fourth school the co-ordinator is a member of the senior management team, although there is no requirement to make regular reports to that team. The co-ordinator holds informal discussions with the headteacher as and when required. This informal method is adopted in several other schools. This approach was used partly to ensure that unnecessary meetings were not held and partly to give both the headteacher and the co-ordinator maximum flexibility. It is difficult at this stage to evaluate the extent to which the school co-ordinator should be required to be a formal part of the management structure of the school. What is important is that both the headteacher and the co-ordinator understand exactly what the channels of communication are and when they should be used.

One of the unique aspects of the school co-ordinators role, and one that makes it extremely difficult to fulfil successfully, is that the co-ordinator has a responsibility to co-ordinate activities between schools and not just within the school. The co-ordinator has a responsibility to the project as well as to the school, and this requires that the co-ordinator works closely with the project director and the other school co-ordinators. This external aspect of the role clearly places considerable demands on school co-ordinators,

Technical and Vocational Initiative

both in terms of time and in terms of the skills they need in order to do the job successfully. In view of this, it may not be entirely appropriate for schools to view the co-ordinator as another head of department or another member of the senior management team. This is not to say that school co-ordinators should receive special treatment. It is simply to acknowledge that the school co-ordinator's role is a new one. It is not fully developed or even fully understood. The implications of attempting to fulfil internal academic and pastoral duties, external academic and pastoral duties, and both internal and external liaison need to be worked through with the school co-ordinator and the project director. Because of the strains of carrying out their responsibilities several school co-ordinators have found themselves faced with one of the classic dilemmas of management: how to reconcile the competing claims of those activities, which are necessary to ensure that the school functions smoothly on a day-to-day basis with activities necessary to make the innovation successful. In this TVEI project, as in most others, these pressures are exacerbated by the way in which co-ordinators have been appointed, since all of them already carried posts of responsibility within the school and were required to continue with those responsibilities as well as carrying out the duties of school co-ordinators.

The responses of schools to TVEI

Preliminary findings from the evidence collected during the evaluation of the second year of the project indicate that many of the organisational and managerial problems have been overcome, but that the extent to which the project has succeeded in having a significant impact in terms of the criteria discussed earlier varies greatly. This can be illustrated by the following three examples.

School A: The internal opposition to the project is no longer a feature of school life, although the ideas of TVEI are not universally accepted. The teachers involved in the project have tended to work together but in relative isolation from the rest of the staff, except for those in the Computer Studies Department, where informal contacts have been developed. The TVEI team, encouraged by the head, has become a little more ambitious in developing new curriculum material and methods. However, in the words of the head, 'They are only scratching the surface. The secret is the quality of the staff. A good teacher will always be looking to improve. Others, even if you give them the world, will go back to what they were doing before. There are only a limited number of really good teachers to go round.' The head also suggested that the teachers' industrial action, especially in a relatively small school could and did effectively prevent meetings that were necessary for the development of TVEI. Many aspects of the project, therefore, remained isolated and contained.

School B: There had also been some opposition to TVEI in this school. However, there had been some staff changes with new staff being appointed; staff who were originally part of the TVEI team being replaced by others from inside the school with different strengths; and a senior member of staff returning to the school after a successful fellowship at a university to study the possibilities of developing TVEI in Modern Languages. In this school the requirement to earmark 30 per cent of the timetable for TVEI in years 4 and 5 was a very real constraint since it limited the placing of other options on the timetable, as well as causing some difficulties for the timetabling of first and second year courses. Nevertheless, developments have taken place in the curriculum area with new methods and materials being tried. This was especially true in the use of computers across the curriculum and in Modern Languages. The topic of computers was the focus of an in-service day for the school, which helped to inform staff about TVEI and to provide opportunities for more colleagues to become familiar with the approaches being adopted in the TVEI course. Here, then, TVEI is being accommodated within the school. It is accepted in some areas, tolerated in others and ignored elsewhere. On the whole the response of the staff is a conservative accommodation of a project not yet fully understood.

School C: The staff of the school were already working in cross-curriculuar ways and the school was fairly open to the extent that it had many visitors. The boundaries, both physical and intellectual, were relatively permeable. TVEI ideas and materials were beginning to spread into the remainder of the curriculum through the use of school inservice days. The overall policy was to involve as many people as possible in teaching TVEI, to encourage crosscurricular co-operation and to integrate TVEI into the general work of the school. As a result, staff were becoming more confident in developing and using open-learning techniques in a variety of contexts. This often involved the adaptation of TVEI teaching strategies for other purposes on other, not dissimilar, courses as well as the use of TVEI funded equipment. In short, the general response to TVEI in this school tended to be one of 'opportunistic adaptation'.

CONCLUSIONS

In this chapter it has been argued that TVEI emerged as one of a number of responses to some fundamental concerns about the nature of secondary education. It appeared on the educational scene at a time when schools were confronted by falling rolls, diminishing resources and low morale and when teachers found themselves in a philosophical climate that required them to legitimise and evaluate teaching in ways not directly related to mainstream educational thought. Furthermore, embodied in the aims and criteria for TVEI projects, a radical and wide ranging critique of secondary education in Britain can be found.

This critique forms the basis of a rationale for the involvement of seven schools within one LEA in a TVEI project. The basic criteria of TVEI have been accepted as a starting point, albeit in a modified and limited form. Nevertheless, those within the project see themselves as moving towards meeting these criteria over the lifespan of the project. This movement is facilitated by the establishment of a management structure, which is both peculiar to, and particular to the TVEI project, although it might be argued that if schools are to move towards a modular curriculum, or other forms of non-subject based teaching, a similar management structure might be needed.

This management structure, with the role of the school co-ordinator central to it, has been regarded by some as the key to understanding the responses of schools to their TVEI projects. Saunders (1986) has suggested, for example, that where the school climate is supportive (approved by senior management) of TVEI, then school co-ordinators are more likely to be able to develop strategies for undermining resistance and suspicion among staff. Where, on the other hand, there is a lack of commitment to change on the part of senior staff, then the considerable burden of TVEI administration and insufficient influence of co-ordinators combines to limit the extent of internal change.

The findings reported indicate that the level of commitment to change by senior staff is not the only, or the most crucial, element determining the extent of internal change, since the senior staff in all seven schools were committed to TVEI. Two other factors emerge. The first is the extent to which the school co-ordinator has a clearly defined position in the hierarchy of the school, which confers upon him or her direct access to the school's major decision-making processes. Given that schools are basically hierarchical in nature, at least as far as policy-making is concerned, it is necessary that the school co-ordinator can be given or can establish ways of working that enable him or her to have an influence on school policy across departments. The second factor is the extent to which the school co-ordinator, or somebody in the senior management team working with the co-ordinator, can devise strategies to minimise the isolation of teachers within secondary schools. Where schools are organised on a subject basis, a teacher's first point of professional reference is likely to be the subject department and this may also form the significant social group. The interaction between departments will be limited and may decrease according to the degree of dissimilarity between them. Thus there may be more interaction between members of History and Geography Departments than between History and Physics Departments. At the same time teaching is, for the most part, an isolated and isolating activity, taking place, as it does, between individual teachers and groups of children within enclosed classrooms. It has been argued (Beckhard and Harris, 1979) that for innovation to be successful it has to be associated with a substantial level of social and professional interaction. In some schools in this project, such interaction was encouraged by the distribution of resources for staff development or for pupils' clubs. More formally, equipment, buildings and learning materials have been used elsewhere in the curriculum. This use of TVEI resources has proved to be particularly effective. Thus, the responses of schools to TVEI (whether or not they easily fit the threefold typology of isolated containment, conservative accommodation and opportunistic adaptation) depend to a

Technical and Vocational Initiative

significant extent on the way these changes are mediated through the management structure of the school.

CONCLUSION

Liz Bondi

The studies presented in this volume examine and illustrate various aspects of the relationship between education and society. In the introduction, it was asserted that education is 'in recession' (Hewton, 1986a) in three senses: in the economic sense of the limitation or withdrawal of public funds for education; in the demographic sense of the decline in pupil numbers; and in the social-psychological sense of an erosion of faith in the ability of education to fulfil its role in contemporary society. The empirical chapters have examined some of the consequences of these trends for the provision of education and some of the associated social issues. To conclude the volume, this chapter attempts to draw out some common themes and to identify areas requiring further research.

It has been amply demonstrated that the economic, demographic and social-psychological pressures on educational provision have precipitated conflicts among the various groups involved in, or affected by, the service. Several chapters trace the development of such conflicts, showing how underlying tensions become exacerbated, how different groups pursue their goals and how the issues concerned are eventually resolved. These findings, whether relating to the reorganisation of school accommodation or aspects of the curriculum, have implications for policy-making and political action at all levels of educational provision. For example, it is clear from Chapters 1, 2 and 3 that any attempt to reorganise school provision is likely to prompt vociferous opposition from groups who are capable of pursuing their goals tenaciously and imaginatively. Equally, the scope for local communities to ensure that

Conclusion

their views influence the policy-makers in the manner they intend is limited. Chapter 2 demonstrates that these kinds of conflict are inevitable within existing policy-making arrangements both in England and Wales and in Scotland.

In other ways, what emerges most strongly from these case studies is the sheer variety of experiences and outcomes: similar issues evolve in different ways and to different effect in different places. Contrast for example, the use made by parents of procedures for consultation in Fife (Chapter 3) and in Portsmouth (Chapter 1): in the latter the great majority ignored the opportunities offered by questionnaires and those that did participate came into conflict with one another; in the former a substantial proportion of parents attended public meetings and, on the whole, joined forces to oppose the plans of the education authority. Consider also the contrast between the capitulation of local politicians to parental opposition in Fife (Chapter 3) and the resistance to similar opposition in Dundee (Chapter 2). Some of these, and other, variations may be traceable to relatively straightforward factors, such as the political party in power in the district, county or regional council, or the social class composition of the local population. But explanations are often less clear cut and must frequently rely on a wide variety of local and national factors to account for the development and outcome of a particular issue. In order to refine such analyses, there is clearly a great need for more comparative (or comparable) studies that can identify more precisely the key causal factors and that can explain why the politics of educational provision vary from place to place.

The prevalence of conflict in educational provision is, in part, generated by uncertainty induced by rapid change. At the time of writing, Green Papers have been issued on (a) the introduction of a national curriculum; (b) arrangements for schools to opt out of local authority control and to receive funding directly from central government; (c) 'open enrolment', which would require schools to admit pupils up to their physical capacity; and (d) the delegation of substantially greater financial responsibility to headteachers and school governors. These proposals are expected to become the subject of an Education Bill, the enactment of which is already being heralded by proponents and critics alike as the greatest educational reform since 1944. Whether or not the legislation lives up to this reputation, its impact will demand much attention. Several chapters in this

Conclusion

volume address issues that are likely to be of continued importance, such as parental choice (Chapter 4), school closures (Chapters 1 and 2), technical education (Chapter 10), education in a multicultural society (Chapters 6 and 7), the character of the teaching force (Chapter 9) and geographical variations in educational policy and provision (Chapter 5). These studies also highlight the 'distance' between legislation and implementation: exhortations by central government to rationalise provision or increase parental choice have not always had the intended results, while policies regarding new technology in education have been interpreted in different ways (Chapter 5). Thus, in addition to research on the impact of legislative changes on the provision of education there is also a need to refine upon more abstract understandings of the processes involved in making and implementing policies.

The organisation of this volume distinguishes between the provision of education and the social consequences of education. The former is changing rapidly and looks set for further upheavals. Those responsible for initiating both contemporary and past reforms in the organisation of educational provision have frequently justified their actions in terms of educational outcomes. In particular, successive reforms, including the 1944 Act, comprehensive reorganisation and the current pursuit of greater choice in education, have been advocated in terms of improving the quality of education, raising standards and increasing opportunities. However, in many respects these reforms have had remarkably limited effects. For example, the impact of comprehensive reorganisation on educational attainment has been widely and inconclusively debated. Whether eventually declared to have raised or lowered standards among any particular group, perhaps the most striking feature of this reform is the very modest character of any net effect. Thus, alongside research on the rapidly changing politics of educational provision, there is clearly a need for research addressing the lack of change in patterns of educational attainment. Chapters 7 and 8 offer useful pointers for such research. Both tackle long-standing issues in the sociology of education by refining existing research and by offering new insight into underachievement among, respectively, black and socially disadvantaged young people. At the same time, however, the two studies employ very different methodologies, namely participant observation (Chapter 7) and multivariate statistics (Chapter 8). The

Conclusion

similarities between these studies suggests that such approaches should not be treated as mutually exclusive. Indeed, the two projects indicate that research on these familiar and persistent issues may best be advanced by the complementary use of qualitative and quantitative methods. The studies presented in this volume have been conceived and executed from a variety of disciplinary perspectives, including politics, sociology and geography. In practice, all are multi-disciplinary: it is not possible to undertake effective research focusing solely on the politics, sociology or geography of education. Thus, attempts to explain policy decisions in education must consider the social and geographical context alongside political processes. Conversely, attempts to explain geographical patterns in education invariably lead to examination of social and political factors. The research reported here illustrates some of the ways in which social, political and geographical considerations can be combined. However, the interactions between the politics, sociology and geography of educational provision and educational outcomes remain rich areas for study. It is hoped that this contribution suggests some avenues and offers some direction for such research.

REFERENCES

Adler, M. (1985) Falling rolls and rising conflict, unpublished paper presented to the Scottish Educational Research Association Conference, St. Andrews

Adler, M., Petch, A. and Tweedie, J. (1987) The origins and impact of the Parents' Charter. In D. McCrone (ed.), The Scottish Government Yearbook, Unit for the Study of Government in Scotland, University of Edinburgh

Adler, M. and Raab, G. (1988) The impact of parental choice on admissions to secondary schools in Edinburgh and Dundee. Journal of Education Policy (forthcoming)

Aitkin, M.A. and Longford, N.T. (1986) Statistical modelling issues in school effectiveness studies. Journal of the Royal Statistical Society, Series A, 149, 1-26

American Council on Education (1983) American Universities and Colleges, de Gruyter, New York

Apple, M.W. (1982a) Reproduction and contradiction in education: an introduction. In M.W. Apple (ed.), Cultural and Economic Reproduction in Education, Routledge and Kegan Paul, London

------ (ed.) (1982b) Cultural and Economic Reproduction in Education, Routledge and Kegan Paul, London

Arbena, J. (1985) Funding big-time intercollegiate athletics: fifty years of the Clemson IPTAY Club. Paper presented to the 13th meeting of the North American Society for Sports History, La Crosse, Wisconsin

Arnstein, S. (1969) A ladder of citizen participation. Journal of the American Institute of Planners, 35, 216-24

Astley, W.G., Axelsson, R., Butler, R.J., Hickson, D.J. and Wilson, D.C. (1982) Complexity and cleavage: dual

References

explanations of strategic decision making. Journal of Management Studies, 19, 457-375

Audit Commission (1986) Towards Better Management of Secondary Education, HMSO, London

Bacon, R. and Ellis, W. (1976) Britain's Economic Problem: Too Few Producers, Routledge and Kegan Paul, London

Bacon, W. (1978) Public Accountability and the Schooling System - A Sociology of School Board Democracy, Harper and Row, London

Bailey, S. (1982) Central city decline and the provision of education services. Urban Studies, 19, 263-79

Bailey, S. (1984) The costs of sixth form rationalisation. Policy and Politics, 12, 53-69

Bale, J. (1982) Sport and Place, University of Nebraska Press, Lincoln

------ (1985) Towards a Geography of International Sport, Occasional Paper 8, Department of Geography, Loughborough University

------ (1986) Athletic aliens in academe. In J. Mangan and R. Small (eds) Sport, Culture and Society, Spon, London

------ (1987) Alien student-athletes in American universities: locational decision-making and sojourn abroad. Physical Education Review, (in press)

Baldridge, J.V. and Burnham, R.A. (1975) Organisational innovation: individual, organisational and environmental aspects. Administrative Science Quarterly, 20, 165-75

Ballinger, L. (c. 1981) In Your Face! Sports for Love and Money, Vanguard, Chicago

Barber, E., Altbach, P. and Myers, R. (eds) (1984) Bridges to Knowledge: Foreign Students in Comparative Perspective, Chicago University Press, Chicago

Barnes, J. (ed.) (1975) Educational Priority vol. 3: Curriculum Innovation in London's EPAs, HMSO, London

Barnes, J.H. and Lucas, H. (1975) Positive discrimination in education: individuals, groups and institutions. In J. Barnes (ed.) Educational Priority vol. 3: Curriculum Innovation in London's EPAs, HMSO, London

Baron, H.M. (1971) Race and status in school spending: Chicago, 1961-1966. Journal of Human Resources, 6, 3-24

Barrett, S. and Fudge, C. (1981) Examining the policy-action relationship. In S. Barrett and C. Fudge (eds) Policy and Action: Essays on the Implementation of Public Policy, Methuen, London

Becker, H. (1963) Outsiders: Studies in the Sociology of

References

Deviance, New York, Free Press
Beckhard, R. and Harris, R.T. (1979) Organisational Transitions: Managing Complex Change, Addison Wesley
Beezley, W. and Hobbs, J. (1983) Nice girls don't sweat: women in American sport. Journal of Popular Culture, 16 (4), 42-53
Bell, R. and Grant, N. (1977) Patterns of Education in the British Isles, Allen and Unwin, London
Bernstein, B. (1962) Social class, linguistic codes and grammatical elements. Language and Speech, 5, 221-40
------ (1977) Class and pedagogies: visible and invisible. In J. Karabel and A.H. Halsey (eds) Power and Ideology in Education, Oxford University Press, Oxford
------ (1982) Codes, modalities and the process of cultural reproduction. In M.W. Apple (ed.), Cultural and Economic Reproduction in Education, Routledge and Kegan Paul, London
Birmingham Centre for Contemporary Cultural Studies (1981) Unpopular Education, Hutchinson, London
Black, D. (1980) Inequalities in Health, DHSS/HMSO, London
Blunkett, D. and Green, G. (1983) Building from the Bottom: The Sheffield Experience, (Fabian tract 491) Fabian Society, London
Boaden, N. (1971) Urban Policy Making: Influences on County Boroughs in England and Wales, Cambridge University Press, London
------, Goldsmith, M., Hampton, W. and Stringer, P. (1982) Public Participation in Local Services, Longman, London
Boddy, M. (1984) Local councils and the financial squeeze. In M. Boddy and C. Fudge (eds) Local Socialism?, Macmillan, London
Bondi, L. (1986) The geography and politics of contraction in local education provision: a case study of Manchester primary schools. Unpublished Ph.D. thesis, University of Manchester
------ (1987) School closures and local politics: the negotiation of primary school rationalisation in Manchester. Political Geography Quarterly, 6, 203-24
Borgatta, E. and Jackson, D. (1980) Aggregate Data Analysis: an Interpretation, Sage Publications, London
Boseley, S. (1987) Baker proposes to offer parents chance to pick schools. The Guardian, 1 May, and Baker confirms popular schools to expand. The Guardian, 2 May
Boudon, R. (1973) Education, Opportunity and Social

References

Inequality, John Wiley, London
Bourdieu, P. (1972) Cultural reproduction and social reproduction. In Brown, R. (ed.) Knowledge, Education and Cultural Change, Tavistock, London
------ and Passeron, J.L. (1977) Reproduction in Education, Society and Culture, Sage, Beverley Hills
Bowles, S. and Gintis, H. (1976) Schooling in Capitalist America, Routledge and Kegan Paul, London
Bradford, M.G., Bondi, L., Burdett, F.J, Petch, J. and Quirk, B. (1988) Education, Place and Locality: Explanations of the Spatial Variation in Education, Routledge, London (in press)
Brady, E. (1986) Foul shots in the land of 'Who shot JR'. USA Today, 28 March
Bramley, G. and Evans, A. (1981) Guide to the block grant. Municipal Journal, 89, 44-4 and 80-1
Briault, E. and Smith, F. (1980) Falling Rolls in Secondary Schools, NFER, Windsor (in two parts)
Broadfoot, P. (1986) Power relations and English education: the changing role of central government. Journal of Education Policy, 1, 53-62
Brooksbank, K. and Ackstine, A.E. (1984) Educational Administration, 2nd edn, Councils and Education Press, London
Brown, K.M. (1985) Turning a blind eye. Sociological Review, 33, 670-90
Brown, P. and Ferguson, S. (1977) To close or not to close: an educational question. Proceedings of PTRC Seminar. Policy Analysis for Urban and Regional Planning, PTRC, London
------ (1982) Schools and population change in Liverpool. In W.T.S. Gould and A.G. Hodgkiss (eds) The Resources of Merseyside, Liverpool University Press, London
Burdett, F.J. (1985) An organisational approach to the geography of public provision: the making of innovative policies by local education authorities. Unpublished PhD thesis, University of Manchester
------ (1987a) The creation of local education authority policies for computers in schools. In Kent, A. (ed.), Computer Assisted Learning in Social Sciences and Humanities, Blackwell, Oxford
------ (1987b) Local education authority policies for computers in education. Journal of Computer Assisted Learning, 3, 30-9
------ and Bradford, M.G. (1987) An organisational

313

References

approach to the geography of innovation by local authorities: the importance of scrutiny, conflict and centralisation. Environment and Planning C (in press)
----- and Bradford, M.G. (1988) The geography of educational policy innovation: an organisational approach. In M.G. Bradford, L. Bondi, F.J. Burdett, J. Petch and B. Quirk, Education, Place and Locality: Explanations of the Spatial Variation in Education, Routledge, London (in press)
Burgess, R.G. (1986) Sociology, Education and Schools, Batsford, London
Burnhill, P.M. (1984) The 1981 Scottish school leavers survey. In D. Raffe (ed.), Fourteen to Eighteen: the Changing Pattern of Schooling in Scotland, Aberdeen University Press, Aberdeen
Byrne, D., Williamson, B. and Fletcher, B. (1975) The Poverty of Education, Martin Robertson, London
Cady, E. (1978) The Big Game: College Sports and American Life, University of Tennessee Press, Knoxville
Central Advisory Council for Education (England) (CACE) (1967) Children and their Primary Schools: a Report, (the Plowden Report), HMSO, London
Central Policy Review Staff (1977) Population and the Social Services, HMSO, London
Chartered Institute of Public Finance and Accountancy (1986) Performance Indicators in the Education Service: a Statement, London
Coleman, J. (1968) The concept of equality of educational opportunity. Harvard Educational Review, 38, 7-22
Cox, K.R. (1979) Location and Public Problems, Basil Blackwell, Oxford
Crompton, K. (1987) A Curriculum for Enterprise: Pedagogy or Propaganda. School Organisation, 7, 5-11
Cyert, R.M. and March, J.G. (1963) A Behavioural Theory of the Firm, Prentice Hall, New Jersey
Dale, R. (1983) Thatcherism and education. In J. Ahier and M. Flude (eds), Contemporary Education Policy, Croom Helm, London
------ (ed.) (1985) Education, Training and Employment, Pergamon Press, Oxford
Danziger, J.N. and Dutton, W.H. (1977) Technological innovation in local government: the case of computers. Policy and Politics, 6, 27-49
David, M.E. (1977) Reform, Reaction and Resources, NFER, Windsor

References

------ (1983) Sex, education and social policy: A new moral economy. In S. Walker and L. Barton (eds), Gender Class and Education, Falmer, Lewes
Davies, B. and Ferlie, E. (1982) Efficiency-promoting innovation in social care. Policy and Politics, 10, 181-205
Davies, J. (1974) The Evangelistic Bureaucrat, Tavistock, London
Davies, L. (1984) Pupil Power: Deviance and Gender in School, Lewes, Falmer
Dearlove, J. (1973) The Politics of Policy in Local Government: the Making and Maintenance of Public Policy in the Royal Borough of Kensington and Chelsea, Cambridge University Press, London
De Mellow, R.A. (1979) Postcodes in the 1981 Census of Scotland. Newsletter 41, British Urban and Regional Information Services Association, Bristol
Dennis, N. (1970) People and Planning, Faber and Faber, London
Dennison, W.F. (1983) Doing Better for Fewer: Education and Falling Rolls, Longman (for the Schools Council), York
------ (1984) Educational Finance and Resources, Croom Helm, London
------ (1985) Managing the Contracting School, Heinemann, London
Department of Education and Science (1977) Education in Schools: A Consultative Document (Cmnd 6869), HMSO, London
------ (1977) Circular 5/77 'Falling numbers and school closures', London
------ (1977) Circular 14/77 'Local education authority arrangements for the school curriculum', London
------ (1979) Local authority arrangements for the school curriculum, HMSO, London
------ (1980) Circular 2/80 'Procedures affecting proposals made under Sections 12-16 of the Education Act 1980', London
------ (1981) Circular 2/81 'Falling rolls and surplus places', London
------ (1986) Report by Her Majesty's Inspectors on the effects of local authority expenditure policies on education provision in England - 1985, HMSO, London
Department of the Environment Inner Cities Directorate (1983) 1981 Census: Urban Deprivation, Information

References

Note 2, HMSO, London
Donnison, D., Chapman, V., Meacher, M., Sears, A. and Urwin, K. (1975) Social Policy and Administration Revisited, Allen and Unwin, London
Douglas, J.W.B. (1964) The Home and the School, MacGibbon and Kee, London
------ Ross, J.M. and Simpson, H.R. (1968) All Our Future, Peter Davies, London
Downs, G.W. (1976) Bureaucracy, Innovation and Public Policy, Lexington, Massachusetts
Duguid, G. and Grant, R. (1983) Areas of Special Need in Scotland, Central Research Unit, Scottish Office, Edinburgh
Dunning, E. (1981) Social bonding and the socio-genesis of violence: a theoretical analysis with special reference to combat sports. In A. Tomlinson (ed.), The Sociological Study of Sport, Brighton Polytechnic, Brighton
Edwards, H. (1984) The collegiate athletics arms race: origins and implications of the 'Rule 84' controversy. Journal of Sport and Social Issues, 8, 97-105
Eggleston, S.J. (1977) The Ecology of the School, Methuen, London
------ (ed.) (1982) Work Experience in Secondary Schools, Routledge and Kegan Paul, London
------ (1986) Multicultural society: The qualitative aspects. Research Papers in Education, 1, 217-36
------ Dunn, D. and Anjali, M. (1986) Education for Some, Trentham Books, Stoke-on-Trent
Eichberg, H. (1984) Olympic sport - neocolonialism and alternatives. International Review for Sociology of Sport, 19, 97-105
Eide, I. (ed.) (1970) Students as Links Between Cultures, Universitetsforlaget, Oslo
Eitzen, S. (1986) How can we clean up big-time college sports? Chronicle of Higher Education, 31 (22), 96
Eversley, D. and Kollmann, W. (1982) Population Change and Social Planning, Edward Arnold, London
Field, F. (ed.) (1977) Education and the Urban Crisis, Routledge and Kegan Paul, London
Finn, D., Grant, N. and Johnson, R. (1978) Social democracy, education and the crisis. In Centre for Contemporary Cultural Studies, On Ideology, Hutchinson, London
Floud, J., Halsey, A. and Martin, F. (1985) Social Class and Education Opportunity, Heinemann, London

References

Flowerdew, R. and Aitkin, M. (1982) A method of fitting a gravity model based on the Poisson distribution. Journal of Regional Science, 22, 191-202

Forbes, J., Lamont, D. and Robertson, I. (1979) Intra-urban migration in Greater Glasgow: a summary report of a study. Central Research Unit, Scottish Development Department, Edinburgh

Forsythe, D. (1983) The Rural Community and the Small School, Aberdeen University Press, Aberdeen

Fowler, G. (1981) The Changing nature of educational politics in the 1970s. In P. Broadfoot, C. Brock and W. Tulasiewicz (eds), Politics and Educational Change, Croom Helm, London

Fudge, C. (1984) Decentralisation: socialism goes local? In M. Boddy and C. Fudge (eds), Local Socialism?, Macmillan, London

Galtung, J. (1984) Sport and international understanding: sport as a carrier of deep culture and structure. In M. Ilmarinen (ed.), Sport and International Understanding, Springer-Verlag, Berlin

Garner, C.L. (1979) Residential mobility in the local authority housing sector in Edinburgh 1963-73. Unpublished PhD thesis, University of Edinburgh

------ (1984) Linking census data to SEDA. Proceedings of the European SIR Users Group meeting, London, Status, Berlin

------ Main, B.G.M. and Raffe, D. (forthcoming) Local variation in school-leaver employment and unemployment within large cities. Centre for Educational Sociology, Edinburgh

Gatherer, W.A. (1981) The local education authority and the curriculum, Educational Policy Bulletin, 9, 179-93

Gautt, P. (1983) unpublished statistics, personally communicated

Geen, A.G. (1981) Educational policy making in Cardiff 1944-1970. Public Administration, 59, 85-108

Glasgow District Council (1983) Social deprivation in Glasgow. Mimeograph

Goldstein, H. (1986) Multilevel mixed linear model analysis using iterative generalized least squares. Biometrika, 73, 43-56

Goudge, T. (1984) A geographical analysis of major college football programs: the parameters of success. Unpublished PhD thesis, Oklahoma State University

Gould, P. (1966) On mental maps. Michigan Inter-University

References

Community of Mathematical Geographers, Discussion Paper, 9

Gray, J., McPherson, A. and Raffe, D. (1983) Reconstructions of Secondary Education: Theory, Myth and Practice Since the War, Routledge and Kegan Paul, London

Grubb, W.N. and Lazerson, M. (1981) Vocational solution to youth problems: the persistent frustrations of the American experience. Educational Analysis, 3, 91-104

Guthrie, J.W. (1970) Educational inequality, school finance and a plan for the '70's. Inequality and Economic Resources, hearings before the select committee on equal educational opportunity of the US Senate, pp. 3451-500

------ (1971) Schools and Inequality. MIT Press, Massachusetts

Guttmann, A. (1978) From Ritual to Record: the Nature of Modern Sports, Columbia University Press, New York

Hadley, R., Dale, P. and Sills, P. (1984) Decentralising Social Services, Bedford Square Press/NCVO, London

------ and Hatch, R. (1981) Social Welfare and the Failure of the State: Centralised Social Services and Participatory Alternatives, Allen and Unwin, London

------ and McGrath, M., (1980) Going Local: Neighbourhood Social Services, Bedford Square Press/NCVO, London

Halsey, A.H. (1972) Educational Priority, Vol. 1: EPA, Problems and Policies, HMSO, London

------ (1975) Sociology and the equality debate. Oxford Review of Education, 1, 9-23

------ Heath, A. and Ridge, J. (1980) Origins and Destinations: Family Class and Education in Modern Britain, Clarendon Press, Oxford

Hambleton, R. (1978) Policy Planning and Local Government, Hutchinson, London

Hambleton, R. and Hoggett, P. (1984) The Politics of Decentralisation: Theory and Practice of a Radical Local Government Initiative, Working Paper 46, School for Advanced Urban Studies, University of Bristol

Hampshire Education Committee (1983) Secondary Education in Portsmouth, Hampshire County Council

Hargreaves, J. (1982) Sport, culture and ideology. In J. Hargreaves (ed.) Sport, Culture and Ideology, Routledge and Kegan Paul, London

Hauser, R.M. (1970) Context and consex: a cautionary tale. American Journal of Sociology, 75, 645-64

References

Heclo, H. (1972) Policy analysis - a review article. British Journal of Political Studies, 2, 83-108
Herbert, D.T. (1976) Urban education: problems and policies. In D.T. Herbert and R.J. Johnston (eds) Social Areas in Cities (vol. 2), Wiley, Chichester
Hewton, E. (1986a) Education in Recession, Allen and Unwin, London
------ (1986b) Policy-making in a cuts culture. Journal of Education Policy, 1, 305-14
Hill, D.M. (1974) Democratic Theory and Local Government, Allen and Unwin, London
Hilsum, S. and Start, K.B. (1974) Promotion and Careers in Teaching, NFER, London
Himsworth, C. (1980) School attendance orders and the sheriff. Journal of the Law Society of Scotland, 25, 450-5
Hollander, T. (1980) A geographical analysis of intercollegiate track and field athletics in the United States. Unpublished MA dissertation, Eastern Michigan University
Holtermann, S. (1975) Areas of urban deprivation in Great Britain: an analysis of 1971 Census data. Social Trends, 6, 33-46
Honey, R. and Sorenson, D. (1984) Jurisdictional benefits and local costs: the politics of school closures. In P. Knox, P. Kirby and S. Pinch (eds), Public Service Provision and Urban Development, Croom Helm, London
Howell, D.A. and Brown, R. (1983) Educational Policy Making: an Analysis, Heinemann, London
Howick, C. and Hassani, H. (1979) Education spending: primary. CES Review, 5, 41-9
------ (1980) Education spending: secondary. CES Review, 8, 23-33
Hunter, C. (1983) Education and local government in the light of central government policy. In J. Ahier and M. Flude (eds) Contemporary Education Policy, Croom Helm, London
Hutchison, D. (1975) Areas of difference: a critique of the work of Byrne and Williamson on regional inequalities in educational attainment. Quality and Quantity, 9, 171-83
Jackson, B. and Marsden, D. (1963) Education and the Working Class, Routledge and Kegan Paul, London
Jacobs, S. (1976) The Right to a Decent Home, Routledge and Kegan Paul, London

References

Jamieson, I. (1986) Corporate hegemony or pedagogic liberation: the schools-industry movement in England and Wales. In R. Dale (ed.) (1986) Education, Training and Employment, Pergamon Press, Oxford

Jarman, B. (1983) Identification of under-privileged areas. British Medical Journal, 286, 1706-9

Jencks, C., Smith, M., Acland, M., Bane, M.J., Cohen, D., Gintis, H., Heyns, B. and Michelson, S. (1973) Inequality: A Reassessment of the Effect of Family and Schooling in America, Allen Lane, London

Jenkins, S. (1985) Somalian finds winning races easiest thing in USA. International Herald Tribune, 24 June

Jenkinson, R. (1974) The geography of Indiana interscholastic and intercollegiate basketball. Unpublished EdD thesis, Oklahoma State University

Jennings, R.E. (1977) Education and Politics: Policy-Making in Local Education Authorities, Batsford, London

Johnston, R. (1984) The world is our oyster. Transactions of the Institute of British Geographers, NS9, 443-59

------ and Taylor, P. (eds) (1986) A World in Crisis? Geographical Perspectives, Blackwell, Oxford

Jones, J. and Stewart, J. (1983) The Case for Local Government, Allen and Unwin, London

Jordan, T. (1975) These are 'All Americans'? Track and Field News, 28 (4), 56

Judd, J. (1987) Baker plan snubbed by parents. The Observer, 3 May

Kelsall, R.K. and Kelsall, H.M. (1971) Social Disadvantage and Educational Opportunity, Holt Rinehart and Winston, London

Kerner, O. (1968) Report of the National Advisory Commission on Civil Disorders, Government Printing Office, Washington

Kidd, B. (1973) Athletics and the big dollar. In J. Murphy (ed.), Sports or Athletics? A North American Dilemma, University of Windsor, Windsor

King, R. (1971) Unequal access in education. Sex and social class. Social and Economic Administration, 5, 167-75

------ (1974) Social class, educational attainment and provision an LEA study. Policy and Politics, 3, 17-35

Kjellberg, F. (1979) A comparative view of municipal decentralisation: neighbourhood democracy in Oslo and Bologna. In L.J. Sharpe (ed.) Decentralist Trends in Western Democracies, Sage, London

Klineberg, O. and Hull, W. (1979) At a Foreign University:

References

an International Study of Adaptation and Coping, Praeger, New York
Kogan, M. (1985) Education policy and values. In I. McNay and J. Ozga (eds) Policy-Making in Education, Pergamon Press (for the Open University), Oxford
Labov, W. (1972) The logic of non-standard English. In P.P. Giglioli (ed.), Language and Social Context, Penguin, Harmondsworth
Lazerson, M. (1971) Origins of the Urban School, Harvard University Press, Cambridge, Massachusetts
Le Grand, J. (1982) The Strategy of Equality, Allen and Unwin, London
Leonard, P. (ed.) (1985) The sociology of community action. Sociological Review Monograph 21, University of Keele
Levy, F., Meltsner, A.J. and Wildavsky, A. (1974) Urban Outcomes: Schools, Streets and Libraries, University of California Press, Berkley
Little, A.N. (1977) What is happening in inner city schools? In F. Field (ed.), Education and the Urban Crisis, Routledge and Kegan Paul, London
Locke, T. and Ibach, B. (1982) Caught in the Net, Leisure Press, New York
Lyons, G. (1981) Teaching Careers and Perceptions. NFER Nelson Publishing, London
Macbeth, A., Strachan, D. and Macaulay, C. (1986) Parental Choice of Schools in Scotland, Department of Education, University of Glasgow
McConnell, H. (1983) Southern major college football: supply, demand and migration. Southeastern Geographer, 23
McCullagh, P. and Nelder, J. (1983) Generalised Linear Models, Chapman and Hall, London
McCulloch, G. (1986) Policy, politics and education: the Technical and Vocational Education Initiative. Journal of Education Policy, 1, 35-52
MacFadyen, I. and McMillan, F. (1984) The Management of Change at a Time of Falling School Rolls, Scottish Council for Research in Education, Edinburgh
McLaughlin, T. (1983) One coach's view of foreigners. Track and Field News, 36 (10), 43
McNay, I. and Ozga, J. (eds) (1985) Policy-Making in Education, Pergamon Press (for the Open University), Oxford
McPherson, A. and Willms, J.D. (1986) Certification, class conflict, religion and community: a socio-historical

References

explanation of the effectiveness of contemporary schools. In A.C. Keckhoff (ed.), Research in Sociology of Education and Socialization, vol. 6, JAI Press, Greenwich, Massachusetts

Maddala, G.S. (1983) Limited Dependent and Qualitative Variables in Econometrics, Cambridge University Press, London

Magnusson, W. (1979) The New Neighbourhood Democracy: Anglo-American Experience in Historical Perspective. In L.J. Sharpe (ed.) Decentralist Trends in Western Democracies, Sage, London

Main, B.G.M. and Raffe, D. (1983) Determinants of employment and unemployment among school leavers: evidence from the 1979 survey of Scottish school leavers. Scottish Journal of Political Economy, 30, 1-17

Mangan, J. and Small, R. (eds) (1986) Sport, Culture and Society, Spon, London

Manners, J. (1975) African recruiting boom. In D. Prokop (ed.), The African Running Revolution, World Publications, Mountain View, California

Manpower Services Commission (1984) TVEI Review, 1984, HMSO, London

March, J.G. and Simon, H.A. (1958) Organisations, Wiley, London

------ and Olsen, J.P. (1976) Ambiguity and Choice in Organisation, Univesitetsforlaget, Bergen

Maxfield, D.W. (1972) Spatial planning of school districts. Annals of the Association of American Geographers, 63, 582-90

Meredith, P. (1981) Executive discretion and choice of secondary school. Public Law, Spring, 52-82

------ (1984) Falling rolls and the reorganisation of schools. Journal of Social Welfare Law, July, 208-21

Merson M. and Bell, L. (1985) Technical and Vocational Education Initiative Metropolitan Borough of Solihull Evaluators' Report 1984/85, University of Warwick

------ (1986) Technical and Vocation Education Initiative Metropolitan Borough of Solihull Evaluators' Report 1985/86, University of Warwick

Michener, J. (1976) Sports in America, Random House, New York

Mihailich, J. (1982) Sports and Athletics: Philosophy in Action, Rowman and Littlefield, Totowa, New Jersey

Miller Lite (1983) Miller Lite Report on American Attitudes Towards Sports, Miller Brewing Co., Milwaukee

References

Mintzberg, H. (1985) The organisation as political arena. Journal of Management Studies, 22, 133-56

Mladenka, K.R. (1980) The urban bureaucracy and the Chicago political machine: who gets what and the limits of political control. American Political Science Review, 74, 991-8

Morrison, C.M. (1974) Educational Priority, vol. 5, A Scottish Study, HMSO, London

Mortimore, J. and Blackstone, T. (1982) Disadvantage and Education, Heinemann Educational, London

------ and Mortimore, J. (1986) Education and social class. In R. Rogers (ed.) Education and Social Class, Falmer, Lewes

Mosteller, F. and Tukey, J.W. (1977) Data Analysis and Regression, Addison-Wesley, Reading, Massachusetts

Moulden, M. and Bradford, M.G. (1984) Influences on educational attainment: the importance of the local residential environment. Environment and Planning A, 16, 49-66

Munro, N. (1986) 'Carrot and stick' bid to shut schools. Times Educational Supplement (Scotland) 29 August

NCAA (1984) Guide to International Academic Standards for Athletic Eligibility, NCAA, Mission, Kansas

Neave, G. (1984) The EEC and Education, Trentham Books, Stoke-on-Trent

Office for Population Censuses and Surveys (1980) Classification of Occupations, HMSO, London

Osterhoudt, R. (1976) Sport, the university and the inclination for self-destruction. Sport Sociology Bulletin, 5 (2), 1-4

Owen, J.D. (1972) The distribution of educational resources in large American cities. Journal of Human Resources, 7, 26-38

Packwood, T. (1984) School governing bodies: a case of uncertainty. Policy and Politics, 12, 269-80

Pahl, R. (1970) Whose City? Longman, London

------ (1984) Divisions of Labour, Blackwell, Oxford

Parkes, D.L. (1985) Competition ... and competence? Education, training and the roles of the DES and MSC. In I. MacNay and J. Ozga (eds) Policy-Making in Education, Pergamon Press (for the Open University), Oxford

Pattison, M. (1980) Inter-governmental relations and the limitations of central control: reconstructing the politics of comprehensive education. Oxford Review of

References

Education, 6, 63-84
Payne, J. (1974) Educational Priority, vol, 2: EPA Survey and Statistics, HMSO, London
Petch, A. (1986) Parental choice at entry to primary school. Research Papers in Education, 1, 26-47
Peet, R. (1986) The destruction of regional cultures. In R. Johnston and P. Taylor (eds) A World in Crisis? Geographical Perspectives, Blackwell, Oxford
Pettigrew, A.M. (1973) The Politics of Organisational Decision Making, Tavistock, London
Pinch, S. (1985) Cities and Services: the Geography of Collective Consumption Routledge and Kegan Paul, London
Portsmouth Evening News
Pyle, D. (1976) Aspects of resource allocation by local education authorities. Social and Economic Administration, 10, 106-21
Raffe, D. (1983) Education and class inequality in Scotland. In G. Brown and R. Cook (eds), Scotland the Real Divide, Mainstream Publishing, Edinburgh
------ (1984) School attainment and the labour market. In D. Raffe (ed.), Fourteen to Eighteen: the Changing Pattern of Schooling in Scotland, Aberdeen University Press, Aberdeen
Ranson, S. (1980) Changing relations between centre and locality in education. Local Government Studies, 6 (6), 3-23
Raudenbush, S. and Bryk, A. (1986) A hierarchical model for studying school effects. Sociology of Education, 59, 1-17
Regan, D.E. (1979) Local Government and Education, Allen and Unwin, London
Rhind, D. (ed.) (1983) A Census User's Handbook, Methuen, London
Rhodes, R.A.W. (1979) Research into central-local relations in Britain: a framework for analysis. In SSRC, Central-Local Government Relations, London
------ (1981) Control and Power in Central-Local Government Relations, SSRC/Gower, Farnborough
Ribbins, P. and Brown, R. (1979) Policy making in english local government: the case of secondary school reorganisation. Public Administration, 57, 187-202
Richardson, A. (1983) Participation, Routledge and Kegan Paul, London
Riddell, A. (1985) Deprivation - what is it? Scottish

References

Medicine, 5 (2), 14-16
Riley, R. (1974) Ngeno Courting Stardom. Track and Field News, 27 (5), 7
Rist, R.C. (1970) Student social class and teacher expectations: the self-fulfilling prophecy in ghetto education. Harvard Educational Review, 40, 411-51
Roberts, H. (1986) After sixteen: what choice? in R.G. Burgess (ed.) Exploring Society, Longman, London
Robinson, P. (1976) Education and Poverty, Methuen, London
Robson, B.T. (1969) Urban Analysis, Cambridge University Press, Cambridge
Rodda, J. (1984) Kenyan mountain men at peak. The Guardian, 23 March
Rogers, E.M. and Shoemaker, E.F. (1971) The Communication of Innovation, Free Press, New York
Rogers, R. (ed.) (1986) Education and Social Class, Falmer, Lewes
Rooney, J. (1969) Up from the mines and out from the prairies: some geographical implications of football in the United States. Geographical Review, 59, 471-92
------ (1980) The Recruiting Game, University of Nebraska Press, Lincoln
------ (1985) America needs a new intercollegiate sports system. Journal of Geography, 84, 139-43
Roper, L. and Snow, K. (1976) Correlation studies of academic excellence and big-time athletics. International Review of Sport Sociology, 61, 589-98
Rose, H. and Hanmer, J. (1975) Community participation and social change. In D. Jones and M. Mayo (eds) Community Work Two, Routledge and Kegan Paul, London
Ruffett, F. and Chreseson, J. (1984) Secondary Education: The Next Step, Policy Studies Institute, London
Rutter, M.L. and Madge, N. (1976) Cycles of Disadvantage: a Review of Research, Heinemann, London
------, Tizard, J. and Whitmore, K. (eds) (1970) Education, Health and Behaviour, Longman, London
Sage, G. (1980) Sport and American society: the quest for success. In G. Sage (ed.), Sport and American Society: Selected Readings, Addison Wesley, Reading, Massachusetts
Sallis, J. (1986) Was it money, politics, education or just something the Secretary of State had eaten? The Guardian, 10 June
Saran, R. (1973) Policy-Making in Secondary Education - A

References

 Case Study, Oxford University Press, Oxford
SASPAC (1983) User Manual (Release 3.0), Local Authorities Management Services and Computer Committee, London
Saunders, M. (1986) The innovative enclave: unintended effects of TVEI implementations. In TVEI Working Papers, Centre for Applied Research in Education, University of East Anglia
School for Advanced Urban Studies (1983) The Future of Local Democracy (A Response to the White Papers on Rates and Streamlining the Cities), University of Bristol
Scottish Education Department (1981) Circular 1074 'The Education (Scotland) Act 1981', Edinburgh
------ (1985) 'Future strategy for higher education in Scotland: report of the Tertiary Education Advisory Council on its review of higher education in Scotland', HMSO, Edinburgh
------ (1986) Placing Requests in Education Authority Schools. Statistical Bulletin, No. 5/86
Seabrook, J. (1984) The Idea of Neighbourhood, Pluto Press, London
Sexton, P.C. (1961) Education and Income: the Inequality of Opportunity in our Public Schools, Viking, New York
Sharpe, L.J. (ed.) (1979) Decentralist Trends in Western Democracies, Sage, London
Sim, D. (1984) Urban deprivation: not just the inner city. Area, 16, 299-306
Smith, A. (1986) unpublished statistics, personally communicated
Smith, G. (1975) Educational Priority, vol. 4: The West Riding Project, HMSO, London
Snyder, E. and Spreitzer, E. (1981) Sport, education and schools. In G. Luschen and G. Sage (eds), Handbook of Social Sciences and Sport, Stipes, Champaign, Illinois
Society of Education Officers (1975) Management in the Education Service: Challenge and Response, Carter and Halls, Coventry
Sojka, G. (1983) Evolution of the student-athlete in America. Journal of Popular Culture, 16 (4), 54-67
Spaulding, S. and Flack, M. (1976) The World's Students in the United States, Praeger, New York
Stanworth, M. (1981) Gender and Schooling: A Study of Sexual Division in the Classroom, Women's Research and Resource Centre, London. (Reprinted by Hutchinson

References

in 1983)

Starbuck, W.H. (1982) Congealing oil: inventing ideologies to justify acting ideologies out. Journal of Management Studies, 19, 3-27

Stidwell, H. and Bedecki, T. (1986) Training of Commonwealth and Irish track and field athletes in US colleges and universities. In J. Mangan and R. Small (eds), Sport, Culture and Society, Spon, London

Stillman, A. and Maychell, K. (1986) Choosing Schools: Parents LEAs and the 1980 Education Act, NFER/Nelson, Windsor

Strathclyde Regional Council (1986) Adapting to Change (Report of the working group on the implications of falling school rolls), Glasgow

Tapper, T. and Salter, B. (1986) The assisted places scheme: a policy evaluation. Journal of Education Policy, 1, 315-30

Taylor, G. and Ayres, N. (1969) Born and Bred Unequal, Longman, London

Taylor, J. (1986) First degree murder. Times Educational Supplement, 10 October

Taylor, P. (1982) A materialist framework for political geography. Transactions of the Institute of British Geographers, NS7, 15-34

Taylor, P. (1985) Political Geography, Longman, London

Taylor, W. (1981) Contraction in context. In B. Simon and W. Taylor (eds), Education in the Eighties, Batsford, London

Thomas, R.W. and Robson, B.T. (1984) The impact of falling school rolls on the assignment of primary schoolchildren to secondary schools in Manchester, 1980-1985. Environment and Planning A, 16, 339-56

Tomlinson, J. (1986) Crossing the Bridge, Sheffield Papers in Education Management, Sheffield City Polytechnic

Troyna, B. and Smith, D. (eds) (1983) Racism, School and the Labour Market, National Youth Bureau, Leicester

Tunley, P., Travers, T. and Pratt, J. (1979) Depriving the Deprived: a Study of Finance, Educational Provision and Deprivation in a London Borough, Kogan Page, London

Tunna, K. (1985) Opening the black box. Times Education Supplement, 20 September

Tweedie, J. (1986) Parental choice of school: legislating the balance. In Stillmann, A. (ed.) The Balancing Act of 1980: Parents, Politics and Education, NFER, Slough

Tyler, W. (1977) The Sociology of Educational Inequality,

References

Methuen, London
Underwood, J. (1984) Spoiled Sport, Little, Brown and Co., Boston
Van Dyne, L. (1976) Give me your strong, your fleet ... Chronicle of Higher Education, 12 (5), 1-7
Wallace, R. (1986) Technical and Vocational Education, Macmillan, London
Watson, W. (1970) Image and geography. The myth of America and the American scene. Advancement of Science, 27, 71-9
Wedge, P. and Prosser, N. (1973) Born to Fail?, Arrow Books, London
Weston, P., Lamb, J., Burnhill, P. and Garner, C. (1984) Collaborative Research Dictionary 1981, Centre for Educational Sociology, University of Edinburgh
Whannell, G. (1983) Blowing the Whistle: the Politics of Sport, Pluto, London
Willis, P. (1978) Learning to Labour, Saxon House, Farnborough
Willms, J.D. (1985) The balance thesis: contextual effects of ability on pupils' O-grade examination results. Oxford Review of Education, 11 (1), 33-41
------ (1986) Social class segregation and its relationship to pupils' examination results in Scotland. American Sociological Review, 51, 224-41
------ (1987) Comparing schools in their examination performance: policy questions and data requirements. Centre for Educational Sociology, University of Edinburgh
------ and Kerr, P.D. (1987) Changes in sex differences in Scottish examination results since 1986. Journal of Early Adolescence (in press)
Wilson, D.C. and Kenny, G.K. (1985) Managerially perceived influence over interdepartmental decisions. Journal of Management Studies, 22, 155-73
Williamson, W. and Byrne, D.S. (1977) The structure of educational provision: an LEA case study. In P. Raggett and M. Evans (eds), Urban Education, Open University Press, Milton Keynes
------ (1979) Educational disadvantage in an urban setting. In D.T. Herbert and D.M. Smith (eds), Social Problems and the City, Oxford University Press, Oxford
Winningham, G. (1979) Rites of Fall: High School Football in Texas, University of Texas Press, Austin
Wiseman, S. (1964) Education and Environment, Manchester

References

    University Press, Manchester
Wright, C. (1986) School processes - an ethnographic study. In S.J. Eggleston, D. Dunn and M. Anjali (eds), Education for Some, Trentham Books, Stoke-on-Trent
Yin, R.K. (1979) Changing Urban Bureaucracies: how New Practices become Routinised, Lexington, Massachusetts
Young, T. (1986) The sociology of sport: structural marxist and cultural marxist approaches. Sociological Perspectives, 29, 3-28
Ziegler, E. (1979), Isssues in North American Sport and Physical Education, American Association for Health, PE and Recreation, Washington DC

INDEX

Afro-Caribbean 219, 220, 224
Asian 219-21, 223
attainment 10, 14, 222, 226-55 passim, 257, 259, 308

birthrate 1, 22, 52, 62

catchment 23, 26, 27, 33, 37, 39, 76, 83, 87, 114, 116, 123, 125, 128-46 passim, 231, 235, 257-83 passim
Catholic 63, 67, 68, 71, 113, 124, 125
class 7, 8, 10, 11, 14, 64, 65, 72, 78, 104, 114, 123, 134-45 passim, 183, 184, 215, 218, 226-37 passim, 252, 258, 259, 261, 307
community 43, 52-80 passim, 83, 87, 97, 103, 108, 111, 218, 220, 232, 261, 271, 277, 279, 287, 289, 292, 242 also see neighbourhood
computer(s) 151, 152, 161, 164-6, 175 also see microcomputers
consultation 19, 21, 22, 28, 33-5, 39, 43-7, 55-80 passim, 83, 86, 94, 100, 101, 106, 108, 111, 167
Coventry 14, 260, 271, 273, 280, 283
culture/cultural 7, 9, 10, 11, 14, 205-7, 209, 215, 218, 220, 229
curriculum 10, 21, 27, 29, 151, 152, 161, 165, 166, 169, 223, 225, 286-98 passim, 302-6

delegation 52, 75, 77, 80
deprivation 14, 91, 104, 114, 135, 226, 235-55 passim also see disadvantage
disadvantage 9, 47, 57, 257, 258, 260, 287, 308 also see deprivation
Dundee 14, 53, 66-73 passim, 113, 114, 121-47 passim, 307
Dunfermline 83, 87-112 passim

Edinburgh 14, 113, 114, 121-47 passim, 234
Education Act 1944 8, 11, 12

330

Index

Education Act 1980 22, 44, 54
Education (Scotland) Act 1946 115
Education (Scotland) Act 1980 58, 113, 118
Education (Scotland) Act 1981 58, 89, 94, 114, 118
EPA 9
equality of opportunity 7, 8, 10, 14, 21
ethnic minority 14, 214, 218, 219, 224, 259 also see race/racial

falling school rolls 2, 13, 19, 27-30, 34, 52-68 passim, 73, 79, 83, 89, 90, 119, 261, 303, 306
Fife 14, 83, 87, 100, 108, 307
further education 23, 27, 28, 49, 51, 115, 237, 253, 285, 288

gender 11, 239
Glasgow 14, 226-55 passim

Hampshire 19, 21, 27, 29, 30, 41
higher education 135, 139, 237, 253, 285, 288
home background 8, 226-9, 248, 252
housing 63, 64, 68, 90, 101, 102, 108, 114, 119, 133, 134, 138, 139, 144, 145, 231-5, 238, 240, 248, 255, 257, 279

inner city 62, 64, 259-82 passim, 215

Lothian 121-4

Manchester 53, 61-6 passim, 72, 73, 227, 233
Manpower Services Commisssion (MSC) 6, 225, 285, 289-91, 293, 296
microcomputers 151, 152, 164, 167, 169, 175 see also computers
migration 178, 180, 208

neighbourhood 9, 10, 14, 22, 23, 40, 47, 123, 144, 226-61 passim, 270 also see community

organisation theory 3, 14, 152, 154, 161, 167, 176, 177

parental choice 4-6, 14, 29, 53, 89, 96, 113-47 passim, 308
placing requests 91, 93, 113-47 passim
policy making 2, 3, 5, 14, 21, 70, 75, 84, 85, 111, 112, 148-77 passim, 304, 307
policy innovation 3, 148-77 passim, 285
Portsmouth 1, 9, 14, 21, 21, 27-31, 36, 41-7, 307
positive discrimination 4, 9, 14, 248, 258, 261
public expenditure 1, 2, 3, 6, 36, 53, 60, 68, 76, 115, 290

race/racial 7, 10, 11 also see ethnic minority
recession 1, 5, 213, 306
rezoning 83, 93, 101, 108-12

school closures 6, 14, 19-51 passim, 52-80 passim, 261, 308

331

Index

school effectiveness 230, 231
sixth-form provision 19-51 passim
social identity 214, 215
social mobility 7
Social Priority 9, 14, 258-83 passim
Strathclyde 79, 80, 234

Tayside 53, 66-72 passim, 121, 124
teachers 5, 6, 9, 14, 21, 27, 32, 34, 37, 44, 45, 49-51, 57, 59, 60, 64, 98, 109, 164, 165, 206, 219-23, 257-83 passim, 290-8 passim, 301, 302

technical education 8, 12, 14
TVEI 4, 6, 12, 15, 285-305 passim

unemployment 7, 9, 12, 135, 139, 213, 214, 221, 225, 238, 242, 254, 288, 289

vocational 14, 214-18, 258, 274, 281, 291, 292, 297
VRQ 228

work experience 214, 224, 288, 291, 297

YTS 224, 289

+LC191 .E38 1988

AUDREY COHEN COLLEGE
50664000149387
/Education and society : studies in the
LC191 .E38 1988 C.1 STACKS 1988

EDUCATION AND SOCIETY: Studies in the Politics, Sociology and Geography of Education

Edited by L. Bondi, Department of Geography, University of Edinburgh and M.H. Matthews, School of Geography, Lanchester Polytechnic

Falling school enrolments and financial constraints have prompted many education authorities to re-assess and rationalize existing school systems. However making changes which are consistent with the education services' aim of providing an equal standard of education for all, regardless of locality, is proving difficult. This book examines the most contentious issues in contemporary education. The political, social, educational and geographical impact of changes in the provision of educational services are discussed and illustrated through a wide range of case studies. Issues are examined from a number of different perspectives, amongst them those of the parent, the educational administrator and the organisational theorist, with the result that the book is able to evaluate which changes are most consistent with the requirements of each group.

ROUTLEDGE SERIES IN GEOGRAPHY AND ENVIRONMENT
Edited by Alan Wilson, Nigel Thrift,
Michael Bradford and Edward W. Soja

Urban Housing Provision and the
Development Process
David Drakakis-Smith

David Harvey's Geography
John L. Paterson

Planning in the Soviet Union
Judith Pallot and Denis J.B. Shaw

Catastrophe Theory and Bifurcation
A.G. Wilson

Regional Landscapes and
Humanistic Geography
Edward Relph

Crime and Environment
R.N. Davidson

Human Migration
G.J. Lewis

The Geography of Multinationals
*Edited by Michael Taylor and
Nigel Thrift*

Urbanisation and Planning in the
Third World: Spatial Perceptions
and Public Participation
Robert B. Potter

Office Development: A
Geographical Analysis
Michael Bateman

Urban Geography
David Clark

Retail and Commercial Planning
R.L. Davies

Institutions and Geographical
Patterns
Edited by Robin Flowerdew

Uneven Development and
Regionalism
Costis Hadjimichalis

Managing the City: The Aims and
Impacts of Urban Policy
Edited by Brian Robson

International Geopolitical Analysis
*Edited and translated by Pascal
Giret and Eleanore Kofman*

Analytical Behavioural Geography
R.G. Golledge and R.J. Stimson

Money and Votes: Constituency
Campaign Spending and Election
Results
R.J. Johnston

The Uncertain Future of the Urban
Core
Edited by Christopher M. Law

Mathematical Programming
Methods for Geographers and
Planners
James Killen

The Land Problem in the Developed
Economy
Andrew H. Dawson

Geography Since the Second World
War
*Edited by R.J. Johnston and
P. Claval*

The Geography of Western Europe
Paul L. Knox

The Geography of
Underdevelopment
Dean Forbes

Regional Restructuring Under
Advanced Capitalism
Edited by Phil O'Keefe

Multinationals and the
Restructuring of the World
Economy
Michael Taylor and Nigel Thrift

The Spatial Organisation of
Corporations
Ian M. Clarke

The Geography of English
Politics
R.J. Johnston

Women Attached: The Daily Lives
of Women with Young Children
Jacqueline Tivers

The Geography of Health Services
in Britain
Robin Haynes

Politics, Geography and Social
Stratification
*Edited by Keith Hoggart and
Eleonore Kofman*

Planning in Eastern Europe
Andrew H. Dawson

Planning Control: Philosophies,
Prospects and Practice
*Edited by M.L. Harrison and
R. Murdey*